Global Construction Data

Global construction data is vital for contractors, governments, international organisations, policy makers, academic researchers and statisticians. As the global population of the world expands, the sustainability of the built environment raises the political agenda and the need to manage infrastructure and buildings in both urban and rural contexts becomes ever more pressing. How much more can the built environment grow and how can it be managed sustainably?

This edited volume addresses how we can find a possible way through the inconsistencies between national construction data sets to devise a consistent approach to national construction data to further the global sustainability agenda and inform policy making. This search begins in Part I, which looks at the methods and definitions used in construction statistics in different countries. Part II considers examples of different types of construction data from the cost of materials, measuring work on high rise buildings and existing stock. In Part III, the authors consider construction data internationally, beginning with the problem of comparing data in different countries using exchange rates and purchasing power parities (PPPs), comparing innovation processes in different countries and looking at the provision of building design internationally. In Part IV, the international theme is continued by comparing accounting practices and company performance in different countries and concludes with an international comparison of construction industries.

This book raises awareness of the significance of the construction industry globally and the importance of data to measure it. It informs the discussion of the best ways of handling the consequences of policies affecting the built environment and the effect of the built environment on the rest of the economy and society. It is essential reading for international economists, construction industry consultants, policy makers, construction statisticians and academics.

Stephen Gruneberg is an Honorary Professor in the Bartlett School of Construction and Project Management at University College London (UCL).

About CIB and the CIB series

CIB, the International Council for Research and Innovation in Building and Construction, was established in 1953 to stimulate and facilitate international cooperation and information exchange between governmental research institutes in the building and construction sector, with an emphasis on those institutes engaged in technical fields of research.

CIB has since developed into a worldwide network of over 5000 experts from about 500 member organisations active in the research community, in industry or in education, who cooperate and exchange information in over 50 CIB Commissions and Task Groups covering all fields in building and construction related research and innovation.

www.cibworld.nl/

This series consists of a careful selection of state-of-the-art reports and conference proceedings from CIB activities.

R&D Investment and Impact in the Global Construction Industry
K *Hampson* et al
ISBN: 9780415859134. Published: 2014

Public Private Partnerships A *Akintoye* et al.
ISBN: 9780415728966. Published: 2015

Court-Connected Construction Mediation Practice A. *Agapiou and* D. *Ilter*
ISBN: 9781138810105. Published: 2016

Advances in Construction ICT and e-Business S. *Perera* et al
ISBN: 9781138914582. Published: 2017

Clients and Users in Construction K. *Haugbolle and* D. *Boyd*
ISBN: 9781138786868. Published: 2017

Integrating Information in the Built Environments A. X. *Sanchez* et al
ISBN: 9781138706323. Published: 2018

Global Construction Data

Edited by
Stephen Gruneberg

Routledge
Taylor & Francis Group
LONDON AND NEW YORK

First published 2020 by Routledge

2 Park Square, Milton Park, Abingdon, Oxon OX14 4RN
605 Third Avenue, New York, NY 10017

Routledge is an imprint of the Taylor & Francis Group, an informa business

First issued in paperback 2021

Publisher's Note

The publisher has gone to great lengths to ensure the quality of this reprint but points out that some imperfections in the original copies may be apparent.

British Library Cataloguing-in-Publication Data
A catalogue record for this book is available from the British Library

Library of Congress Cataloging-in-Publication Data
Names: Gruneberg, Stephen L., editor.
Title: Global construction data / edited by Stephen Gruneberg.
Description: First edition. | Milton Park, Abingdon, Oxon ; New York, NY : Routledge, 2020. | Includes bibliographical references.
Identifiers: LCCN 2019014803 | ISBN 9781138350403 (hardback) | ISBN 9780429435911 (ebook)
Subjects: LCSH: Construction industry. | Economic indicators.
Classification: LCC HD9715.A2 G569 2020 | DDC 338.4/7624—dc23
LC record available at https://lccn.loc.gov/2019014803

ISBN: 978-1-138-35040-3 (hbk)
ISBN: 978-1-03-217747-2 (pbk)
DOI: 10.1201/9780429435911

Typeset in Goudy
by Apex CoVantage, LLC

Contents

Preface

One major distinction between national income accounts and international statistics on national construction industry data is that a system of national income accounts has been coordinated and now form a cohesive integrated set of accounts for comparing national income data in different countries and data gathering and estimation have been improved in the process. This aids the perception of national income in every country knowing the tables attempt to measure common variables consistently.

This international transformation of national construction industries into a consistent international framework has not yet occurred in the field of construction statistics. Nevertheless, work has been done to make comparisons and to prepare the ground for further developments. For example, in Chapter 4 Langston discusses the concept of a *citiBLOC* and the concept of construction purchasing power parities (PPPs).

And yet there is still much to be said about how different countries arrive at their numerical assessments of the size and scale of their construction industries. In this book, we try to take examples of different types of measures and statistics in order to begin the process of finding a common international base to eventually find an internationally accepted approach to assessing and comparing the activities of the construction industry around the world. We are not there yet.

Definitions of building types, the national institutions of each country and the many different kinds of firms that manage, organise production, design, build and manufacture the component parts and materials are all part of the construction process. These standards vary from country to country and are not easily compared. Often, they are not even found in other countries and do not even translate into the structure of another country's construction industry. A good example is the surveying profession in the UK, which is not found in many other countries. Similarly, the training and role of architects varies widely from one country to another and therefore means that the legal responsibilities of architects and civil and structural engineers also vary from one country to another. It is not even possible to argue that they carry out the same duties and responsibilities in different countries.

Only a small number of aspects of data gathering in construction are discussed in order to initiate a process of bringing together the many different approaches to measuring construction. Eventually, it may be possible to find a consistent, if imperfect, method of estimating construction statistics globally, as has been achieved in the field of national income accounts. Such an approach could be used to form a system of construction data that could be used to identify where changes are taking place within construction activity. It is almost certain to be an untidy exercise, with many valid objections on both practical and theoretical grounds. Nevertheless, even an imperfect system of estimating construction activity may be better than none at all.

The chapters in this book are arranged in four parts. The first deals with the methods used to measure construction industry activity. Part II concerns the measurement of two aspects of residential construction; the first involves measuring the durability of high-rise blocks of flats in Hong Kong, and the second concerns work on existing stock in Europe.

The third part of the book deals with measuring aspects of the construction process itself, such as construction cost management in South Africa and comparing the national willingness of construction industries to innovate and adopt new techniques and technology by examining the level of adoption of Building Information Modelling in different countries. This part concludes with a chapter on aspects of the global market for design in the built environment and differences between various architectural approaches. The final part covers international aspects of measuring construction industry performance and activity and compares aspects of the construction industries of several countries.

In Chapter 1, Noble Francis discusses the logic of the UK construction data set and some of the measurement issues that arise there. This chapter describes the scope of construction data. He points out the weaknesses and limitations of surveys of construction firms and their resulting statistics, often due to the difficulties of asking firms for information they see as commercially sensitive. He explains the production processes that take place on site. He points out most workers in the construction industry are employed by small and medium sized enterprises even on the largest projects as subcontractors on site. He describes how the data is gathered and that the monthly data is based on a sample of firms. The chapter concludes with some practical difficulties encountered in the collection and recording of data.

A similar approach is adopted in Chapter 2 by Gerard de Valence and Jim Meikle, who develop the statistical concepts to define the structure of construction data in the UK, the United States, Canada and Australia, using the construction element of gross fixed capital formation as a measure of construction industry output in all four countries. To place the construction industry in context, De Valence and Meikle begin by defining gross domestic product. They then compare the share of total construction output as a percentage of GFCF in 26 countries in Table 2.3, comparing construction industries internationally. Between 1997 and 2017 of all countries included in Table 2.3, construction represented around 50 per cent of GFCF, ranging from 37.3 per cent of GFCF in Sweden to 63 per cent in Colombia. They conclude their chapter with a discussion of the sources of data in the US, Canada, Australia and the UK.

In Chapter 2, all data was noted in local currencies. This was done to avoid the problems of converting currencies using exchange rates. The problem is that when a currency exchange rate increases, it automatically increases the value of the size of its construction industry in terms of other countries. This clearly makes little sense. In order to overcome objections that follow from this, Craig Langston deals with purchasing power parities, (PPP) in general and construction PPPs in particular in Chapter 3.

PPPs enable comparisons between countries to be made that more accurately reflect the real cost incurred in different countries, relative to other prices in each country. Langston refers to the Law of One Price, which argues that items purchased in different countries tend to be the same price. This occurs due to arbitrage. When goods move towards higher priced markets, this increases supply and lowers prices. At the same time, as supply moves away from lower price markets, prices there increase until eventually the price is the same in both markets, hence purchasing power parity. The implication of purchasing power parity for measuring construction activity in different countries is discussed in Chapter 3.

Langston's aim is to compare methods of measuring construction in different countries that consider the purchasing power of currencies in different countries. For example, we need to know if it is cheaper to purchase construction materials locally or not.

The second part of the book focuses on one type of building, namely residential buildings and considers the problems of measurement and management. The focus of attention is the housing stock in Hong Kong and the difficulties of measuring the life expectancy of residential stock. This is of paramount importance in managing the housing stock especially where it comes under shared ownership in high rise buildings. For this reason, in Chapter 4 Wai Kin Lau and Yung Yau discuss the issues that arise in measuring the survival of residential buildings and the implications of high rise stock in terms of its expected life and redevelopment.

Chapter 5 is concerned with measuring energy performance of residential buildings with a view to increasing energy efficiency by reducing consumption of energy by as much as 60 per cent. In this chapter, Terttu Vainio and Eero Nippala measure the economic performance of residential buildings in several countries. The purpose is to compare the energy efficiency of renovation targets in different economic environments.

In several Eastern European countries, buildings are relatively wasteful in energy terms although energy is relatively expensive, but construction costs are low. It is nevertheless more difficult to achieve targets in northern Europe, where cold winters have tended to force investment in energy-efficiency. In contrast to Eastern Europe, energy in northern Europe is relatively cheap, but construction costs tend to be high.

The following section of the book looks at measuring aspects of the building process and the problems of measuring them in different countries.

In Chapter 6, Abimbola Windapo and Alireza Moghayedi evaluate activities that cause cost overruns in South Africa and whether there are significant differences in the activities causing cost overruns based on project parameters, (such as client type, procurement system and form of building structure).

One of the most important changes taking place in construction management is the spread of the use of Building Information Modelling (BIM). In Chapter 7, David Greenwood traces the adoption of BIM in different countries as a measure of the willingness to national construction industries to innovate and adopt new approaches to building made possible by information technology. Several criteria are used to measure the extent to which aspects of BIM have been adopted, including the regulatory framework, education and training the setting up of measurements and benchmarks and the technology infrastructure to support BIM. The level of maturity is then tested against several criteria including the extent to which BIM is managed, integrated and ultimately optimised. As many as 21 countries are compared in term of their adoption of BIM. However, far from providing a clear picture of the degree of adoption of BIM in different countries, an inconsistent picture emerges of the adoption of BIM in different countries. This makes for a much more complex account of how new technology permeates the construction industry and BIM is only an example of one technological advance and its progress in developing new ways of working.

Chapter 8 develops a comprehensive picture of the global market for architectural services. Unfortunately, data and statistical information about the economic activity of the architectural profession across the globe is by and large scant and fragmented. Very little data has been collected or analysed regarding international architectural practices and cross-border activities.

In Chapter 8, Peter Raisbeck surveys current national and state regimes for the distribution of information regarding the market for architectural services. This chapter provides an alternative perspective offered by the architectural profession to that offered by the social science of economics. The chapter describes the extent to which information infrastructure related to architects exists in different national jurisdictions, such as those in the United States, UK and Europe. This is contrasted with professional service markets in China, India and Africa. The chapter discusses a range of aggregated data related to architectural firms including revenues, profit, labour force statistics, gender balance, rates of pay and working hours. Chapter 8 also discusses global ranking systems of large architectural firms to build up a picture of the global market for architectural services. It demonstrates that the data associated with the global market in architectural services has a socio-technical agency or influence and shows that global data related to architectural services has either a normative, dynamic or strategic agency. The use to which global architectural data is put and the agency that is conferred upon it, points to the paradoxes and contradictions across the global market for architectural services.

The final section of the book consists of two chapters, which describe construction activity from different points of view. The first is concerned with the measurement of financial performance using the accounts of firms. The second compares construction performance in different countries, using measures of construction output. In Chapter 9, Alex Murray and Alexandr Kulakov discuss the make/buy decisions that underpin the business model that is widely adopted in the construction sector. In other words, the predominance of subcontracting in construction is, in essence, the result of decisions to buy-in the services of other firms rather than produce in-house. This has implications for contractors, which enable them to operate with very lean assets and yet produce very large turnovers. This is clearly explained by Murray and Kulakov, and they show this not to be just a local phenomenon but one spread throughout the world.

They examine the performance of contractors in the G8 economies of the USA, Japan, Russia, France, Germany, Canada, Italy and the UK, focusing on the US, Japan, France and the UK. They use the three-part Du Pont system to analyse how firms operate. This brings together the large turnover of firms together with their small profit margins, which together provides a sufficient return on the capital employed that enables them to survive in a high-risk business environment.

In the final chapter, Stephen Gruneberg describes the UK Benchmark model, which uses data from official UK construction statistics in combination with UN data on national income and gross fixed capital formation to devise a global comparable measure of national construction industry output and comparable growth rates.

Taken as a whole, this book covers several theoretical and practical aspects of global construction statistics and their uses. It demonstrates the diversity of approaches and points in the direction of a need to co-ordinate the measurement of national construction industries in the same way national income accounts form a basis for increasing the understanding of construction data. As the unstoppable rise of the global economy continues and as international cooperation is increasingly sought to mitigate the adverse effects of construction activity, the more policy makers and decision takers are able to measure the impact on the standard of living and the quality of life of the changes brought about by investment in the built environment the better.

The finger of blame is often pointed at the construction industry but investment in the built environment is a response to the growth in population and the increase in income of that population. Nevertheless, it is only a matter of time before uninhabited, remote, wild, unspoilt, regions of the world will no longer exist at the present rate of degradation of the natural environment. In order to understand the changes that are taking place, there is a need to measure the activities of the construction sector throughout the world. The impact of construction has national, regional and global impacts that do not respect national boundaries and the pollution and spillover effects caused cannot be isolated, restricted or contained within the borders of a country. International co-operation is needed, and construction data is necessary to inform policy and action.

This book would not have been possible without the help of Ed Needles and Patrick Hetherington of Taylor and Francis. Their support has been invaluable as has the effort put in to this book by the contributing authors, all of whom have surpassed expectations. Nevertheless, it must be said that any weakness or errors are entirely the fault of myself. It has been a long march, but it has produced a volume that paves the way for others to follow in the years to come.

Stephen Gruneberg

Part I

Measuring construction activity as a whole

1 Measuring construction activity in the UK

Noble Francis

Introduction

The construction industry is one of the key sectors of the UK economy, covering not only the production of buildings and structures but also their repair, maintenance and improvement. The importance of the construction industry to the UK economy cannot be underestimated. It not only contributes directly through the income and employment generated but it also contributes indirectly through enabling other areas of the economy with facilities such as housing, schools, hospitals, offices, shops, factories, warehouses and a variety of different infrastructure (Gruneberg and Francis, 2019). To be able to fully understand the construction industry, it is vital to appropriately define and be able to measure the size, structure and fluctuations in construction. However, measuring the construction industry is more complex than for other sectors of the economy for a variety of reasons.

Many sectors of the UK economy, such as basic manufacturing, produce a standardised product, such as the number of a certain type of automobile. This is known as the volume and is easily measurable over a period of time, often on a daily or weekly basis. The number of units of production can then be compared over time to see how the rate of production may have changed over time. The value indicates either the change in the cost of production over time or the change in selling price. However, construction is often more complex, and the majority of construction is a process making a bespoke product on every occasion. It covers a vast array of areas from housing and commercial buildings to infrastructure and industrial buildings with specific needs for the client based around both new and existing facilities.

Construction covers many different types of products and services with teams of different types of firms that are brought together for only one specific project or programme of projects. It includes the services needed to design facilities, the production of materials and building components, the trades and management needed to assemble buildings and structures on site. A broad definition of construction also includes the employment of architects, surveyors, civil and structural engineers, plant and tool hire, construction product manufacturers and their distribution networks. The construction sector is often seen as one sector but, in fact, it covers a wide variety of work across many different areas.

In addition, activity is often sub-contracted out to smaller and specialist contracting firms, which adds an extra layer of complexity, when measuring construction activity within a particular period of time. For instance, a contractor will know the value of contracts it has won and will need to deliver. However, this is only an early indicator of activity on the ground, as not all projects go ahead. However, despite the difficulties inherent in measuring the UK construction industry, it is essential to be able to measure the activity within construction to be able to fully understand it.

Defining the UK construction sector

Construction is a process involving architects and professionals, contractors, merchants and distributors, plant and tool hire in addition to construction materials and product manufacturers. Product manufacturers produce all the materials and products that go into the construction of a facility. Builders' merchants and distributors act as wholesalers and retailers of building materials and products as well as offering finance and credit. Tool and plant hire firms exist to provide additional capacity for heavy machinery or tools that are needed on-site to complete projects but are not owned by the contractor or sub-contractors, as they may be too costly for a contractor to own if they are likely to be underutilised resources when firms are working on other types of projects afterwards.

On large projects, there may be more than one major contractor operating as a member of a joint venture due to the large scale of production involved and the necessity to spread the burden of risk. The major contractors are likely to sub-contract work out to those with skills in specific areas, specialist contractors and civil engineering firms. As with machinery and tools, direct employment of those with specialist skills would mean significant periods of unproductive inactivity when these skills were not required. Subcontracting out specialist skills and activities ensures that the main contractors do not suffer the burden of unproductive cost when there is a period of inactivity. At the same time, it frees up the specialist firms to find work with other main contractors, which is an efficient way of using the resources of construction firms by making it possible to have continuity of work instead of periods of idleness. The nature of construction and the reliance on subcontracting to deal with risk and the potential for underutilised resources depending on the project means that the construction industry is dominated by a large number of small firms, which are taken on with other subcontractors as well as sub-subcontractors working for subcontractors working on large projects.

For some construction products, used in large quantities, main contractors may purchase products directly from manufacturers in order to take advantage of economies of scale or savings of size. Economies of scale exist where the purchaser can obtain a product at a lower price by purchasing large quantities through buying in bulk to reduce the cost per unit.

UK construction data

Many private sector organisations such as trade associations, which are membership organisations, or economic research consultancies provide monthly or quarterly trade surveys and data in the construction industry. However, these surveys tend to suffer from several issues for those wishing to conduct research on the size and structure of the construction industry as well as monitoring, analysing and forecasting activity within it. First, the surveys from independent organisations tend to only cover the change in activity within a specific part of the construction sector such as small and medium-size enterprises (SME) contracting, civil engineering or construction product manufacturing. Second, these surveys do not measure the size of the sector but tend to focus only on changes in activity within a specific area. Third, these surveys often only cover a small sample of firms within the part of the construction supply chain they are covering, and responses are often skewed towards larger firms that have greater resource available to fill in response questionnaires on a regular basis. Fourth, the surveys tend to measure and report a net balance of firms, which is the number of firms reporting an increase after subtracting the number of firms reporting a decrease. As a result, it is not reporting the extent of the change. Rather, it is using the net number of firms reporting an increase to indicate the direction of change overall for the sector and using that change as a proxy for the extent of the increase or decrease. A proxy is a variable that is used to represent a similar variable that is difficult to measure. By using the net balance of firms, all firms are given an equal weighting, and this can be problematic. If, for example, the industry contains two construction firms, with one firm enjoying an increase in construction activity of £100 million and with the other firm enduring a fall in activity of £1 million, the net balance of firms would indicate that activity had remained flat whereas industry activity had, in fact, risen by £99 million. Finally, industry surveys are not based on effective random sampling across the population of firms. Rather, they depend on voluntary self-selecting membership participation, which introduces several potential biases into the results.

Government construction data

The Department for Business, Energy and Industrial Strategy (BEIS), a UK government department, measures activity across all industries in its Business Population Estimates (BPE). This includes all UK firms that are registered to pay Value Added Tax (VAT) in addition to an estimate of the activities of small firms that are below a threshold required to be VAT registered and thus do not have to pay VAT. These generally cover people, who are self-employed (BEIS, 2018). BEIS measures the number of firms, turnover, employment and other variables by UK industry. The key benefit of this data is that it provides an insight into the basic structure of the industry. The majority of the focus on the construction industry by government and media tends to be on the largest firms but the sector is actually dominated by SMEs, defined as firms employing less than 250 employees (see Figure 1.1).

It is, in general, the population of SMEs, which carry out the productive transformation of materials and products into finished buildings. Of the more than 2 million people employed in construction in 2017, 86 per cent were employed

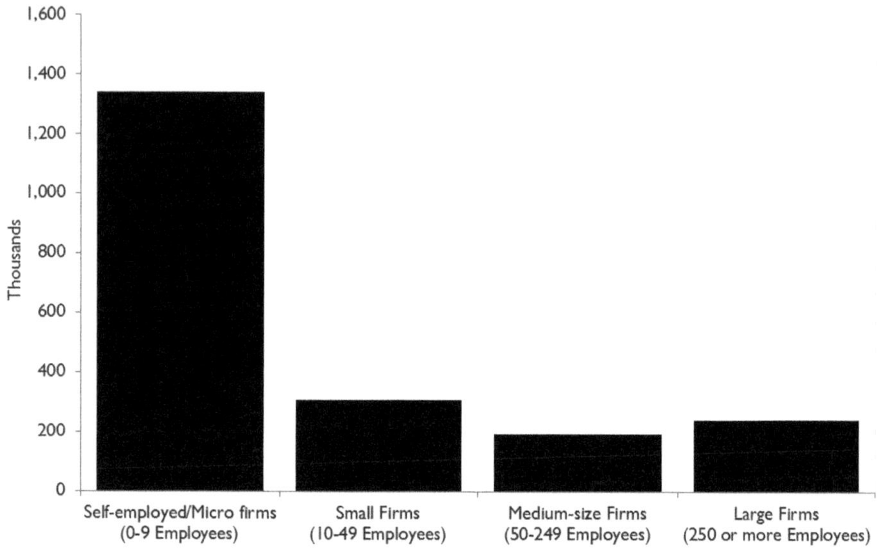

Figure 1.1 Employment by Size of Construction Firm in 2017

Source: Table 1.5, BEIS Business Population Estimates (2018)

by SMEs while large contractors only employed the remaining 14 per cent of the total construction workforce during 2017, mainly co-ordinating the work of the many specialist firms involved on site. The high proportion of work carried out by SMEs is also because the 34 per cent of total construction that is repair, maintenance and improvement of existing buildings and structures tends to be dominated by small firms. Of the almost 66 per cent of construction activity that is new construction work, main contractors often dominate turnover but operate primarily for the purpose of winning projects and managing the sub-contractors who actually undertake the activity and bear the majority of the risk.

The Business Population Estimates (BPE) data are useful to illustrate the general level of activity and the structure of contracting turnover. In addition, the consistency of the data across all UK industries ensures that it is also useful for comparing the activity of contractors with other areas such as agriculture, manufacturing and services. However, the data suffer from three key issues. First, the definition of construction covers only the number of firms and employment of the contractors, those firms that operate on the construction site itself. Yet, this is only one part of the whole construction supply chain. Defining construction as only including contractors on site ignores the contribution of the supply chain of all the building components and materials and the design as well as other specialisms. Second, the frequency of the data is only annual and, as a result, provides construction economists with relatively few data points on which to conduct research. As a result, the data give little insight into the key changes that often occur in a volatile industry. Third, given that the construction industry covers such a wide variety of activities, from building and maintaining housing, health and education facilities, commercial and industrial buildings as well infrastructure, the BEIS data gives little insight into the different areas in which activity is occurring.

ONS construction data

The independent Office for National Statistics (ONS) also provides an alternative source of data that cover activity within the construction sector in two different forms. The first set of data is taken from its Annual Business Survey (ABS) and is designed to help in calculating the total value of the output of all industries in the whole economy utilising the variable, Gross Value Added (GVA). The GVA of an industry is the value that only the specific industry adds to the economy so it excludes the inputs used, as these will be included in another sector. Within UK construction, the GVA is the selling price of construction output after subtracting the costs of materials, merchanting, plant and tool hire, designers and engineers. It is the turnover minus the total amount spent on goods and contractors' own sub-contracted services. The benefit of using GVA is that it avoids double counting. If the value of construction used the aggregate sales or firms' turnover, for example, it would include the value of construction products twice in determining the value of the UK economy, initially within UK manufacturing and then within UK construction. As the national income is a measure of the total income arising in all sectors of the economy, this would consequently result in an overestimation of the size of the whole economy.

Table 1.1 illustrates the GVA in the UK construction supply chain during 2017, which was £131.5 billion. 67 per cent of this GVA was provided by building contractors, which included major contractors, specialist contractors, civil

Table 1.1 GVA and Employment in UK Construction in 2017

	Gross Value Added	*Employment*	*Number of Firms*	*Capex*	*Turnover*
	£ Million			*£ Million*	*£ Million*
Construction products manufacturing	21,501	337,300	23,818	2,084	60,159
Building contractors	87,854	1,423,000	292,447	6,349	239,825
Materials and products distribution	9,383	190,000	10,221	688	48,248
Construction plant hire	4,213	42,000	4,187	1,005	6,324
Building professional services	8,586	98,000	22,911	603	10,609
Total Construction	**131,537**	**2,090,300**	**353,584**	**10,729**	**365,165**

Source: Tables B, C, F, G UK Annual Business Survey, Office for National Statistics (2018a)

engineering contractors and the subcontractors in the construction trades. The importance of utilising GVA rather than turnover is clear from Table 3.1 which shows the GVA of contractors was £87.9 billion, while the total turnover or sales of contractors was £239.8 billion. Of total construction GVA in the UK 16 per cent is provided by manufacturers of construction products with materials and products distribution providing 7 per cent of the GVA in the construction supply chain, while architects and professionals provide a further 7 per cent.

The ABS data on construction GVA highlight the value of production in the construction supply chain and illustrates the value added by each part of the supply chain on an annual basis. However, it tells us little about the type of work undertaken in construction and how the fortunes of the sector vary throughout the year. In the medium-term, the GVA data do not indicate which sectors of the industry suffer the greatest falls due to cuts in government spending or as the industry enters a recession or, conversely, which sectors benefit the most due to government policies or during periods of substantial UK economic growth.

ONS construction output survey

The most extensive and frequent coverage of the construction industry is provided by the ONS with a specific survey on construction output. It consists of data covering both the volume and value of construction activity across all key construction sectors and sub-sectors in Great Britain. These data are used at a general level to determine the construction GVA highlighted above. The series originated in 1940 and have been compiled by various government departments in its current form since 1955 on a quarterly and annual basis. Responsibility for the construction output series was taken over by the ONS in 2008. It also added monthly construction output to the frequency of construction output data provided in 2010. These data and time series are the most comprehensive available on the construction industry and are used by the ONS itself when determining the size of and change in the UK economy. The ONS data are also used by the European Commission's statistical office, government departments, the Bank of England, economic analysts and forecasters, media and construction industry observers and academics.

On a monthly basis, the ONS asks companies that are classified as operating within construction to estimate each month their output, which it defines as the amount chargeable to customers for building and civil engineering work done in the relevant period excluding VAT. In addition to this, the ONS asks firms to include the value of work done on their own initiative on buildings such as dwellings or offices for eventual sale or lease and of work done by their own operatives on the construction and maintenance of their own premises. It also asks construction firms to include the value of goods made by businesses themselves and used in the work (ONS, 2018b).

As activity within the UK construction sector is often subcontracted out to smaller firms and specialist firms that may also be included in the survey, to avoid overestimating activity within the construction sector by double counting, contractors filling in the ONS survey of construction activity are asked to exclude activity by their sub-contractors and specialist contractors.

According to the ONS, the construction sector is defined as all firms classified to construction in the Standard Industry Classification (SIC) 2007 (ONS, 2007). This is in line with way in which industries are classified in the EU and the USA, which are the European Union industrial classification system, NACE and the United Nations International Standard Industrial Classifications, ISIC, respectively. The key benefit of this is that it provides a standard framework and consistency for the construction output data in principle when ensuring comparability at the European and global level. In addition, utilising SIC code classifications ensure that it is consistent for comparing industries within the same country. The ONS excludes property developers from the survey on the basis that most of their work is contracted out to firms that still fall within the sector. The ONS assumption of excluding firms classified as property developers on the basis that all major house builders sub-contract out the majority of the construction work may be valid but most do construction-related work to an extent and directly engage with teams employed in site management, skilled trades and other production functions that may be expected to fall within the scope of construction output.

The firms within the survey are selected from the government's Inter-Departmental Business Register (IDBR). The Inter-Departmental Business Register (IDBR) is a database of 2.6 million businesses across all sectors of the UK economy and provides the main sampling frame for surveys of businesses carried out by the ONS and other government departments across all industry sectors (ONS, 2018c). It is an important data source for analyses of business activities. The IDBR does not, however, include the smallest of UK businesses, which are those without employees and with a turnover below the threshold for paying tax.

The constraint of utilising firms within the SIC codes covering construction firms means that it does not include architects and other professionals such as quantity surveyors and planners. This is because these occupations are classified in the services sector rather than in the construction sector, although they are clearly important to facilitating construction activity. The exclusion of professional services firms presents its own set of issues when interpreting construction output time series, given that an increase in the number of design-and-build contracts means that contractors expect to undertake increasing amounts of the design work that previously would have been undertaken by consultants and architects employed directly by the client. This work would not be collected as construction output, but how this shift in practice has impacted on the level of design work undertaken directly or contracted out by contractors and how this may have impacted on the measure of construction output is unclear.

In addition, it does not include activity by construction occupations that may occur within other industry sectors. For instance, if civil engineers working for a water company undertake construction work in-house then it is not included in the ONS construction output data as the firm carrying out the construction work is classified within the water sector and the ONS estimates the employment and activity within the SIC category for water supply, sewerage, waste management and remediation activities. A similar principle would apply to construction activity undertaken in-house by local authorities and housing associations, which build and maintain social and affordable homes. Including this activity in the ONS construction output data would lead to double-counting. However, if the same activity were to be contracted out to a firm classified within construction then the ONS would estimate it as occurring within the infrastructure sector.

Furthermore, large firms may conduct activity across different sectors of the economy. Many large construction firms in the UK have increasingly conducted work within facilities management and support services over the last twenty years as they have attempted to diversify away from the volatile construction sector into areas in which activity is more stable. Facilities management and support services companies include activities for other firms that are sub-contracted out and includes activities as diverse as day-to-day maintenance and safety testing of facilities, cleaning offices, probation services for government and serving meals in schools. The ONS assigns an SIC to each business within the large company and then the SIC of the company is determined by which business provides the highest GVA. However, this also raises a key issue as the SIC of the large company may change over time depending on the fortunes of the businesses within the company and this reclassification of large companies may affect construction output figures. For instance, the reclassification of a large firm that was originally classified as support services to the SIC for construction in 2015 led to a structural break in the data, boosting activity particularly in the infrastructure sector by over £1 billion.

The construction output data were first produced by the statistics division of the UK government department, the Ministry of Works, in 1940 (Hansard, 1940). It produced a Quarterly Return of Employment and Output, based upon survey data that required respondents to supply the number of operatives and the value of construction output across different construction sectors. The Ministry of Works underwent changes of department until 1970 and was brought into the Department of Environment (DoE). During 1997, the Department of Environment and Department of Transport (DoT) merged to form the Department of Environment, Transport and the Regions (DETR). In 2001, responsibility for construction statistics moved to the Department of Trade and Industry (DTI), which became the Department of Business Enterprise and Regulatory Reform (BERR) during 2007. The most recent significant transfer of construction output data was in 2008 when the independent ONS took over responsibility for all construction data. Initially, the ONS utilised the previous methodology but, from January 2010, constructed a new construction output series that was in line with the methodology that the ONS uses in measuring activity in other industries (Crook and Sharp, 2010).

The construction output data pre-2010 and post-2010 are provided by the ONS as a continuous data series. However, there are significant concerns that the data contain a structural break, a shift in the data series during 2010 that is not explained by other data covering the construction industry. For example, the shift in use of methodology in determining construction output data occurred after the worst financial crisis in over 35 years that occurred in 2008 and subsequently construction output fell by 13 per cent during 2009. According to the new, revised ONS methodology, construction output rose by 9 per cent in 2010, recovering over half of the output lost in the recession while, simultaneously, employment within the construction industry fell by 6 per cent during 2010 (Gruneberg and Francis, 2019). Despite this, it is still useful for those interested in construction research to have a continuous series for data analysis as long as data issues such as these are considered within the context of the research.

The ONS construction output data are currently collected through a monthly survey from 8,000 firms that are sampled from the IDBR's 230,000 construction firms. Returns for businesses that do not respond are imputed and the data are weighted to generate estimates for the full population and the entire construction industry. Because the size of these construction firms varies, the survey of the population is stratified as follows: all firms that employ more than 100 or employ between 10 and 99 and have an annual turnover of £60 million or greater are included. Random samples are taken for firms employing zero to four employees, five to nine employees and 10 to 99 employees with a turnover of less than £60 million.

The survey requests data from construction firms on the value of output to the nearest £1,000 for work in construction sectors and sub-sectors that is chargeable to clients in the reference period in England, Scotland and Wales. As a result, the ONS construction output data is based on a survey covering only Great Britain. It does not cover work in Northern Ireland. The data for Northern Ireland are covered in a separate survey of 700 firms (NISRA, 2019a) called the Quarterly Construction Enquiry (NISRA, 2019b) carried out by the Northern Ireland Statistics and Research Agency (NISRA).

The ONS construction output survey asks respondents for values that include the following; work on buildings to be sold later (speculative work, in particular house building and commercial offices), work done by firms on their own business premises, fixtures, equipment and tools made by firms and used in construction as well as materials used by businesses, overheads and profits; labour costs on a firm's own payroll. However, the survey excludes payments made to sub-contractors, payments to architects and other consultants, fixtures, equipment and tools the business made for sale, materials the business sold, value of land and VAT. The ONS collects the values for work in the following 11 types of construction output:

- Private new housing
- Public new housing
- Private housing repair, maintenance and improvement
- Public housing repair, maintenance and improvement
- Infrastructure
- Infrastructure repair and maintenance
- Public non-housing
- Public non-housing repair and maintenance
- Private commercial

- Private industrial
- Private non-housing repair and maintenance

In construction output, the ONS treatment of repair and maintenance of existing facilities differs considerably between the housing and non-housing sectors. For private and public housing, the repair, maintenance and improvements sectors cover activity that includes changes to the home that improves and adds value to the property such as adding an extension or converting the loft into an additional office or bedroom. This is in addition to the basic repairs and maintenance of the home. However, for the repair and maintenance of public non-housing, private non-housing and infrastructure, only fixing something that is broken or maintaining the facility to an existing standard is included such as replacing a single glazed window in an office with similar glass or fixing a pothole. Any construction activity that added value to the non-housing facility would be covered within new work, even if it replaced a single pane window with double glazing in an office or the resurfacing a road.

Within the construction sector, measuring work done in a specific period is extremely challenging. Within manufacturing and retailing, firms have data on production and sales on a daily or a weekly basis. However, in construction, data may not be readily available or even available at all to firms filling in the ONS questionnaire. As a result, firms may use a proxy variable, for example, the value of new contracts received during the time period, the value of invoices raised or the value of invoices that been paid. This means that the ONS construction output may, in practice, be an aggregate of slightly differing measures.

Due to cost constraints and the burden on respondents, the monthly ONS construction output survey is not a census but is based on a sample of the industry that is then inflated to form a total for the entire construction industry. As a result, any outliers within the data would be exaggerated in the overall total. To take account of this possibility, the ONS assesses the survey responses for outliers and if the ONS suspects that there is an outlier then it may contact the firm to check the details of the response. If outliers appear to be in the construction output responses, the ONS uses an approach called the one-sided Winsorisation method (Lewis, 2007) to detect possible outliers. This involves determining thresholds for the construction output data beyond which values are considered outliers. Any values above the thresholds are reduced towards the threshold. Where businesses fail to respond to the survey, construction output values for the firm are estimated from a pattern of responses from similar types of businesses.

If firms do not respond to the survey, the ONS imputes a value for the firm, (ONS, 2018b). The type of imputation used depends on whether the non-response of the business is for a firm that has only just joined the sample for the first time or if it has been on the sample for one or more periods. If the firm has only just joined the sample, the ONS constructs a response based upon other firms. For every business in the population, the ONS weights the data from the sample of businesses to provide estimates for the full population. The weight is given by the average population register turnover divided by the average sample register turnover.

The ONS also adjusts for seasonal effects, which are effects that consistently appear in a month or quarter each year, such as Christmas or Summer for example. The purpose of this is to allow researchers to compare construction activity in a certain month or quarter with other months or quarters in the same year. For instance, a considerable proportion of the UK construction industry closes between Christmas and New Year. Consequently, without an adjustment for this, construction output in each December would almost always be lower than in November but this would reveal little about building activity occurring within the sector during this period. If an adjustment is made for a substantial proportion of the construction industry closing down between Christmas and New Year, then it facilitates a comparison of December's activity with that of November of that year or any month in any year. The seasonal adjustment, using historic trends over time, provides a clearer view of the underlying trends. The ONS uses a seasonal adjustment method called X-13ARIMA-SEATS, which was developed by the United States Census Bureau (US Census Bureau, n.d.) and is recommended for use by Eurostat, the European Commission's statistical agency (Eurostat, 2015). It should be noted that, as the monthly UK data have only been available since 2010, the seasonal adjustment for each month is currently based upon a small sample in an industry where activity is often volatile. The Eurostat statistical agency recommends that five years is the minimum time span needed to establish a seasonal pattern in monthly data for seasonal adjustment and, by the beginning of 2019, the ONS had almost nine years of monthly data. Nevertheless, significant revisions to seasonal patterns in the construction output data may occur until the seasonal adjustment has been developed in the longer-term.

The ONS construction output data is provided in value terms, called current prices and on a volume basis, called constant prices. Over time, the current prices data may increase due to rises in the volume of production, the price of production or, most often, both. Data in constant or real terms is vital, particularly for construction forecasters, to measure and forecast the actual volume of activity occurring, omitting the effects of price rises. A change in construction activity may be due to a combination of a change in the volume of production and price inflation. In order to establish the extent of the real change in output, the ONS needs to estimate the price of construction and inflation, or deflation, in construction prices over time. This is one of the most challenging aspects of dealing with the ONS construction output data.

Until recently price and cost indices were used to adjust for inflation in construction based on bills of quantities. However, changing procurement practices have meant that bills of quantities have declined in usage over the last twenty years and were rarely used in construction during 2018. As a result, the sample for estimating price inflation had deteriorated to the extent that it was no longer statistically robust (Yu and Ive, 2015; UK Statistics Authority, 2011a). The responsibility for construction price and cost indices was taken in-house by the ONS in April 2015. The distinction between real construction output and construction price inflation in Great Britain is very important, as can be seen in Figure 1.2. The volume of construction output, in constant prices, is the most useful for construction economists, many of whom use it as the basis for forecasting real construction output.

While current prices data are available for 11 sectors, the data in constant prices are only available for nine sectors (see Figure 1.3) due to the difficulties in estimating price inflation in different areas of non-housing repair and maintenance and improvements (RM&I).

Although the ONS only surveys firms on their construction output in current prices across 11 sectors and provides data in constant prices in nine sectors, the ONS does model the construction output data to provide users with construction output by sector and sub-sector in current prices on a quarterly basis. The purpose of this is that some of the construction sectors may be too generic to be useful. For example, within infrastructure, the ONS provides quarterly data split between water, sewerage, roads, rail, electricity and harbours. To estimate the splits of construction output, the ONS uses construction new orders data. This is provided by Barbour ABI (ONS, 2018d), who measure the number and value of construction contracts. This provides a value of orders at postcode level and by type. However, the relationship between construction contracts and the activity on site is not straightforward, given that the workload is spread over time, particularly on large projects and varies from contract to contract.

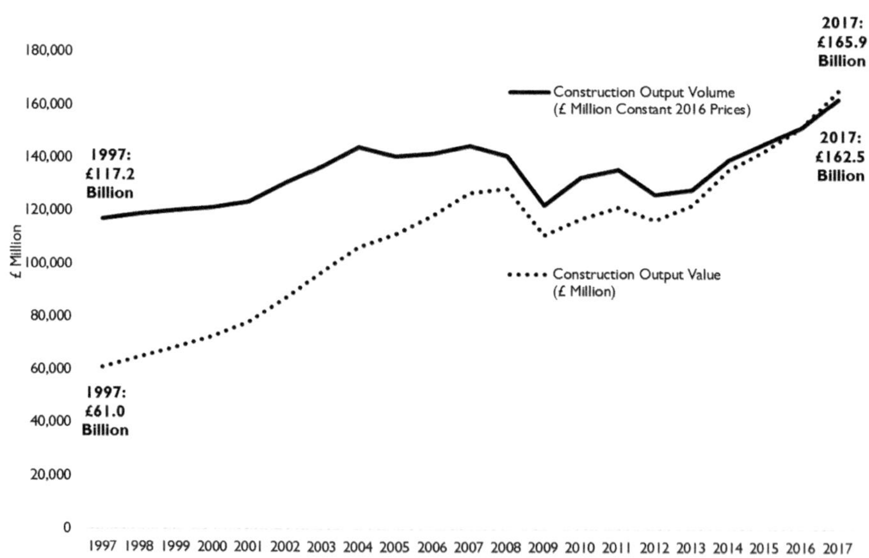

Figure 1.2 Construction Output Volume and Value in Great Britain between 1997 and 2017

Source: Table 2a, ONS Construction Output (2019)

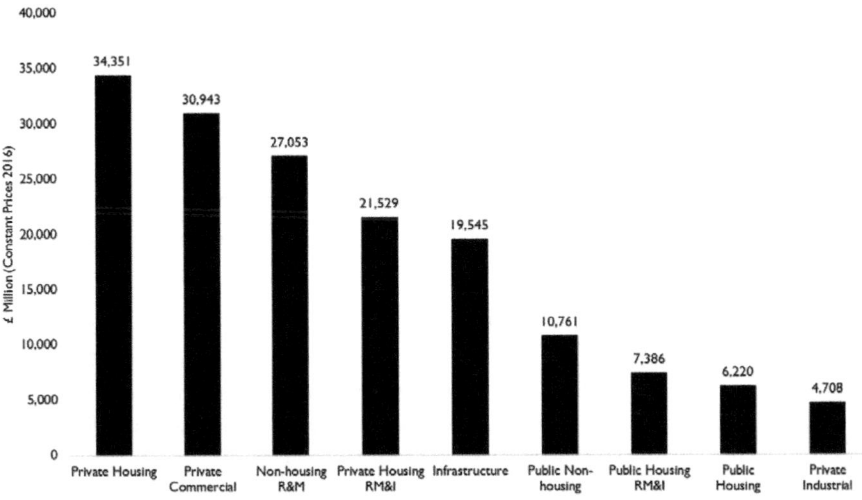

Figure 1.3 Construction Output Volume by Sector in Great Britain in 2017

Source: Table 2a, ONS Construction Output (2019)

The ONS projects forward values of orders in sub-sectors based on an average time lag between orders and output on projects in each sub-sector. The orders series does not cover repair and maintenance where there is considerably less information available. There are considerable issues in utilising this modelled approach. New orders may be cancelled or delayed and, therefore, the work is not carried out or not at the expected time respectively. The average time lag between orders and output is likely to distort the value of output in sectors, where there is generally a consistent lag but with exceptional cases of one-off very large projects. This is particularly the case with many parts of the infrastructure sector, such as the water, rail and energy sub-sectors, where most of the construction activity is determined under consistent five-year spending plans under the auspices of a regulator overseeing private company investment. However, in each of these sub-sectors, one-off major projects with an estimated cost of the £4.2 billion Thames Tideway Tunnel, the £16 billion Transport for London Crossrail railway line (renamed The Elizabeth Line) and the £19.6 billion nuclear reactor at Hinkley Point C are highly likely to have a considerably longer time gap between contracts being signed and activity on the ground when compared with projects, where companies have long-term relationships and contracts in place for repetitive but smaller projects.

Concluding remarks

Most macroeconomic variables were determined at a time when the economy was dominated by agriculture, manufacturing and financial services. In these activities, there are specific generic units that are relatively straightforward to measure. However, measuring construction output is a challenging activity. It is not one industry but a combination of several different types of activity, in which construction work on each project is bespoke. New teams are brought together on each project or programme of projects in different parts of the country in different construction markets. Despite this, it is vital that construction output is measured as accurately as possible in a manner that reflects the size, structure and changes in the sector.

The ONS has a clear definition of what it is measuring in terms of construction. However, the ONS faces considerable challenges in measuring activity within the industry within this definition. Furthermore, the definition is limited for a variety of reasons highlighted in this chapter and this implies that the direct value of construction to the UK economy is considerably underestimated. In addition, in viewing the construction industry in a similar manner to other sectors that provide a product to consumers ignores the large indirect impact of the construction industry, in which it operates more analogously to the financial sector in that it enables other sectors to operate and grow.

The lack of statistics that appropriately reflect the value and importance of the construction industry from a direct and indirect point of view undermines a full understanding of the construction supply chain as well as its benefits to the UK economy. It also hinders evidence-based policy by focusing investment, both public and private, on areas that merely have a higher short-term rate of return or direct benefit. In addition, if the structure of construction changes in the medium-term with a greater focus on technology, advanced and off-site manufacturing techniques, the measurement of construction and its value to the UK economy may be even more difficult to determine.

References

BEIS (2018). *Business Population Estimates for the UK and Regions, 2018: Methodology & Quality Note*. Available at: https://assets.publishing.service.gov.uk/government/uploads/system/uploads/attachment_data/file/746602/OFFICIAL_SENSITIVE_-_BPE_2018_-_methodology_note_FINAL_FINAL.pdf

Crook, T. and Sharp, G. (2010). Development of construction statistics, *Economic & Labour Market Review*, 4(3). Available at: www.ons.gov.uk/ons/rel/elmr/economic-and-labour-market-review/no – 3 – march-2010/development-of-construction-statistics.pdf

Eurostat (2015). *ESS Guidelines on Seasonal Adjustment*. Available at: https://ec.europa.eu/eurostat/documents/3859598/6830795/KS-GQ-15-001-EN-N.pdf/d8f1e5f5-251b-4a69-93e3-079031b74bd3

Gruneberg, S. and Francis, N. (2019). *The Economics of the Construction Industry*, Newcastle upon Tyne, Agenda.

Hansard (1940). *Ministry of Works and Buildings*. Available at: hansard.millbanksystems.com/commons/1940/oct/24/ministry-of-works-and-buildings

Lewis, D. (2007). Winsorization for estimates of change and outstanding issues with the implementation of Winsorization for level estimates. *13th Meeting of the National Statistics Methodology Advisory Committee*, Office for National Statistics (UK). Available at: www.ons.gov.uk/ons/guide-method/method-quality/advisory-committee/2005-2007/thirteenth-meeting/winsorisation-for-estimates-of-change.pdf

NISRA (2019a). *Construction Output Statistics – Methodology*, Northern Ireland Statistics and Research Agency. Available at: www.nisra.gov.uk/publications/construction-output-statistics-methodology

NISRA (2019b). *Construction Output Statistics*, Northern Ireland Statistics and Research Agency. Available at: www.nisra.gov.uk/statistics/economic-output-statistics/construction-output-statistics

ONS (2007). *UK Standard Industrial Classification of Economic Activities 2007 (UK SIC 2007), Newport*, Office for National Statistics. Available at: www.ons.gov.uk/ons/guide-method/classifications/current-standard-classifications/standard-industrial-classification/index.html

ONS (2011). *Output in the Construction Industry, Investigation into Lagged Responses*, Office for National Statistics, Newport. Available at: http://webarchive.nationalarchives.gov.uk/20160105160709/www.ons.gov.uk/ons/rel/construction/output-in-the-construction-industry/investigation-into-lagged-response/index.html

ONS (2018a) *Annual Business Survey, Office for National Statistics*. Available at: www.ons.gov.uk/file?uri=/businessindustryandtrade/business/businessservices/datasets/uknonfinancialbusinesseconomyannualbusinesssurveysectionsas/current/abssectionsas.xls

ONS (2018b). *Annual Business Survey 2017*, Office for National Statistics, Newport. Available at: www.ons.gov.uk/file?uri=/businessindustryandtrade/business/businessservices/datasets/uknonfinancialbusinesseconomyannualbusinesssurveysectionsas/current/abssectionsas.xls

ONS (2018c). *Inter-Departmental Business Register (IDBR)*, Office for National Statistics, Newport. Available at: www.ons.gov.uk/aboutus/whatwedo/paidservices/interdepartmentalbusinessregisteridbr

ONS (2018d). *Construction Development: Improvements to Regional and Sub-Sector Level Estimates*, June 2018. Available at: https://www.ons.gov.uk/businessindustryandtrade/constructionindustry/articles/constructiondevelopmentimprovementstoregionalandsubsectorlevelestimatesjune2018/2018-06-04/pdf

ONS (2019). *Construction Industry*, Office for National Statistics, Newport. Available at: www.ons.gov.uk/businessindustryandtrade/constructionindustry www.ons.gov.uk/businessindustryandtrade/constructionindustry/methodologies/constructionoutputqualityandmethodologyinformation

UK Sections (2018). *Business Population Estimates 2018*. Available at: https://assets.publishing.service.gov.uk/government/uploads/system/uploads/attachment_data/file/746600/OFFICIAL_SENSITIVE_-_BPE_2018_-_detailed_tables.xls

UK Statistics Authority (2011a). *Review of an Error in the Published Estimate of Output in Construction*, UK Statistics Authority. Available at: www.statisticsauthority.gov.uk/news/review-of-an-error-in-the-published-estimates-of-output-in-construction/

UK Statistics Authority (2011b). *Assessment of Compliance with the Code of Practice for Official Statistics: Construction Price and Cost Indices*, UK Statistics Authority. Available at: www.statisticsauthority.gov.uk/wp-content/uploads/2015/12/images-assessment-report-95-construction-price-and-cost-indices_tcm97-38289.pdf

US Census Bureau (n.d.). *The X-13ARIMA-SEATS Seasonal Adjustment Program*, United Stated Census Bureau. Available at: www.census.gov/srd/www/x13as/

Yu, M. and Ive, G. (2015). A review of construction cost and price indices in Britain, in Best, R. and Meikle, J. (eds.) *Measuring Construction: Prices, Output and Productivity*, London, Routledge.

2 Construction output as gross fixed capital formation

Gerard de Valence and Jim Meikle

Introduction

National statistical agencies get a moment in the spotlight when releasing economic data for gross domestic product (GDP) but, underneath the simple percentage change in GDP that gets all the attention, there are many layers of data about the flow of economic activity through the economy. One of those layers is output at the industry level, the production of goods and services measured as value added by the identifiable industries within the economy, as defined by the United Nations *System of National Accounts* (UN, 2008a). One of those industries is called construction, which covers building and infrastructure work carried out by contractors or sometimes in-house by infrastructure firms such as water companies. Also, households undertake construction work in less developed countries and even in advanced economies, where it may form a small proportion of building work but is nevertheless significant. Construction as a share of GDP varies widely around the world. However, there is a rough framework where rapidly growing emerging economies have a high ratio of construction value added to GDP, often well over 10 per cent and slower growing developed economies where the share is less than 10 per cent (Girardi and Mura, 2014).

Everywhere, the work done on building and construction is a major contributor to economic activity, measured as total industry output and employment and thus to GDP. However, for many people employed in or associated with an industry, the output and activity statistics for that industry are probably more widely known and used than the headline number for GDP. Those statistics frame the view that people then use in their research and analysis on the state of the industry, within the boundaries defined through the selection of data sources. Where those boundaries are and how the data is collected and presented are technical questions that receive less attention. Those questions are the ones addressed here.

The chapter starts with the measurement of Gross Domestic Product (GDP) and then focuses on one of its components known as Gross Fixed Capital Formation (GFCF). This is total spending on investment over the previous period, and this is where construction output is found and thus the contribution of construction expenditure to GDP in a country (Gruneberg and Folwell, 2013). Building and construction, the other components of GFCF and the structure of the supply and use tables that GDP is calculated from are detailed. This leads into the country sections, where the specific data used to calculate construction GFCF is identified in the United States (US), Canada, Australia and the United Kingdom (UK). Similarities and differences between the methods used in those countries are identified and discussed in the final section.

There are several different measures of construction output used in producing Construction GFCF, which is a composite number like GDP itself, and these are reviewed before a discussion of their relative strengths and weaknesses. How the separate measures for residential building, non-residential building and engineering construction are sourced and combined is covered, as are the statistical techniques applied to those measures. This then leads into a discussion of inclusions and exclusions in the data. The conclusion covers what we know and don't know about construction output.

A note on presentation is required. Documents are cited in the usual way, but national statistical agencies have extensive web sites and when used as a source links are given in the endnotes. The names of surveys and statistical publications are italicised and the relevant catalogue or table number given. Finally, in the country sections, when used, all monetary values are in the local currency.

Construction in the expenditure approach and capital account

If there is a single number that defines an economy it is GDP, typically given as a country's annual total output of goods and services and its aggregate demand for those goods and services. However, GDP is not directly measured or observed, it is built up from measurements of components of an economy, which are combined to get to the aggregate number for GDP, (Vanoli, 2005). Those components are households, businesses and private sector organisations, and government and the public sector.

Compounding this, there are three different aggregates used in estimating GDP: the income measure adds wages, salaries and profit shares of the economy; the production measure adds the contribution of the different industries to the economy; and the expenditure measure adds the spending of households, business and government together. Known as the triple identity the three measures are used to check the accuracy of GDP and, although never the same, any major differences between them point to problems somewhere in the process of collecting and analysing the data used to produce the national accounts. The three approaches are shown in Table 2.1 and arrive at slightly different estimates for

Table 2.1 The three approaches to GDP

Production Account	GDP by the output approach is gross value added
Expenditure Approach	GDP by the expenditure approach is consumption + gross capital investment + net exports
Income Account	GDP by the income approach is compensation of employees + gross operating surplus + gross mixed income

an economy because they follow different methodologies. How a set of national accounts is presented, with the data points defined and laid out following an agreed template, is based on the United Nations *System of National* Accounts (UN, 2008a).

The expenditure approach adds household spending on consumption to business and government investment in fixed assets (those used in production) and trade with the rest of the world as net exports. This gives the formula for GDP as C+I+G+NX, or consumption plus investment plus government plus net exports equals total expenditure. For macroeconomic policy the expenditure approach provides a means to assess the effects on consumers (households) and producers (firms) of economic conditions, or changes in those conditions. In developed economies their spending, on consumption and investment, typically accounts for over 80 per cent of GDP. The expenditure approach is also included in many countries' annual budget papers, and changes in key variables like consumption, investment, prices and trade flows included in the account are widely reported. Table 2.2 shows the components of the expenditure approach, included is GFCF, which is total investment in buildings, structures, plant, equipment, software and R&D. Investment in buildings and structures is measured as construction work done, so this is where the output of the construction industry appears in the national accounts, the only industry to be individually identified in those accounts.

One of the insights of national accounting is that money not spent on consumption can be saved and spent on investment that enhances the economy's productive capacity:

> In the national accounts, investment is the purchase of machinery, software, infrastructure and buildings, and inventories. Together these are called gross capital formation (GCF). When changes in inventories is excluded, with only the purchases of buildings, structures, software and machinery included, the result is known as gross fixed capital formation (GFCF). This measures

Table 2.2 How the capital account by type of asset and sector is displayed

Gross fixed capital formation Assets	*Non-financial corporations*	*Financial corporations*	*General Government*	*Households*
Dwellings				
Other buildings and structures				
Machinery and equipment				
Weapons systems				
Cultivated biological resources				
Intellectual property				
Costs of ownership transfer of non-produced assets				

Source: System of National Accounts (UN, 2008a: 203).

> total expenditures on products intended for use in future production, "gross" means the expenditure is measured without deducting the consumption of fixed capital (the wear and tear).
>
> (Lequiller and Blades, 2014: 25)

GFCF is defined as the 'net acquisition of produced fixed assets', which are assets intended for use in the production of goods and services in the future (for more than a year). Net acquisitions means that GFCF deducts sales of fixed assets on the second-hand market from purchases of fixed assets, and produced assets were traditionally physical, material assets like buildings and machinery. However, during revisions of the SNA in 1993 and 2008 intangible assets like software were included as investment in intellectual property, so GFCF now has two types of assets, material and intellectual. Material fixed assets are: dwellings (excluding land); other buildings and structures (excluding land); transport equipment; and other machinery and equipment. GFCF in dwellings and other buildings and structures does not include the value of the land on which they are situated because land is not a produced asset. Intellectual property fixed assets include: R&D; mineral exploration; computer software and databases; and entertainment, literary and artistic originals. Different countries have different approaches to these intangible assets and the inclusion of expenditure on software, R&D and trademarks are investment.

The figures for these components of GFCF are found in the *Capital Account*, one of the supporting tables of data that GDP is based on. Here GFCF is broken down into its constituents, across the four institutional sectors the economy is divided into by the *System of National Accounts*, as shown in Table 2.2.

In the long run, the investment measured by GFCF determines economic growth and the level of labour productivity and thus incomes and living standards. The GFCF of households is the purchase of dwellings (excluding land) and of business the spending on plant, equipment, buildings, and structures and intellectual property. The GFCF of general government is physical infrastructure (transport, power etc.), social infrastructure (schools, hospitals etc.) and military defence systems. However, the GFCF of the business sector is the largest single component of investment, and changes in the amount of business investment have a big influence on the business cycle and are highly correlated with the beginning and end of economic cycles (Kohlscheen et al., 2018). Investment in buildings and structures is around half of total GFCF in the countries covered in Table 2.3.

Table 2.3 demonstrates the importance of construction, in most countries accounting for around 50 per cent of total GFCF when dwellings and other buildings and structures are combined. But where do these estimates of construction work done, or industry output, come from? It is implicitly understood that countries follow the SNA when preparing and presenting their national accounts, but what does this mean in practice? To answer those questions the processes and procedures followed by the statistical agencies in four countries are outlined in the sections on the US, Canada, Australia and the UK. These agencies have

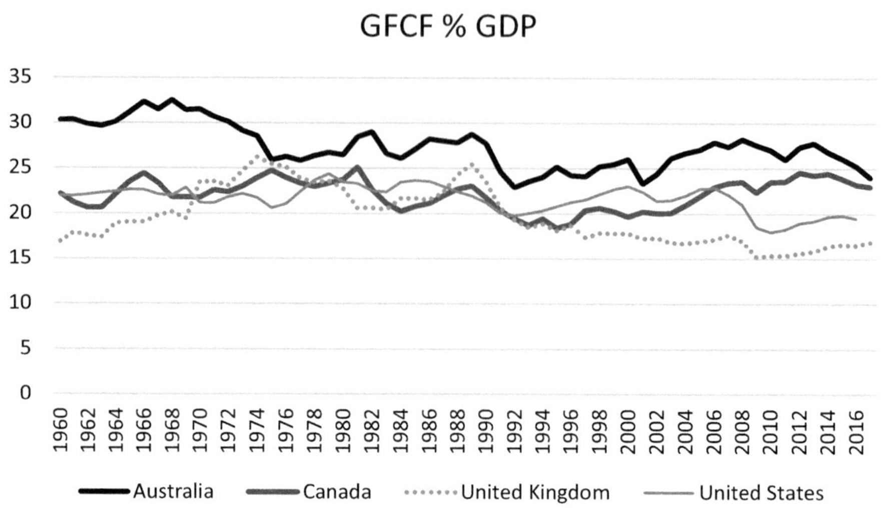

Figure 2.1 GFCF as per cent of GDP

Source: World Bank (2019)

Table 2.3 Percentage shares of total GFCF, average by country 1997–2017

Country	*Dwellings*	*Other buildings and structures*	*All construction*	*Machinery and equipment*	*Intellectual property*
Austria	19.8	29.6	49.4	33.9	16.5
Canada	28.0	32.7	60.7	25.81	13.4
Colombia	16.5	46.5	63.0	23.8	1.3
Czech Rep.	12.6	31.0	43.6	44.8	11.1
Denmark	22.5	23.8	46.3	32.92	20.8
Estonia	12.8	40.3	53.1	40.6	6.0
Finland	26.2	28.0	54.2	24.9	20.7
France	27.3	26.8	54.1	24.1	21.5
Germany	28.3	20.4	48.7	34.9	16.4
Greece	29.5	25.9	51.4	35.5	8.9
Ireland	26.7	23.3	50.0	28.7	21.3
Israel	28.9	19.8	58.7	30.8	20.5
Italy	25.8	25.6	51.4	35.2	13.2
Japan	14.8	30.6	45.4	28.4	20.6
Korea	15.2	38.6	53.8	30.7	15.5
Latvia	10.4	39.1	49.5	43.3	6.6
Netherlands	23.9	27.6	51.6	28.4	19.8
New Zealand	25.6	26.4	52.0	34.8	13.2
Norway	19.0	43.6	62.6	24.9	12.5
Portugal	22.7	35.1	57.8	30.2	10.7
Slovak Rep.	11.1	33.6	44.7	44.8	7.7
Slovenia	13.4	35.6	49.0	38.3	12.2
Spain	30.9	30.2	61.1	28.6	9.9
Sweden	15.1	22.2	37.3	34.7	27.7
United Kingdom	20.1	33.2	53.3	25.9	20.4
United States	20.1	22.5	42.6	25.7	23.6

Source: ONS, 2017: 13. The table shows the average spend on each of the assets as a percentage of GFCF over the 20 years 1997 to 2017. Column for All Construction added.

been developing a more detailed version of their input-output tables, which have been used for many years to track the value of flows between industries and have over the last few years started producing supply and use tables, which track flows of products between industries. These supply and use tables have become an important source of data for estimating GFCF. A discussion on the similarities and differences between these countries processes and methodologies follows.

Balancing the different measures of GDP

Supply and use tables are the building blocks for national accounts and are used to ensure GDP is balanced for all three approaches (production, expenditure and income) and together they provide the annual benchmarks and quarterly estimates. They allow calculation of GDP by the three approaches outlined above and are used to achieve consistency in the economic aggregates by linking value added, inputs, outputs and final demand. Because the income, production and expenditure measures of GDP can all be calculated from the supply and use tables, a single estimate of GDP can be produced. The cells in the table are the lowest level of data in the system and show the flows of economic activity needed to get to GDP and GFCF. These are:

1 Composition and value of goods and services entering final demand
2 Outputs and incomes generated in the production process
3 Intermediate transactions that form inputs into these processes

The supply and use tables reconcile how the supply of products by domestic production or imports are used, for intermediate consumption, final consumption, capital formation, change in inventories or exports. The supply and use framework has columns for industries and rows for products, presented as a matrix. The industries are defined in a Standard Industrial Classification (UN, 2003; see de Valence (2019) for construction in the SIC), and the products are defined in the Central Product Classification (UN, 2015), an international standard that classifies products based on the physical characteristics of goods or on the nature of the services rendered. Construction is industry E in the SIC, subdivided first into contractors and trade services, then into the more detailed categories of groups, classes and subclasses. The tables provide an integrated framework of the total supply of goods and services from domestic and foreign producers, called 'products', available for use in the economy. Table 2.4 shows how rows and columns in the supply and use tables are displayed.

Table 2.4 How rows and columns in the supply and use tables are displayed

Supply table		*Use table*	
	Industry output		Industry consumption
Output by product		Products consumed	

The products produced and consumed in the Central Product Classification are subdivided into a hierarchical, five-level structure. At the highest level are sections, which subdivide products into broad groupings such as "Agriculture, forestry and fishery products" (section 0) or "Community, social and personal services" (section 9). The classification is then organized into successively more detailed categories, which are two-digit divisions, three-digit groups, four-digit classes, and five-digit subclasses. Construction and construction services are section 5. Construction, in division 53, covers the physical outputs of construction activities of buildings and civil engineering works. Construction services, in division 54, cover the trade services provided in constructing buildings and structures, subdivided into general and specialized construction services.

Typically, the main source of data to generate the product breakdown of GFCF is a survey asking businesses detailed questions about the type of capital items they purchase and dispose of. This produces annual estimates for each industry and a profile for the industry of spending across the asset categories of machinery and equipment, construction and intellectual property (IP) within the Central Product Classification. This data in the rows is then reconciled in the supply and use tables with the industry data in the columns, a process known as balancing, shown in Table 2.5. Reconciliation is done through iteration, until industry inputs and outputs equal product demand and supply and is reached when the income, expenditure and production approaches all produce the same estimate of current price GDP. Construction data from Government and other organisations is gathered from statutory and regulatory reports.

These supply and use statistics measure the production of products by industry, the flows of products purchased by each industry, the distribution of sales for each product and the incomes earned from production in each industry. When estimates for GFCF components are described as 'derived', it means they are based on these tables, with the current estimate an adjustment of the table's values using new data from business surveys and administrative data like building permits (approvals) and commencements. For the construction component of GFCF, all four of the countries included here produce versions of such derived estimates.

The difference between the construction industry and the construction product is important. By using products as the basic building blocks, GFCF is a different measure of construction output to the industry-based measure of output as value added, because GFCF includes construction work done by organisations and firms not classified as construction contractors or special trades in the SIC. Industries like the real estate industry do construction work and industries such

Table 2.5 Balancing supply and use of products with inputs and outputs

For industries	*For products*
Inputs from the use table equals outputs from the supply table	Supply from the supply table equals demand from the use table

as utilities (water, sewerage, gas and electricity), transport (airports, rail) and telecommunications undertake construction work without hiring contractors. This output for own use is added to the supply table for the enterprises in the industries they reside in. GFCF is recorded in the use table at the same value, meaning that this transaction is balanced in terms of its impact on total supply and total use.[1]

United States

The measurement of economic activity in the US is detailed in the *Concepts and Methods of the U.S. National Income and Product Accounts* (NIPA, 2017). Construction expenditure for the private sector comes from the Private Fixed Investment statistics and for the public sector is found in Government Gross Investment. The underlying data set for both is the Census Bureau's monthly construction statistics.

Government Gross Investment is spending by government on fixed assets, most of which is in a category called structures, or building and construction work done. It includes production of fixed assets by government for own use and investment by federal, state and local government enterprises. The federal data comes from the budget and for structures is the value of work put in place by or for the government and its agencies. At the state and local level, the data is based on a five-yearly economic census and an annual sample through a *Survey of State and Local Finances*. For state and local gross investment, the estimates for structures, which account for over three-quarters of their total, are based on Census Bureau monthly construction statistics.

For the private sector in the *National Income and Product Accounts*, gross private fixed investment includes non-residential fixed investment in structures, equipment and intellectual property and residential fixed investment in structures and equipment. This investment in structures by private business is building and engineering construction work done, thus industry output for the US private sector. Gross private fixed investment appears in the Domestic Income and Product Account (Account 1) and in the Domestic Capital Account (Account 6) as a component of gross domestic investment. What are included as structures is listed in Table 6.1 in the national income and product accounts (NIPA, 2017), which:

- Includes construction of new non-residential and residential buildings
- Includes improvements (additions, alterations and major structural replacements) to non-residential and residential buildings
- Includes certain types of equipment (such as plumbing and heating systems and elevators) that are considered an integral part of the structure
- Includes non-building construction (such as pipelines, railroad tracks, power lines and plants and dams and levees)
- Includes mobile structures (such as office trailers at construction sites and temporary trailer classrooms) and manufactured homes

- Includes petroleum and natural gas well drilling and exploration, including "dry holes"
- Includes digging and shoring of mines
- Includes brokers' commissions on sales of new and existing non-residential structures and includes brokers' commissions and other ownership transfer costs on sales of new and existing residential structures
- Includes net purchases (purchases less sales) of existing structures from governments
- But excludes maintenance and repair of non-residential and residential buildings
- And excludes demolition costs not related to the construction of new structures

In this system, non-residential structures covers all new non-residential building and engineering construction, improvements and equipment that is part of the structure (such as plumbing, heating and electrical systems), and residential structures is new construction of single-family and multifamily housing units, improvements (additions, alterations and major structural replacements) and some types of equipment (such as heating and air conditioning equipment). In NIPA, Table 5.4 data is presented on the dozens of different types of building and construction projects and their associated expenses that are included in the total. This data comes from a range of sources, but the most important is the Census Bureau Monthly Construction Spending, which collects the core data on work done and, through *The Value of Construction Put in Place Survey*, provides monthly estimates of the total dollar value of construction work done in the U.S.:

> Value put in place is measured as the sum of the cost of materials installed or erected; cost of labour supplied by contractors and by project owners; and a proportionate share of the cost of construction equipment rental, contractors' profit, cost of architectural and engineering work, miscellaneous overhead and office costs chargeable to the project on the owners' books, and interest and taxes paid during construction.
>
> (NIPA, 2017: 6–9)

How value put in place is measured is through a monthly *Construction Progress Reporting Survey*. Owners of selected projects report on the value of work done each month from project start through completion and the survey collects data on expenditures for four types of construction: privately-owned non-residential construction, state and local public construction, privately-owned multi-family and federal construction projects. The survey currently covers about 6,500 private non-residential; 10,500 state and local; 1,500 multi-family; and 700 federal projects each month. According to their website,[2] the final *Construction Spending* data is a combination of directly measured data from this survey and interpolation and extrapolation of survey estimates to extend coverage. The *Construction Survey* accounts for 65 per cent of the total monthly value of construction output, with estimates used for the other 35 per cent of work done.[3] With maintenance and repair of non-residential and residential buildings not included in the definition, or data, a substantial but unknown amount of actual work done is missing from these estimates of total work done.

The value of non-residential work done is extrapolated from the Bureau of Economic Analysis (BEA) benchmark input-output accounts, based on value put in place from the monthly construction survey. For investment in new single-family structures the value of work done is based on housing starts and average construction costs. Both the annual and quarterly estimates are based on the Census Bureau's monthly construction statistics on the value of new construction put in place using data from its monthly survey of new residential construction, with costs estimated separately for units built to be sold or rented and for units built by an owner or on contract. The Census Bureau then applies a 'construction progress pattern':

> The estimated cost of all single-family units started is then distributed into monthly value put in place by applying fixed 12-month patterns of monthly construction progress. The patterns vary somewhat depending on the particular month the unit is started; in general, the progress pattern assumes that about 16 percent of the project is completed in the first month, about 23 percent in the second month, about 20 percent in the third month, about 15 percent in the fourth month, about ten percent in the fifth month, and the remainder is distributed in declining amounts over the succeeding seven months.
>
> (NIPA, 2007: 6–28)

The sampled industry data and the modelled estimates that provide the monthly *Value of Construction Put in Place* are then used to find the gross private fixed investment and gross government investment estimates for structures. The principal source data used for both government and private gross fixed investment estimates are the BEA benchmark input-output accounts, which are based on the Census Bureau's *Economic Census*, supplemented by their annual and monthly surveys. These benchmark accounts detail the flow of goods and services from each industry to other industries and final users and are prepared at five-year intervals based on the *Economic Census*. The benchmark accounts determine the structure and level of GDP in the *National Income and Product accounts*.

For structures, the benchmark year input-output estimates are based on the *Economic Census* and the Census Bureau's monthly survey of construction spending. The estimates of structures for non-benchmark years use the monthly construction spending data to extrapolate the benchmark-year estimates, assuming constant proportion for periods after the benchmark year (i.e. the relative shares of residential and non-residential construction in the benchmark estimates remain unchanged). The *Economic Census* is conducted every five years by the Census Bureau, covering the whole U.S. economy except agriculture and government, which are covered by their own censuses. The benchmark year also underpins the

National Income and Product Accounts, where construction output appears in the GDP Expenditures Approach as investment in structures. According to the BEA:

> Annual and quarterly estimates of investment in most structures are extrapolated using the Census Bureau's *Value of Construction Put in Place* report. This report combines survey data, regulatory report data, and trade source data to estimate construction spending. For example, housing starts and sales data from the Survey of Construction are used to estimate residential single-family construction, and data from the Construction Progress Reporting Survey are used for most non-residential construction spending. Brokers' commissions, which are capitalized and included in residential housing investment, are extrapolated using Census Bureau data on new home sales and prices and trade-source data on existing home sales and prices.
>
> (Landefeld et al., 2008: 204)

In GDP, this construction spending is found in GFCF as non-residential and residential construction. At the highest level of reporting, in the national accounts, this is construction output. It is gross output, measured without deduction of consumption of fixed capital, which is a measure of capital used up in production (gross private fixed investment less consumption of fixed capital equals net private fixed investment). In the US, it excludes maintenance and repair of non-residential and residential buildings and structures. However, the US version of the 2008 revision of the SNA added a new category called construction intellectual property, which mainly breaks out purchases of software by firms classified to the construction industry.

Canada

The Canadian System of National Accounts (Statistics Canada, 2008)[4] details production of income, generation of income, distribution of income and use of income for six major institutional sectors. The expenditure account with GFCF is below in Table 2.6, showing the long run average share of GDP of consumption as 76 per cent of GDP and investment contributing 24 per cent, divided between Government with four per cent and Business with 19 per cent. Between 2006 and 2017 the main components of construction averaged 17 per cent of GDP, made up of seven per cent residential, six per cent non-residential and four per cent government fixed investment (identified by Statistics Canada as primarily spending on buildings and structures).[5] In Table 2.6 below these long-run averages do not add to 100 per cent, and the business components are shown separately.

Canadian GDP is first reported in the production account, which is the first account in the Canadian system. Output is a measure of goods and services produced, and intermediate consumption is goods and services consumed when generating output goods and services, with net value added the difference between the two: output less intermediate consumption. Gross domestic product is the sum of all value added in the economy, found in the Canadian *Supply, Use and*

Table 2.6 Average share of GDP of GFCF components in Canada

GDP	*2006–17 Avg share*	
Final consumption expenditure	76	
Gross fixed capital formation	24	
Business gross fixed capital formation	19	
Residential structures		7
Non-residential structures		6
Machinery and equipment		4
Intellectual property products		2
General government gross fixed capital formation	4	

Source: Statistics Canada. Table 36-10-0222-01 Gross domestic product, expenditure-based GDP at current prices.

Input-Output Tables,[6] which are set up on a year-by-year basis rather than in time series.

All these statistics are annual and 'are produced with a lag of up to three years after the reference year. It takes this much time to assemble the large and detailed database that is used to compile the supply and use tables'. The monthly estimates of real GDP by industry are calculated first for the years with annual supply and use estimates of gross value added available (the benchmark years) and then the years that follow, up to and including the current year. The monthly series derived for each industry in the first step are extended forward into the current years based on the movement of the monthly output volume indicators in those years collected by surveys.[7]

The main construction statistics publication is the monthly *Investment in Building Construction*, which 'represents the spending value of building construction by households, enterprises and governments for buildings, excluding the value of land'. It is based on data from the *Building Permits Survey*, plus starts and completions data from the Canada Mortgage and Housing Corporation for the residential sector. The monthly *Building Permits Survey* collects data on the 'value of permits issued by Canadian municipalities for both residential and non-residential buildings and the number of residential dwellings authorized. The survey also measures the number of dwelling units demolished, type of project, type of work and the total building area. It covers 2,400 Canadian municipalities and 95 per cent of the population. The *Building Permits Survey* collects information about construction intentions, which are then matched with Canada Mortgage and Housing Corporation data on housing starts and with the *Public and Private Investment Survey* data for the non-residential sector.

For *Investment in Building Construction*, non-residential building activity is 'modelled based on building permits issued by municipalities and confirmed where possible by Statistics Canada analysts'. Non-residential buildings are defined by type of asset and grouped into commercial, industrial and institutional components. All projects have a delay (the time between a permit being received and work beginning) and duration (the length of time it normally takes to complete a particular type of project) and the coefficients for these work put-in-place patterns distribute the value of building permits according to project length. The work put in place coefficients are used to distribute the value of construction investment over the project's duration.

Statistics Canada also publishes *Residential Construction Investment* quarterly, covering spending by individuals, enterprises and governments on the construction of new residential dwellings, renovation work and the acquisition costs. 'All investment for residential buildings (single, doubles, rows and apartments) as well as all renovations' are captured for eventual inclusion in the Canadian System of National Accounts. The four-step process used to incorporate the delay and duration aspects of building projects, and the calculation of the work put in place coefficients, outlines the methodology followed. How this modelling works is explained in Statistics Canada (n.d.) *Investment in New Residential Building Construction (Work put in place) Methodology* paper.

Residential investment is calculated by combining the number of housing starts and completions from Canada Mortgage and Housing Corporation with a provincial average value of projects from the *Building Permit Survey*. Work put in place patterns are then assigned to each province and each type of dwelling. The estimate for work put in place is found through a four-step process. The first and second steps are to get the monthly *Building Permits* survey, which gathers building permits information covering 95 per cent of the Canadian population, and calculate the realization rate, which is the proportion of newly authorised units from the *Building Permits Survey* that will be started in the current month. Projects are then given a starting cost based on the average permit value and the realisation rate for the previous four months.

In step three, projects are given a duration using the number of housing starts and completions from Canada Mortgage and Housing Corporation, which gives a count for the number of active projects in a province in the month. The last step is to apply the work put in place coefficients and use those estimated monthly numbers to arrive at a work done estimate. The work put in place coefficients determine how long it will take to complete a project, and since 2018 are based on a ten-year average from the US *Value of Construction Put in Place Survey*. This duration adjusted number of residential units being built is then multiplied by the starting cost (as found through calculating the realisation rate) to get the value of work put in place, or construction output. Residential investment is this estimate for work done on units started in a quarter, plus the work done on housing starts from previous quarters not yet completed.

The quarterly *Residential Construction Investment* takes the building permits data from the monthly *Investment in Building Construction* to incorporate into the national accounts and GDP figures, which underlines again the importance of construction data in overall GDP. The estimates for the value of non-residential work put in place are modelled each month as the building permits data is processed: 'Month to month, quarter to quarter and year to year trend analyses are conducted on the estimates nationally, by province and by type of structure in order to analyse large changes in the data. Such data movements are validated by examining the permit micro data, by consulting other data sources and by consulting internal stakeholders.'

There is also a Canadian *Annual Capital and Repair Expenditures Survey, which* collects data on the intentions for capital expenditures in the next year and expenditures for the previous two years. It uses 'a stratified random sample survey of business establishments classified both geographically and to their version of the North American Industry Classification System (NAICS) Canada 2012, with a cross-sectional design'. The survey covers machinery and equipment, non-residential building construction, non-residential engineering construction and repair and maintenance. 'The estimates for the construction sector (NAICS 23) are generated entirely from administrative data from Canada Revenue Agency and Institute de la Statistique du Québec, on the Cost of Acquisition for NAICS 23.' Engineering construction data is also collected through a survey of oil and gas capital expenditure.

For industries, the sampling error and response rate are combined into a quality rating code that ranges from A to F, where A is excellent quality and estimates with an F are not published. The GFCF data for Construction is an A and repair and maintenance is graded B. Also, like other agencies Statistics Canada has been reviewing and upgrading their systems and introduced a new survey model called the Integrated Business Statistics Program in 2013. Since 2015, the *Annual Capital and Repair Expenditures Survey* has used the new system.

Despite the importance of repair and maintenance, none of the other countries discussed here survey repair and maintenance (R&M) directly as Canada does with the *Annual Capital and Repair Expenditures Survey*. The extra level of detail is revealing. The long run average share of construction is 61 per cent of total capital expenditure, of which nine per cent is repair, while machinery and equipment is 39 per cent with repair 17 per cent, shown in Table 2.7. When these capital expenditures by business on construction and machinery and equipment repair are added together they were three per cent of Canadian GDP in 2016, and the share of repair in GDP ranged from three to four per cent over the period 2006 to 2016 (latest data). The other countries collect data on residential R&M and additions and alterations, but not business expenditure.

Between 2006 and 2016 construction R&M averaged 9 per cent of total capital expenditure, or around 1.2 per cent of GDP, ranging between 1 per cent of GDP

Table 2.7 Capital expenditures in Canada

Per cent of total	*2006–16 Avg share*
Capital, construction	61
Capital, machinery and equipment	39
Repair, construction	9
Repair, machinery and equipment	17

Source: Statistics Canada. Table: 34-10-0035-01 Capital and repair expenditures, non-residential tangible assets.

in 2006 and 1.3 per cent in 2012. In 2016, Canadian GDP was $2.1 trillion and construction repair was $25 billion. This data is important because it is the best guide available on the direct contribution of business spending on repair and maintenance of the built environment to GDP in a developed OECD economy.

Australia

In the national accounts, gross output is the value of goods and services produced in a period, including production that remains incomplete at the end of that period. Both nominal and volume measures of output are used, the former providing estimates at current prices and the latter deflated estimates with the effect of price changes removed. Nominal gross output is defined as the total value of goods and services produced at basic prices, which is the amount received by the producer from sales, including any subsidies received and excluding taxes on production. Nominal value added is the difference between nominal gross output and nominal intermediate inputs, which is the value of all goods and services used as inputs to the production process (ABS, 2006).

While the nominal, current price estimates of value of work done reflect both price and volume changes, chain volume estimates measure changes in value after the direct effects of price changes have been eliminated and therefore only reflect real volume changes. The base year of the chained price index is moved forward each year, so the current period is also the equivalent of current prices, however the prices used in the volume estimates are their consumer and producer price indexes, produced through the supply and use tables. Data is given as trend and seasonally adjusted, and the ABS also publishes current prices. The deflated volume measures are obtained from the nominal measures using chained Laspeyres indexes to remove the effect of price change. (Construction price indexes have been discussed by Yu and Ive, 2015; Diewert, 2009; de Valence, 2001, Drew et al., 2016 among others).

Building and construction output is industry value added, published quarterly as *Construction Activity: Chain Volume Measures* (ABS 8782). First estimates for the previous quarter are published as *Construction Work Done, Australia* (ABS 8755). In *Construction Activity: Chain Volume Measures* are estimates of building and engineering construction work done during the last quarter and revised estimates for previous quarters. This is industry output. The data these estimates are based on come from two quarterly surveys of work done, the *Building Activity Survey* (ABS 8752) and the *Engineering Construction Survey* (ABS 8762) respectively. Each survey covers 'approximately 95% of the value of work done during the current quarter'. The publication lag is four months, for example the September quarter is released in January. The preliminary estimates have a publication lag of two months, with the September quarter data released in November.

Chain volume estimates of the value of work done are presented in original, seasonally adjusted and trend terms, with separate columns for work commenced, work done and completions. Data on the value of work done is for the private sector only and includes new residential buildings and some alterations and additions, non-residential building and engineering construction activity. The two primary sources for construction output data in Australia are the *Engineering Construction Survey* and the *Building Activity Survey*, both quarterly. The *Building Activity Survey* collects data relating to all stages (commenced, under construction, completed) of residential and non-residential building activity undertaken in the reference quarter. Value of work done in the reference quarter is calculated by subtracting the total work done to the end of the previous quarter from the total work done to the end of the current quarter. The ABS classifies four types of work: new building; alterations and/or additions to an existing building; refurbishment (alterations and additions primarily for non-residential building); and conversions (of non-residential buildings to residential buildings). Data from the surveys are the value of work done, work yet to be done and work not yet commenced.

The ABS calls each individual project a 'job' and surveys between 34,000 and 43,000 building jobs in various stages of construction. Building jobs included in a quarterly survey are those selected in previous quarters which have not been completed or commenced at the end of the previous quarter and new jobs selected in the current quarter. Once selected, a job is included in the survey until completed or abandoned. The survey sample includes residential building jobs valued at $50,000 or more and non-residential building jobs valued at $250,000 or more. All identified projects of $5 million or more are included in the survey, along with the sample of projects selected.

Other data is modelled. Residential building jobs between $10,000 and $50,000, non-residential building jobs between $50,000 and $250,000, new houses over $1 million, and alterations and additions to residential over $500,000 are modelled, based on their building approval details. There is a separate collection for *Building Approvals* (ABS 8731), which are permits issued by local and other government certifying authorities:

> the value of building work approved are derived by aggregating the estimated 'value of building work when completed' as reported on building approval documents provided to local councils or other building approval authorities. Conceptually these value data should exclude the value of land and landscaping but include site preparation costs associated with building activity. These estimates are usually a reliable indicator of the completed value of 'houses'. However, for other buildings they can differ significantly from the completed value of the building as final costs and contracts have often not been established before council approval is sought and gained.[8]

The ABS then notes that 'there may be instances where value reported does not reflect the building completion value'. The reported value might be builder's costs or may include the cost of site preparation and landscaping. Some data providers do not use value on approval documents, 'instead deriving a value based on floor area and type of structure'. A further complication is tax, with residential purchasers paying a value added tax (the Goods and Services Tax), which is included in the price, but non-residential building and engineering construction is generally exempt. Therefore, total building and total construction includes the non-deductible tax payable on residential building.

The *Engineering Construction Survey* uses the same basic methods as the *Building Activity Survey*. From around 43,000 business units a sample of about 1,970 is selected, covering both private and public sectors. Data collected is the value of all new projects commenced during a quarter, the value of work done on all projects during a quarter and the value of work yet to be done on all projects underway at the end of a quarter. There are 13 types of work, with heavy industry divided into another five. There is also a quarterly *Private New Capital Expenditure and Expected Expenditure* survey (ABS 5625). These surveys become the basis of construction GFCF. From the ABS Explanatory Note:

> Data on the value of work done on the construction of new residential buildings, alterations and additions to residential buildings, private sector non-residential buildings and the value of engineering construction activity are the major sources of data which are used to compile the national accounts estimates for private gross fixed capital formation on dwellings, and other buildings and structures. However, there are some adjustments to the survey data which are made in the process of compiling these national accounts series. Allowances are made for the value of activity which is out of scope of the Building Activity Survey and the Engineering Construction Survey. Such activity includes work done on projects which fall below the size cut-offs used for the Building Activity survey and also the value of building work done which is undertaken without obtaining a building permit, either because such a permit is not required or because the requisite permit is not obtained. The national accounts estimates also make allowances for purchases (less sales) of buildings and other structures from (to) the public sector.[9]

The data from all these surveys is finally published in *Construction Work Done, Australia*, (ABS 8755.0), where it becomes an input to the National Accounts. Separate data from the *Building Activity, Australia* (8752) and *Engineering Construction Activity* data (8762, available online) are also published. These are source data used to compile the national accounts estimates for private gross fixed capital formation on dwellings and other buildings and structures.

Between the mid-1990s and 2014 Australia experienced a mining and liquefied natural gas (LNG) investment boom (Downes et al., 2014). Investment in resource industries, like coal and iron ore mining and oil and gas extraction and refineries, increased construction GFCF from around 4 per cent of GDP to almost 10 per cent, with total business investment reaching more than 18 per cent of GDP in 2013 at the peak of the mining boom.[10] Mining-related engineering construction included associated railways, ports and harbours, several LNG refineries and pipelines and offshore gas platforms. The ABS includes the value of the actual work done by the reporting unit in a quarter and the value of purchases of machinery and equipment. Imported structures such as buildings and equipment,

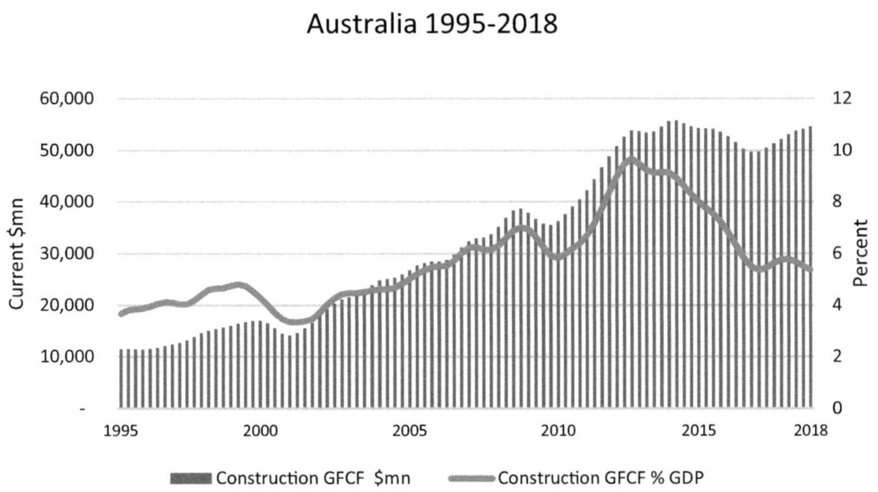

Figure 2.2 Australia's mining boom

Source: ABS 5206.0.

like the gas rigs fabricated overseas, are included in the work done figures after the item is fixed into place. The value of these imports is included in the 'value of work commenced' data in the quarter that work begins on the project's domestic site. The 'value of work yet to be done' category records the total value of the structures to be imported up until the time when the items are transported and installed. Buildings and structures in the capital expenditure survey are in both the *Engineering Construction* and *Building Activity* publications.

Figure 2.2 shows the extraordinary scale of the mining boom in Australia between the mid-1990s and 2014. It also shows how investment today leads to increased output in the future, with a lag of a couple of years between construction and production. Another important point here is that a significant proportion of what was classed as construction consisted of plant and equipment, including offshore oil and gas platforms and onshore refineries costing hundreds of billions of dollars.

United Kingdom

GFCF consists of resident producers' acquisitions, less disposals, of fixed assets during a given period plus certain additions to the value of non-produced assets. Fixed assets are those used in production for more than one year and can be physical items like buildings, machinery, transport equipment, or intellectual property like software or research and development (Eurostat, 2013). Published GFCF tables divide the economy into the five institutional sectors of general government and public corporations, non-financial corporations, financial corporations, households and non-profit institutions serving households. The NACE version of the SIC used in the UK (and EU) includes a unique subdivision, 41.1 *Development of Building Projects*, which includes construction management and project management of construction projects (ONS, 2007). ISIC and the other systems do not include this activity in the construction industry. However, across the EU the share of construction output of SIC 41.1 varies widely and is unevenly and unreliably reported across the 28 countries (de Valence, 2019).

The UK's GFCF estimates are based primarily on business data from the *Quarterly Survey of Capital Expenditure*, which has a sample size of 27,000 businesses in a sample based on employment size (20 to 49, 50 to 99, 100 to 299 and 300 plus). Businesses are classified by industry and stratified by employment, and businesses with an employment size of at least 300 are permanently included in the sample. Those with between 20 and 299 employees are sampled on a rotating basis and those with employment under 20 are not sampled. In addition to the sampled survey, businesses with fewer than 20 employees who undertake large (more than £5 million) capital spending have their capital expenditure included in the estimates. Survey results are weighted using combined ratio estimation, ('strata are combined in the same industry across sampled employment size bands') and then aggregated at industry level. The survey does not cover banking, higher education and new dwellings. Administrative data for government investment is also used in the production of GFCF estimates of government investment.[11]

The main source of data for the Classification of Products by activity (CPA) breakdown of GFCF is the *Quarterly Survey of Capital Expenditure*, which asks businesses detailed questions about the type of capital items they purchase and dispose of. Business investment includes investment by public non-financial corporations and all private sector institutions but excludes expenditure on dwellings and the costs of ownership transfer on non-produced, non-financial assets. The ONS uses reconciled annual estimates for each industry from the supply and use tables to derive quarterly information, which are aggregated from the CPA to asset. For dwellings and other buildings and structures, data on types of building work are combined with the CPA classification:

> For dwellings and other buildings and structures, data on types of building work were combined with the CPA classification in order to permit deflation and more informed balancing than was available using the CPA breakdown alone. This process resulted in a set of proportions which could be applied by industry, asset and institutional sector. There is an ongoing quality assurance process to reconcile the results of this product breakdown in the supply and use tables, and in particular, to reconcile the results of transfer costs on non-produced non-financial assets.
>
> (McLaren and Murphy, 2017: 4)

McLaren and Murphy also describe the nine-step process that turns these CPA products in the supply and use tables into GFCF:

1 Current price data are compiled, unbalanced, by industry, asset, institutional sector and by acquisitions and disposals.

2 A product breakdown is used to pro-rate the estimates described in (1) to the bottom level of the asset and product classification in current prices.
3 The current price data created in (2) are aggregated up the various hierarchies to top-level GFCF. A separate hierarchy is used to aggregate the estimates by highly detailed products to the level at which supply and use balancing is done (112 products). Many of the products used in the supply and use balancing process are not applicable to GFCF, so this process results in estimates for 29 products at this level of detail.
4 The annual 112 product breakdown is balanced in current prices by assessing the supply of these products and where they are used.
5 The annual current price data are returned to the GFCF system, and the quarterly current price estimates are benchmarked to the balanced annuals before being converted back into acquisitions and disposals.
6 Balanced, quarterly, current price estimates for each of the 29 balanced products are pro-rated down the unbalanced patterns of the product, industry and sector hierarchies, before being aggregated up the asset hierarchy to produce a full, balanced current price dataset.
7 Balanced, current price estimates by bottom-level product but at total sector, total industry and by acquisitions and disposals are deflated using specific CPA-level price indices and are then unchained to current year's prices (CYP) and previous year's prices (PYP).
8 The balanced, current price pattern is used to pro-rate the CYP and PYP pattern to all industries and institutional sectors at bottom level, prior to aggregation up the asset hierarchy.
9 The data are now available to be chain-linked at the required levels. (McLaren and Murphy, 2017: 5).

Two recent reports have recommended improvements to the GFCF methodology, the *Independent Review of Economic Statistics* (Bean, 2016) and the *National Statistics Quality Review of the National Accounts and Balance of Payments* (Barker and Ridgeway, 2014). The Bean report noted the number of firms across the economy sampled is very small. In 2014, for the production and construction sectors 6,415 firms completed the long form and 10,340 the short form. About three times those numbers complete the services sector surveys. While this minimises the "burden on respondents" and cuts costs "the fact that the sample is only made up of a small proportion of businesses means that it lacks sufficient granularity if the sample needs to be stratified finely by size, industry or region" (Bean, 2016: 157). As a result of these limitations the ONS has been reviewing their collections and there have been many recent changes in publications and statistical releases.

Comparing GFCF

This analysis focuses on construction output data found in the national accounts produced by statistical agencies in the United States (US), United Kingdom (UK), Australia and Canada. Some similarities and differences between the methods used for both data collection and interpretation are now identified and discussed. All the statistical agencies have been upgrading their survey databases over recent years, particularly for registered businesses and have all been reworking their surveys and started using digital sources of data more extensively. Many of their publications and statistical releases have been recently revised and often renamed, with some discontinued and new ones appearing as the agencies seek efficiencies and develop their datasets.

These four national statistical agencies follow broadly similar methods for collecting and processing the data that is required for estimating construction output. Their systems are based on the internationally agreed *System of National Accounts* (UN, 2008a) and the associated documents for industry and product definitions, so a high degree of similarity can be expected. Also, at the aggregate level of GFCF, construction output is reported for private residential and non-residential building and construction and government expenditure, following the guidelines for presentation of national accounts. However, data sources and the way estimates are prepared vary between the agencies. Two key aspects of these variations are the type of surveys used and the modelling of output.

To estimate construction output a statistical agency needs three pieces of data on a project: when the project started; the size or value of the project when approved; and the monthly value of work done until completion. For private sector projects this data is collected through surveys of construction contractors and subcontractors. The US and Canada spread the spending on a project over time, but use different methods, using the value of a project when approved as the basis. This is reported as a total value (annual or quarterly). Australia collects monthly data and does limited modelling of small projects. This is reported as work commenced, work done, work yet to be done and completed.

The *System of National Accounts* recognises the problem of distributing work done on projects over the time each project takes to complete, but makes no specific recommendation:

> Work-in-progress occurs in all industries, but is especially important in those in which some time is needed to produce a unit of finished output, for example, in agriculture, or in industries producing complex fixed assets such as ships, dwellings, software or films. Work-in progress can therefore take a wide variety of different forms.
>
> (UN, 2008a: 209)

Table 2.8 Statistical surveys

Country	*Surveys*
US	*Value of Construction Put in Place* – monthly, quarterly and annual *Economic Census* – 5 yearly
Canada	*Investment in Building Construction* – monthly, quarterly and annual *Annual Capital and Repair Expenditures Survey*
Australia	*Building Activity Survey* – quarterly and annual *Engineering Construction Survey* quarterly and annual
UK	*Quarterly Acquisitions and Disposals of Capital Assets*

In the US, the principal source data used for both government and private gross fixed investment estimates are the Bureau of Economic Analysis' input-output accounts, supplemented by the Census Bureau's annual and monthly surveys. The Census Bureau's *Value of Construction Put in Place* report combines survey data, regulatory reports and trade sourced data to estimate construction spending. The monthly and quarterly estimates of structures use the construction spending data to extrapolate the benchmark year input-output estimates from the *Economic Census*, conducted every five years. The modelled estimates based on government and industry data are then used to find the private and government investment estimates for structures that are reported as GFCF. Therefore, the estimates for construction in non-benchmark years use monthly construction spending data as an indicator series to extrapolate the benchmark-year estimates from the BEA's input-output accounts, based on value put in place from the *Monthly Construction Survey*. That survey also provides the value of work done on residential building, which is based on housing starts and average construction costs. The Census Bureau has a 'construction progress pattern' that assumes over 75 per cent of a residential project is completed in over five months after commencement, with the remainder distributed in declining amounts over the next seven months.

Statistics Canada's monthly *Investment in Building Construction* is based on their *Building Permits Survey*, plus data from the Canada Mortgage and Housing Corporation database on housing starts, completions, under construction and newly completed. The monthly survey collects information about construction intentions, which are then matched with the Corporation's data on housing starts and with the *Public and Private Investment Survey* data for the non-residential sector. Construction work done is modelled based on the work put in place coefficients used to distribute the value of construction over each project's duration. All projects have a delay and duration and the coefficients for these work put-in-place patterns distribute the value of building permits according to project length.

In Australia, building and construction output is published quarterly as *Construction Activity: Chain Volume Measures*, with estimates of building and engineering construction work done during the last quarter and revised estimates for previous quarters. There are two quarterly surveys of work done, the *Building Activity Survey* (ABS 8752) and the *Engineering Construction Survey*, with each survey claimed to cover 95 per cent of the value of work done in the current quarter. Once selected, a project is included in the survey until completed or abandoned. Estimates for residential building work less than $10,000 and non-residential building work under $50,000 are modelled.

The ONS' GFCF estimates are based on business data from the *Quarterly Acquisitions and Disposals of Capital Assets Survey*, which has a sample size of approximately 27,000 businesses in a sample based on employment. The survey is the source of data for the CPA breakdown of GFCF, with administrative data for government investment also used in GFCF estimates. The ONS uses reconciled annual estimates for each industry from the supply and use tables to derive quarterly information, which are aggregated from the classification of products by activity to classification by asset in GFCF.

Three key points emerge from this review. First, the scope of the four countries' collection of data on construction work done varies considerably. In particular, the inclusion of mining and oil and gas expenditures on machinery and equipment as construction industry output in the US, Canada and Australia boosts industry output to a much greater extent than the UK, where mining and oil and gas expenditure is included as an Intellectual Property Product. On the other hand, the UK includes SIC 41.1 property development. This extends to the NACE version of the *Standard Industrial Classification* used in the European Union and is the main difference between the European SIC version of the construction industry and the rest of the world. Second, Australia is the only country that directly surveys the construction projects selected in their sample from start to finish. The US and Canada rely on monthly approvals (permits) data and a quarterly survey of businesses that includes a small sample of construction contractors and subcontractors. UK (strictly Great Britain) construction output is based on a monthly survey of construction contractors and collects output data on their projects.

The third point is the role of repair and maintenance expenditure in explaining the difference between construction output measured as work done by contractors and subcontractors and construction GFCF, which is significantly higher. Here the data collected in Statistics Canada's *Annual Capital and Repair Expenditures Survey* is unique to Canada. Despite the importance of R&M (discussed elsewhere in this volume), none of the other countries discussed here survey business R&M directly as Canada does.

Conclusion

Within GDP, construction spending is found in GFCF as non-residential and residential construction. At the highest level of reporting, in the national accounts, this is construction output. It is gross output, measured without deduction of consumption of fixed capital, which is a measure of capital used up in production. The US is unusual, in that it does not have a national statistical office and responsibility for generating the data used for calculating GDP and GFCF is spread over three organisations: The Bureau of Economic Analysis, the Census Bureau and the Bureau of Labour Statistics. The three other countries discussed here have a single national statistical agency, the UK's Office of National Statistics, the Australian Bureau of Statistics and Statistics Canada.

Over the last decade or so these agencies have been revising their methodologies and systems based on revised national accounting standards for industry classifications and products (the goods and services produced by an economy). They all run complete supply and use tables and build GFCF from products classified as construction, which is a broader definition than construction industry output because it includes work done internally by organisations not included in the SIC industry 'construction'. Therefore, GFCF is a broader measure of the total contribution of construction to the economy than the output of the SIC construction industry, which only collects work done by contractors and subcontractors (de Valence, 2018b). Using the product approach (through the CPA) results in a different measure of construction output to one based on the production of contractors and subcontractors.

That said, the SIC definition of construction products allows all machinery and equipment, all fixtures and fittings and many fees and charges to be included in the price. This becomes the reported value of a project, of which the actual structural components will only be a percentage, large in the case of typical residential buildings but smaller for non-residential projects and very minor in major resource projects like oil and mining. Because the Australian, Canadian and US economies have important mining, oil and gas industries, the share of construction in GFCF is boosted relative to the UK because these are capital intensive industries and their expenditure on plant and equipment is included as construction. This accounts for some of the difference in GFCF's share of GDP in the UK, which is lower than the other countries.

The US and Canada use the approved value of a project as the basis for distributing expenditure over time to get work done, done in Canada for each project but following a formula in the US. Completion times for projects, particularly major projects, stretch and compress across the building cycle, increasing as industry capacity is absorbed during upswings then shortening during the declining part of the cycle. How sensitive the models are to actual changes in permits, starts and completions is unknown. The SNA recognises valuing 'work in progress' is an issue but does not suggest a solution.

Canadian and US estimates for construction GFCF use monthly construction spending data to extrapolate estimates from the supply and use tables (in the US, input-output accounts) based on work done, or value put in place, from their monthly construction surveys. The UK relies on a quarterly survey, although they have other separate monthly collections on housing starts and construction work done. Australia is singular in following expenditure on projects in the sample through to completion and Canada in collecting repair and maintenance expenditure by business.

In the US version of the 2008 revision of the SNA, intellectual property is included in GFCF, and a new category called Construction IP was introduced. This mainly collects expenditure on software. At a time of rapid development of a wide range of new construction technologies and IP, measuring this expenditure more widely might counter the widespread view that construction is a technological laggard.

Notes

1 Pers. Com. ONS 2019.
2 Available at www.census.gov/construction/c30/about_the_survey.html
3 "in the 1980s, manufacturing shipments of construction materials and other inputs for the construction industry suggested that the industry's output should be growing faster than the estimates produced by using the value of construction put in place as the extrapolator for that industry. After further investigation, the bureau concluded that the put-in-place estimates were too low and adjusted them accordingly." (Landefeld et al., 2008: 211–212).

4 Available at https://www150.statcan.gc.ca/n1/pub/13-606-g/13-606-g2016001-eng.htm
5 Available at https://www150.statcan.gc.ca/n1/pub/13-606-g/2016001/article/14624-eng.htm
6 Available at http://www23.statcan.gc.ca/imdb/p2SV.pl?Function=getSurvey&SDDS=1401
7 Available at https://www150.statcan.gc.ca/n1/pub/13-606-g/2016001/article/14619-eng.htm
8 Available at www.abs.gov.au/AUSSTATS/abs@.nsf/Lookup/8731.0Explanatory%20Notes1Nov%202018?OpenDocument
9 Available at www.abs.gov.au/AUSSTATS/abs@.nsf/Lookup/8782.0.65.001Explanatory%20Notes2Sep%202018?OpenDocument
10 Available at www.rba.gov.au/speeches/2017/sp-dg-2017-11-13.html
11 Available at www.ons.gov.uk/economy/grossdomesticproductgdp/methodologies/quarterlyacquisitionsanddisposalsofcapitalassetssurveyqmi

References

ABS (2006). Australian New Zealand Standard Industrial Classification. Australian Bureau of Statistics, Canberra.

ABS 5206.0. Australian National Accounts: National Income, Expenditure and Product, Australian Bureau of Statistics, Canberra.

Barker, K. and Ridgeway, A. (2014). *National Statistics Quality Review: National Accounts and Balance of Payments*, Office for National Statistics, London.

Bean, C. (2016). *Independent Review of UK Economic Statistics*. Office for National Statistics, London.

de Valence, G. (2001). Construction deflators and measurement of output. ARCOM 2001 Conference, pp. 693–702.

de Valence, G. (2019). Construction in the SIC, in Best, R. and Meikle, J. (eds.) *Accounting for Construction*, Taylor & Francis, London.

Diewert, W. E. (2009). Durables and owner-occupied housing in a consumer price index, in Diewert, W. E., Greenlees, J. S. and Hulten, C. R. (eds.) *Price Index Concepts and Measurement*, University of Chicago Press, Chicago, pp. 445–500.

Downes, P., Hanslow, K. and Tulip, P. (2015). *The Effect of the Mining Boom on the Australian Economy*, Research Discussion Paper 2014–08, Reserve Bank of Australia, Sydney.

Drew, S., Lewis, P. and McLaren, C. (2016). *Chain-Linking Methods Used within the UK National Accounts*, Office for National Statistics, London.

Eurostat (2013). *European System of National and Regional Accounts 2010*, European Union, Brussels.

Girardi, D. and Mura, A. (2014). The construction-development curve: Evidence from a new international dataset, *The IUP Journal of Applied Economics*, XIII(3).

Gruneberg, S. and Folwell, K. (2013). The use of gross fixed capital formation as a measure of construction output, *Construction Management and Economics*, 31(4), 359–368. DOI: 10.1080/01446193.2013.790555.

Kohlscheen, E., Mehrotra, A. and Dubravko, M. (2018). *Residential Investment and Economic Activity: Evidence from the Past Five Decades*, BIS Working Papers No. 726, Bank for International Settlements, Geneva.

Landefeld, J. S., Seskin, E. P. and Fraumeni, B. M. (2008). Taking the pulse of the economy: Measuring GDP, *Journal of Economic Perspectives*, 22(2), Spring, 193–216.

Lequiller, F. and Blades, D. (2014). *Understanding National Accounts: Second Edition*, OECD Publishing. Available at: http://dx.doi.org/10.1787/9789264214637-en

McLaren, C. and Murphy, J. (2017). *National Accounts Articles: Changes to the Gross Fixed Capital Formation Methodology and Processing*, Office for National Statistics, London.

NIPA (2017). *National Income and Product Accounts*, Bureau of Economic Analysis, Washington.

ONS (2007). *Standard Industrial Classification of Economic Activities*, Office of National Statistics, London.

ONS (2017). *An International Comparison of Gross Fixed Capital Formation*, Office for National Statistics, London.

Statistics Canada (n.d.). *Investment in New Residential Building Construction (Work put in place) Methodology*, Investment and Capital Stock Division, Ottawa.

Statistics Canada (2008). *Canadian System of National Accounts*. Statistics Canada, Ottawa.

UN (1993). *System of National Accounts 1993*, United Nations, New York. Available at: http://unstats.un.org/unsd/nationalaccount/docs/1993sna.pdf

UN (2008a). *System of National Accounts 2008*, United Nations, New York. Available at: http://unstats.un.org/unsd/nationalaccount/docs/SNA2008.pdf

UN (2008b). *Standard Industrial Classification of All Economic Activities*, United Nations, New York.

UN (2015). *Central Product Classification*, United Nations, New York. Available at: https://unstats.un.org/unsd/classifications/unsdclassifications/cpcv21.pdf

Vanoli, A. (2005). *A History of National Accounts*, IOS Press, Amsterdam.

World Bank (2019). Online data. Available at: https://data.worldbank.org/indicator

Yu, M. and Ive, G. (2015). R review of construction cost and price indices in Britain, in Best, R. and Meikle, J. (eds.) *Measuring Construction: Prices, Output and Productivity*, Taylor & Francis, Oxford, pp. 79–112.

3 Benchmarking international construction costs

Craig Langston

Introduction

The title of this chapter reflects a preoccupation for practitioners, clients, economists, academics and government departments over many years, namely comparing the cost of construction in one country with the cost of construction in another. It is not just a simple matter of converting actual and/or estimated costs at a given date from one country to another using currency exchange rates. Even within countries, different regions or cities display variations in labour, material and plant costs, productivity ranges based on the availability of resources (including transportation distances) and contractor margins that take heed of market conditions. Furthermore, standards of construction, statutory requirements, local practices and concern for worker health and safety can impact on costs. Collectively, benchmarking international construction costs with a view to identifying value and performance is, and always has been, problematic (Best and Meikle, 2015).

The purpose of this chapter is to shed some light on the various conversion methods that are available for use and, objectively, make recommendations on which method(s) should be commonly adopted in practice. The routine approach for international benchmarking is to convert construction costs into US dollars (USD), so that at least all costs are in the same currency. Most practitioners appear to do this. Yet currency rates can be quite volatile, and therefore conclusions will depend to some extent on the timing of the study.

Purchasing power parity (PPP) is an alternative to currency conversion. The concept has been around since the 16th century, but was developed into its modern form by Gustav (1918) and used by economists ever since. It assumes that, in the absence of transaction costs and official trade barriers, identical goods will have the same price in different markets when the prices are expressed in a given currency (Krugman et al., 2010). Where this doesn't occur, the conclusion is that different countries have different domestic purchasing power.

The use of PPP as an alternative to traditional currency exchange rates is generally regarded as a superior approach (e.g. Rogoff, 1996; Langston and Best, 2005). PPP is an attempt to measure the economic wellbeing of people according to the country in which they reside. While not pretending to be an indicator of living standards, it does reflect the cost of living in-country and therefore forms a new baseline against which construction costs can be interpreted.

PPPs are defined as exchange rates that replace traditional currency exchange rates by taking into account the differences in prices between countries (Pakko and Pollard, 2003). They convert local costs into 'international dollars' compared to a nominated base country. The philosophy behind PPPs is the *Law of One Price* – namely that the cost of a good or service should be the same in different countries – else people would buy goods cheaper from one country and sell them at a profit in another (Baffes, 1991). However, whether the *Law of One Price* holds for any particular item depends on the item meeting four basic criteria (UBS, 2003). They are:

1. The item must be tradable.
2. There are no impediments to trade.
3. There are no transaction costs (such as transport) involved in trade of the item.
4. The item is perfectly homogeneous across all locations.

If all four criteria are met, then the price of the item should be the same in different places at the same time. In that case the cost of an item in currency X should represent the same value as the cost of the same item in currency Y (Best, 2008).

The United Nations sponsored International Comparison Program (ICP) commenced in 1967 and now produces PPPs published by The World Bank Group for most countries on an approximate three-year cycle. These indices have been interpreted and extended to form the Penn World Table (PWT) produced by the University of Pennsylvania. The Eurostat-OECD joint program currently collects more detailed PPP data than the ICP, but for a much smaller set of countries. Indices for both ICP and Eurostat-OECD PPPs are expressed as a proportion of per capita gross domestic product. The Union Bank of Switzerland (UBS) has also been producing PPP data since 1970, again approximately on a three-year cycle. They use a basket of goods and services and express their data in three forms (using a base for Switzerland, United States or the Euro-zone respectively). One criticism of these programs is the time delay between data collection and publication. Another criticism is the cost of the process (Langston and Best, 2005). These PPPs relate to a country and tend to ignore the differences that exist between regions or cities within national borders.

Over the last decade or so, attention has turned to the development of indices that are industry-focused, and more recently data has been compiled related to certain cities. Turner and Townsend, a large multi-national firm of quantity surveyors and project consultants, published surveys of international construction costs since 2009 comprising local prices and conversion to USD. In 2013, for the first time, they additionally presented cost data in the form of PPPs based on a new 'exchange rate' called *citiBLOC*, which was developed as part of a major study of 337 high-rise projects of 20 storeys or more (completed between 2003 and 2012) throughout the five largest cities in Australia and the United States, representing two-thirds of the known population of such buildings in these locations (Langston, 2014). By pricing a representative basket of construction-related items covering labour, material and plant, a standard basket price in each city (in local currency terms) can be determined. The cost of this basket equals one *citiBLOC*. Thereafter, the cost of a project can be divided by the cost of the basket to obtain the equivalent number of baskets required to pay for the construction. Although the unit of measure is 'baskets', not currency, the answer is a comparative index that has no geographical boundaries. For example, if Project A in Los Angeles was 5 baskets/m^2 and Project B in New Delhi was 4 baskets/m^2, then the construction cost in Los Angeles would be 25 per cent more than New Delhi.

The *citiBLOC* approach grew alongside Turner and Townsend's surveys to effectively become an international locality index at the granularity of cities. Table 3.1 illustrates the approach for Sydney, Australia.

Perhaps the best way to describe PPP-adjusted values is to say that they express local prices in terms of purchasing power by weighting them according to a standard basket of relevant construction items (comprising common material, labour and plant items) that are made or otherwise available in-country. Imported goods and services should be avoided. The higher the PPP-adjusted value, the higher are the relative costs of building in one location over another. The PPP 'exchange rate' alone does not provide that information, in the same way that

Table 3.1 Representative construction items for *citiBLOC*

Item	*Standard Description*	*Unit*	*Quantity (weighting)*	*Local Currency (ex-tax)*
Material *(supply only including CBD delivery)*				
A	32 MPa ready-mixed concrete (1 m^3 = 35.31 cu. feet)	m^3	45	11,144
B	Steel in 250 x 25.7kg/m 'I' beam (17.3 lb/foot)	t	6.8	9,350
C	10mm clear tempered glass (1 m^2 = 10.76 sq. feet)	m^2	44	10,472
D	13mm thick gypsum plasterboard (½" thick)	m^2	1,300	10,140
E	100 × 50mm sawn softwood stud (1 m = 3.28 feet)	m	2,750	9,873
Labour *(charge-out rate including on-costs)*				
F	Electrician	hr	150	9,900
G	Carpenter	hr	185	10,915
H	Painter	hr	200	10,400
I	Unskilled labour	hr	275	10,863
Plant *(third party hire rate including operator and fuel)*				
J	50 t mobile crane	day	5	10,200
	Average price per item (i.e. 1 *citiBLOC*):			**10,326**

SYDNEY, AUSTRALIA (2012)
Current Market Conditions:
☑ very competitive (low profit) ☐ normal ☐ overheated (high profit)
Source: Langston, 2014, 2016.

the USD exchange rate does not that information either. However, when the local prices are divided by these exchange rates, the result is an equivalent or "international" value.

By pricing a representative basket of construction-related items covering labour, materials and plant, a standard basket price in each city (in local currency terms) can be computed and act as a locality index: hence the use of the term "citiBLOC". Thereafter, the cost of a project can be divided by the cost of the representative basket to obtain the equivalent number of baskets required to pay for the construction. Although the unit of measure is 'baskets' not currency, the answer is an indicator of cost performance that has no geographical boundaries. For example, if Project A in Los Angeles was 5 baskets/m^2 and Project B in New Delhi was 4 baskets/m^2, then the construction cost in Los Angeles would be 25 per cent more than in New Delhi. Langston and Best (2005) first used the coefficient of variation (CoV) as a test for the *Law of One Price*. The thinking was that the method with the lowest CoV best reflected purchasing parity. They compared general PPPs produced by UBS and the World Bank, as well as USD currency conversion and the Big Mac Index. They found the latter was as good as any other method in some cities, but not in others. Hong Kong was a case in point, where the price of the Big Mac was about half of its expected value. This highlighted that the hamburger is not really a standard commodity across the world, but if one could be found there would be some confidence that its use in international cost comparisons would be superior to more costly and time-consuming methods. Large discrepancies were also found between the more established indices, particularly over the accuracy of the ICP data for Bangkok. Exchange rates were generally more volatile and displayed the greatest dispersion, suggesting that PPPs were more appropriate for use in practice.

Langston (2016) extended the notion of CoV testing by applying it to the data publicly available in Turner and Townsend (2013). Five different exchange rates were investigated, based on labour and material prices, composite prices, *citiBLOC* indices, the Big Mac Index and USD currency conversion respectively. He found that across the 23 surveyed cities, *citiBLOC* had the lowest CoV and hence better modelled the *Law of One Price* (i.e. where CoV theoretically equals zero).

Method

Turner and Townsend (2018) is the latest survey of construction prices and embraces 46 cities. Over the last five years, they have used an identical framework for presenting their data. This makes it possible to objectively compare 2013 and 2018 costs and to see if the same conclusions reported in Langston (2016) can be replicated. The updated investigation doubles the number of cities, as can be observed in Table 3.2. Cities are ranked herein according to their cost of living, using information compiled independently via the Expatistan website (www.expatistan.com/cost-of-living). The higher the index the more expensive is the cost of living in a city compared to a nominated base (set in this study as Sydney, Australia).

Table 3.2 Surveyed locations

City	*Country*	*Currency*	*Expatistan*^
Amsterdam*	The **Netherlands**	EUR	0.89
Bangalore**	Republic of **India**	INR	0.67
Beijing	People's Republic of **China**	CNY	0.81
Belfast	**United Kingdom**	GBP	0.75
Birmingham	**United Kingdom**	GBP	0.79
Bogotá	Republic of **Columbia**	COP	0.65
Brisbane	Commonwealth of **Australia**	AUD	0.85
Buenos Aires	Argentine Republic (**Argentina**)	ARS	0.63
Dar es Salaam	United Republic of **Tanzania**	TZS	0.67
Doha*	State of **Qatar**	QAR	0.92
Dubai*/Abu Dhabi	**United Arab Emirates**	AED	0.88
Dublin*	Republic of **Ireland**	EUR	1.00
Edinburgh	**United Kingdom**	GBP	0.81
Ho Chi Minh City*	Socialist Republic of **Vietnam**	VND	0.64
Hong Kong*	**Hong Kong** SAR, People's Republic of China	HKD	1.04
Houston	**United States** of America	USD	0.78
Istanbul	Republic of **Turkey**	TRY	0.62
Jakarta	Republic of **Indonesia**	IDR	0.63
Johannesburg*	Republic of **South Africa**	ZAR	0.70
Kampala*	Republic of **Uganda**	UGX	0.65
Kigali	Republic of **Rwanda**	RWF	0.63
Kuala Lumpur*	**Malaysia**	MYR	0.64
London*	**United Kingdom**	GBP	1.08
Madrid	Kingdom of **Spain**	EUR	0.74
Melbourne	Commonwealth of **Australia**	AUD	0.88
Moscow*	**Russian** Federation	RUB	0.67
Munich**	Federal Republic of **Germany**	EUR	0.83
Muscat*	Sultanate of **Oman**	OMR	0.70
Nairobi	Republic of **Kenya**	KSH	0.67
New York City	**United States** of America	USD	1.10
Paris	French Republic (**France**)	EUR	0.95
Perth	Commonwealth of **Australia**	AUD	0.83
San Francisco**	**United States** of America	USD	1.16
Santiago	Republic of **Chile**	CLP	0.69
Säo Paulo*	Federative Republic of **Brazil**	BRL	0.68
Seattle	**United States** of America	USD	0.94
Seoul*	Republic of Korea (**South Korea**)	KRW	0.78
Shanghai*	People's Republic of **China**	CNY	0.74
Singapore*	Republic of **Singapore**	SGD	0.94
Southampton	**United Kingdom**	GBP	0.76
Sydney*	Commonwealth of **Australia**	AUD	1.00 (base)
Tokyo*	**Japan**	JPY	0.90
Toronto*	**Canada**	CAD	0.85
Warsaw*	Republic of **Poland**	PLN	0.64
York	**United Kingdom**	GBP	0.78
Zurich	Swiss Confederation (**Switzerland**)	CHF	1.14

* cities common to Turner and Townsend (2013)
** ditto, but similar city (e.g. Los Angeles replaced with San Francisco)
^ Expatistan is a broad-based 'cost of living' index (accessed 2 June 2018)
Source: Turner and Townsend, 2018.

The first phase of the investigation compares USD and *citiBLOC* PPP exchange rates. As was done previously, three types of construction cost data are again used. Mean cost/m^2 for various building types (comprising residential, commercial, industrial, retail, hotels, hospitals, schools, carparks and airports) are compared. Then, unit rates for labour, material and plant are compared. Finally, unit rates for composite work items comprising a mix of supply and install activities are compared.

CoV is calculated as standard deviation divided by mean and expressed as a percentage. Values below 20% typically demonstrate very low variance, values between 20% and 50% are considered good given the nature of the base data, while values over 50% suggest the prices are either erroneous or heterogeneous.

The second phase of the study compares five different exchange rates. As was done previously, these exchange rates were based on a basket of labour and material unit rates (*L+M*), a basket of composite work items (*Composite*), a basket of equally weighted labour, material and plant costs (*citiBLOC*), a McDonalds hamburger index (*Big Mac*) and USD exchange rates (*Currency*). They are explored in turn.

Results

In the first instance, average construction prices for various building types in each city, expressed in both USD and PPP terms per square metre of gross floor area, are used to determine CoV. Table 3.3 shows these building types and computes the CoV across two datasets matching cities common with Turner and Townsend (2013) and extended in Turner and Townsend (2018). Langston (2016) previously found that of the 27 building types listed, 25 of them (i.e. 93%) had a CoV that is lower for *citiBLOC* PPP than USD conversion. This is observed to increase to 100% (for both n=23 and n=46) using 2018 data. Again, all but one of these values has a CoV between 20% and 50%.

A range of labour, material and plant items in each city is similarly used to determine CoV. The results are provided in Table 3.4. Langston (2016) previously found that of the 17 items listed, 12 of them (i.e. 71%) had a CoV that is lower for *citiBLOC* PPP than USD conversion. This is observed to be 100% for labour and plant and 63.64% (n=23) and 36.36% (n=46) for material using 2018 data. However, over half of the items had a CoV between 50% and 100%, indicating higher volatility at this level of work breakdown. The reason material prices favour USD over PPP conversion is suspected to be due to the larger proportion of cities from developing countries in the extended database (n=46) that have a higher reliance on imported construction products with embodied foreign labour in their manufacture.

Finally, a range of composite items (i.e. involving supply and install activities) in each city is similarly used to determine the CoV. These outcomes are contained in Table 3.5. Langston (2016) previously found that of the 19 items listed, 14 of them (i.e. 74%) have a CoV that is lower for *citiBLOC* PPP than USD conversion. This is observed to be 73.68% (n=23) and 84.21% (n=46) using 2018 data. Most items had CoVs between 20% and 50%.

Table 3.3 Coefficients of variation (average cost/m^2)

Building type (Turner and Townsend, 2013, 2018)	*Common (n=23)*		*Extended (n=46)*	
	% (USD)	*% (PPP)*	*% (USD)*	*% (PPP)*
Residential				
Individual detached/terrace house medium standard	67	**46**	61	**43**
Individual detached house prestige	77	**53**	67	**47**
Townhouses medium standard	66	**44**	58	**42**
Apartments low rise medium density	59	**34**	55	**36**
Apartments high rise	57	**31**	54	**34**
Aged care/affordable units	76	**54**	63	**46**
Commercial				
Offices – business park	52	**24**	52	**30**
CBD offices – up to 20 floors medium (A-Grade)	57	**22**	56	**25**
CBD offices – high rise prestige	56	**24**	54	**24**
Industrial				
Warehouse/factory units – basic	59	**48**	53	**45**
Large warehouse distribution centre	52	**36**	47	**37**
High tech factory/laboratory	57	**32**	53	**36**
Retail				
Large shopping centre including mall	56	**29**	51	**29**
Neighbourhood incl. supermarket	57	**33**	54	**35**
Prestige car showroom	54	**39**	52	**37**
Hotels				
3 star travellers	45	**26**	42	**27**
5 star luxury	40	**25**	40	**30**
Resort style	45	**42**	40	**39**
Hospitals				
Day centre (including basic surgeries)	57	**41**	50	**34**
Regional hospital	63	**40**	59	**34**
General hospital (e.g. city teaching hospital)	65	**44**	55	**36**
Schools				
Primary and secondary	55	**35**	52	**35**
University	54	**26**	52	**31**
Carparks				
Multi storey above ground	53	**34**	48	**33**
Multi storey below ground	73	**47**	63	**42**
Airports				
Domestic terminal, full service	49	**43**	42	**33**
Low cost carrier, basic service	48	**42**	40	**32**
Proportion lowest CoV (%)	0.00	**100.00**	0.00	**100.00**

Bold figures indicate lowest CoV

Table 3.4 Coefficients of variation (labour, material and plant)

Item (Turner and Townsend, 2013, 2018)	*Common (n=23)*		*Extended (n=46)*	
	% (USD)	*% (PPP)*	*% (USD)*	*% (PPP)*
Labour (cost/hour)				
Group 1 tradesman (e.g. plumber/ electrician) #	98	**69**	91	**62**
Group 2 tradesman (e.g. carpenter/ bricklayer) #	96	**66**	89	**59**
Group 3 tradesman (e.g. carpet layer/ tiler/plasterer) #	92	**64**	89	**59**
General labourer #	97	**70**	97	**65**
Site foreman	89	**57**	87	**54**
Proportion lowest CoV (%)	0.00	**100.00**	0.00	**100.00**
Material (cost/unit)				
Concrete 30 MPa (m^3) #	**36**	46	**35**	43
Reinforcement bar 16mm (tonne)	**26**	34	**23**	34
Concrete block 400 x 200mm (thousands)	81	**63**	78	**57**
Standard brick (thousands)	**62**	65	**57**	59
Structural steel beams (tonne) #	35	**35**	36	**34**
Glass pane 10mm tempered (m^2) #	51	**47**	47	**41**
Softwood timber for framing 100 x 50mm (m) #	44	**42**	**38**	46
13mm plasterboard (m^2) #	47	**36**	44	**41**
Emulsion paint (litre)	54	**53**	**56**	80
Copper pipe 15mm (m)	**49**	51	**50**	55
Copper cable (3C+E) 2.5mm PVC (m)	87	**83**	**77**	77
Proportion lowest CoV (%)	36.36	**63.64**	**63.64**	36.36
Plant (cost/day)				
Hire 50 tonne mobile crane + operator #	51	**24**	54	**22**
Proportion lowest CoV (%)	0.00	**100.00**	0.00	**100.00**

 # items are used to construct citiBLOC PPP
Bold figures indicate lowest CoV

Overall, PPP-adjusted prices have lower CoVs than USD-adjusted prices, and therefore PPPs adhere more closely to the *Law of One Price*. Currency conversion, on the other hand, generally has higher CoVs, and although the approach is still valid when pricing construction works located in another country, it is not appropriate when benchmarking international project cost performance.

PPP is shown to be preferable compared to currency conversion. But *citiBLOC* PPP is not the only choice available. Three further PPP methods are added, so a total of five cost conversion strategies can be compared against each other. Once again, the method with the lowest CoV represents the best available option.

The L+M PPP is calculated based on local prices for the 5 labour items and the 11 material items provided earlier in Table 3.4. Labour and materials are

Table 3.5 Coefficients of variation (composite work items)

Item (Turner and Townsend, 2013, 2018)	*Common (n=23)*		*Extended (n=46)*	
	% (USD)	*% (PPP)*	*% (USD)*	*% (PPP)*
Excavate basement (m^3)	86	**76**	76	**67**
Excavate footings (m)	68	**60**	68	**56**
Concrete in slab (m^3)	36	**33**	40	**28**
Reinforcement in beams (tonne)	**28**	34	**28**	31
Formwork to soffit of slab (m^2)	77	**44**	71	**45**
Blockwork in wall (m^2)	68	**35**	76	**37**
Structural steel beams (tonne)	40	**31**	44	**31**
Pre-cast concrete wall (m^2)	**42**	60	61	**57**
Curtain wall glazing including support system (m^2)	52	**32**	59	**35**
Plasterboard 13mm thick to stud wall (m^2)	51	**45**	51	**43**
Single solid core door including frame/ hardware (no.)	**53**	60	55	**54**
Painting to walls, primer + two coats (m^2)	60	**47**	54	**43**
Ceramic tiling (m^2)	48	**25**	57	**28**
Vinyl flooring to wet areas (m^2)	**26**	44	**39**	51
Carpet medium tufted (m^2)	**35**	56	**33**	57
Lighting installation (m^2)	48	**41**	53	**48**
Copper pipe 15mm to wall (m)	62	**38**	54	**30**
Fire sprinklers (m^2 serviced area)	61	**38**	54	**39**
Air conditioning including main plant (m^2 serviced area)	50	**30**	53	**31**
Proportion lowest CoV (%)	26.32	**73.68**	15.79	**84.21**

Bold figures indicate lowest CoV

combined using the proportion of labour and material costs in each *citiBLOC* (plant cost is distributed evenly between them). Similarly, a composite PPP is calculated based on local prices for the 19 items provided earlier in Table 3.5. Finally, prices for a McDonalds Big Mac hamburger (considered a default global commodity) are used to provide a non-construction alternative, sourced largely from www.economist.com/content/big-mac-index.

An equivalent cost/m^2 for buildings in each city is computed by taking the mean local price for each of the categories listed in Table 3.3 (i.e. residential, commercial, industrial, retail, hotels, hospitals, schools, carparks and airports). While it is obvious that this resultant cost/m^2 does not apply to any building type, the average of all types is done so as to add more stability to the accuracy of in-country prices. This cost/m^2 is then divided by the relative PPP (i.e. L+M, Composite, *citiBLOC*, Big Mac and Currency, compared to the base for Sydney of 1). The results are shown in Table 3.6 (n=23) and Table 3.7 (n=46). Each is categorised into upper (25%), middle (50%) and lower (25%) quartiles using the indices from Expatistan (listed earlier in Table 3.2) that depict a cost of living from expensive (San Francisco = 1.16) to good value (Istanbul = 0.62).

Table 3.6 Average cost/m² (various conversion methods, n=23)

City	*Local Currency*	*citiBLOC*	*L+M*	*Composite*	*Big Mac*	*Currency*
Expensive (upper quartile)						
San Francisco	3,488	3,303	3,473	3,214	3,897	4,569
London	2,518	4,546	4,356	3,996	4,657	4,458
Hong Kong	29,521	5,317	**4,720**	4,267	^**8,496**	**4,958**
Dublin	2,513	4,129	3,172	4,030	3,754	3,919
Sydney (base)	3,311	3,311	3,311	3,311	3,311	3,311
Singapore	2,982	4,174	3,465	3,470	3,034	2,960
Mid-range (middle quartile)						
Doha	7,919	5,289	3,881	3,424	3,894	2,850
Tokyo	313,370	4,103	4,010	**6,007**	4,865	3,698
Amsterdam	2,114	4,308	3,969	3,063	3,158	3,298
Dubai/Abu Dhabi	6,877	**5,408**	3,687	3,354	2,898	2,455
Toronto	3,131	3,318	3,034	3,846	2,820	3,205
Munich	2,019	3,523	3,089	3,321	3,016	3,149
Seoul	1,965,743	4,503	4,206	4,208	2,636	2,362
Shanghai	5,596	3,687	2,153	2,253	1,619	1,145
Johannesburg	13,380	2,454	1,669	2,994	2,631	1,452
Muscat	600	5,285	3,131	3,607	3,145	2,014
Säo Paulo	4,767	3,896	3,080	3,192	1,705	1,934
Good value (lower quartile)						
Bangalore	46,225	4,200	2,188	2,142	**1,515**	**939**
Moscow	72,802	3,703	3,316	2,337	3,304	1,633
Kampala	4,241,835	2,943	**1,299**	2,967	2,319	1,525
Kuala Lumpur	4,366	3,075	1,890	2,913	2,862	1,451
Warsaw	3,960	3,203	2,675	2,764	2,313	1,526
Ho Chi Minh City	19,029,238	**2,437**	1,620	**2,041**	1,727	1,093
	CoV (%)	***22.38***	*30.09*	*25.71*	*45.50*	***46.00***
	Range	***2,971***	*3,421*	*3,966*	***6,981***	*4,019*

^ *Big Mac price in HK is a clear outlier*
Bold figures indicate highest and lowest cost/m², CoV or range

Table 3.8 summarises the comparison of methods, and as previously discovered in Langston (2016), clearly shows that *citiBLOC* has the lowest CoV for both n=23 and n=46 datasets. In fact, the difference between the two datasets is negligible. However, only *citiBLOC* falls below the maximum target based on the mean CoV of the five conversion methods for each city. Ignoring the outlier for Big Mac in Hong Kong, currency conversion has the highest values for CoV, range and comparison to base. When subdivided into expensive (upper quartile), mid-range (middle quartile) and good value (lower quartile), the CoV for *citiBLOC* is even lower – averaging close to or under 20% (see Table 3.9).

Table 3.7 Average cost/m² (various conversion methods, n=46)

City	*Local Currency*	*citiBLOC*	*L+M*	*Composite*	*Big Mac*	*Currency*
Expensive (upper quartile)						
San Francisco	3,488	3,303	3,473	3,214	3,897	4,569
Zurich	3,434	2,988	2,732	3,328	3,117	4,591
New York City	3,644	3,080	3,289	2,823	4,072	4,773
London	2,518	4,546	4,356	3,996	4,657	4,458
Hong Kong	29,521	5,317	**4,720**	4,267	^**8,496**	**4,958**
Dublin	2,513	4,129	3,172	4,030	3,754	3,919
Sydney (base)	3,311	3,311	3,311	3,311	3,311	3,311
Paris	2,095	4,096	3,750	3,262	3,267	3,267
Singapore	2,982	4,174	3,465	3,470	3,034	2,960
Seattle	2,937	2,972	3,278	2,816	3,282	3,848
Doha	7,919	5,289	3,881	3,424	3,894	2,850
Tokyo	313,370	4,103	4,010	**6,007**	4,865	3,698
Mid-range (middle quartile)						
Amsterdam	2,114	4,308	3,969	3,063	3,158	3,298
Dubai/Abu Dhabi	6,877	**5,408**	3,687	3,354	2,898	2,455
Melbourne	2,941	2,919	2,883	3,086	2,941	2,941
Toronto	3,131	3,318	3,034	3,846	2,820	3,205
Brisbane	2,935	3,268	3,103	3,074	2,935	2,935
Munich	2,019	3,523	3,089	3,321	3,016	3,149
Perth	2,733	3,239	3,255	3,588	2,733	2,733
Edinburgh	1,830	4,196	3,878	4,090	3,384	3,239
Beijing	5,858	3,822	2,273	2,384	1,694	1,199
Birmingham	1,853	4,180	4,070	4,108	3,428	3,281
York	1,831	4,102	4,004	4,085	3,386	3,241
Houston	2,367	2,925	2,865	2,858	2,645	3,101
Seoul	1,965,743	4,503	4,206	4,208	2,636	2,362
Southampton	2,047	4,063	3,960	3,830	3,785	3,623
Belfast	1,629	4,569	4,215	4,475	3,013	2,884
Madrid	1,728	3,691	3,273	3,650	2,581	2,695
Shanghai	5,596	3,687	2,153	2,253	1,619	1,145
Johannesburg	13,380	2,454	1,669	2,994	2,631	1,452
Muscat	600	5,285	3,131	3,607	3,145	2,014
Santiago	1,7017,832	4,106	2,847	3,038	2,310	2,195
Säo Paulo	4,767	3,896	3,080	3,192	1,705	1,934
Bangalore	46,225	4,200	2,188	2,142	1,515	**939**
Good value (lower quartile)						
Moscow	72,802	3,703	3,316	2,337	3,304	1,633
Dar es Salaam	2,177,070	2,378	1,602	2,904	**1,468**	1,270
Narobi	90,426	**1,939**	1,247	2,899	1,875	1,150
Kampala	4,241,835	2,943	1,299	2,967	2,319	1,525
Bogatá	3,674,074	2,555	1,769	2,362	1,989	1,603
Kuala Lumpur	4,366	3,075	1,890	2,913	2,862	1,451
Warsaw	3,960	3,203	2,675	2,764	2,313	1,526
Ho Chi Minh City	19,029,238	2,437	1,620	**2,041**	1,727	1,093
Jakarta	12,620,370	3,722	2,734	3,822	2,083	1,225
Buenos Aires	24,626	4,039	2,051	4,871	1,937	1,702
Kigali	1,067,571	2,779	**1,194**	2,122	2,668	1,620
Istanbul	3,264	3,069	2,466	2,955	1,791	1,094
	CoV (%)	**22.39**	*30.34*	*23.28*	*39.27*	**43.51**
	Range	**3,469**	*3,526*	*3,966*	**7,028**	*4,019*

^ *Big Mac price in HK is a clear outlier*

Bold figures indicate highest and lowest cost/m², CoV or range

Table 3.8 Comparison summary (various conversion methods)

Method	*CoV*	*Range*	*Compared to Base*
Common (n=23)			
L+M	30.09%	3,421	3.32%
Composite	25.71%	3,966	19.78%
citiBLOC (preferred)	22.38%	2,971	-10.27%
Big Mac (not recommended)	45.50%	**6,981**	**110.84%**
Currency (not recommended)	**46.00%**	4,019	21.38%
Maximum target	^24.23%	0	0.00%
Extended (n=46)			
L+M	30.34%	3,526	6.49%
Composite	23.28%	3,966	19.78%
citiBLOC (preferred)	**22.39%**	**3,469**	**4.77%**
Big Mac (not recommended)	39.27%	**7,028**	**112.26%**
Currency (not recommended)	**43.51%**	4,019	21.38%
Maximum target	^22.78%	0	0.00%

Shaded figures indicate lowest values and **bold** figures indicate highest values
^ *mean of CoV across the five conversion methods for each city*

Table 3.9 *citiBLOC* summary (by quartile)

Quartile	*CoV*	*Range*	*Compared to Base*
Common dataset (n=23)			
Expensive (upper quartile)	18.56%	2,014	−39.17%
Mid-range (middle quartile)	22.23%	2,954	−10.79%
Good value (lower quartile)	18.88%	1,763	−46.76%
Mean	19.89%	2,244	−32.24%
Extended dataset (n=46)			
Expensive (upper quartile)	21.10%	2,345	−29.18%
Mid-range (middle quartile)	18.46%	2,954	−10.79%
Good value (lower quartile)	20.75%	2,100	−36.58%
Mean	20.10%	2,466	−25.51%

Discussion

Focusing further on the *citiBLOC* indices, we see that each of upper, middle and lower quartile data compute a regression line (line of best fit) that is quite flat. There is considerable volatility and a low r^2 value in each case, which may have more to do with the accuracy of Expatistan's cost of living index used to rank the cities. Each quartile is presented in Figure 3.1 (n=23 and n=46).

Figure 3.2 graphically illustrates index volatility of the equivalent cost/m^2 values for each of the 46 cities in Turner and Townsend (2018). They are listed in order of decreasing cost of living from left to right. The overall trend lines for cost/m^2

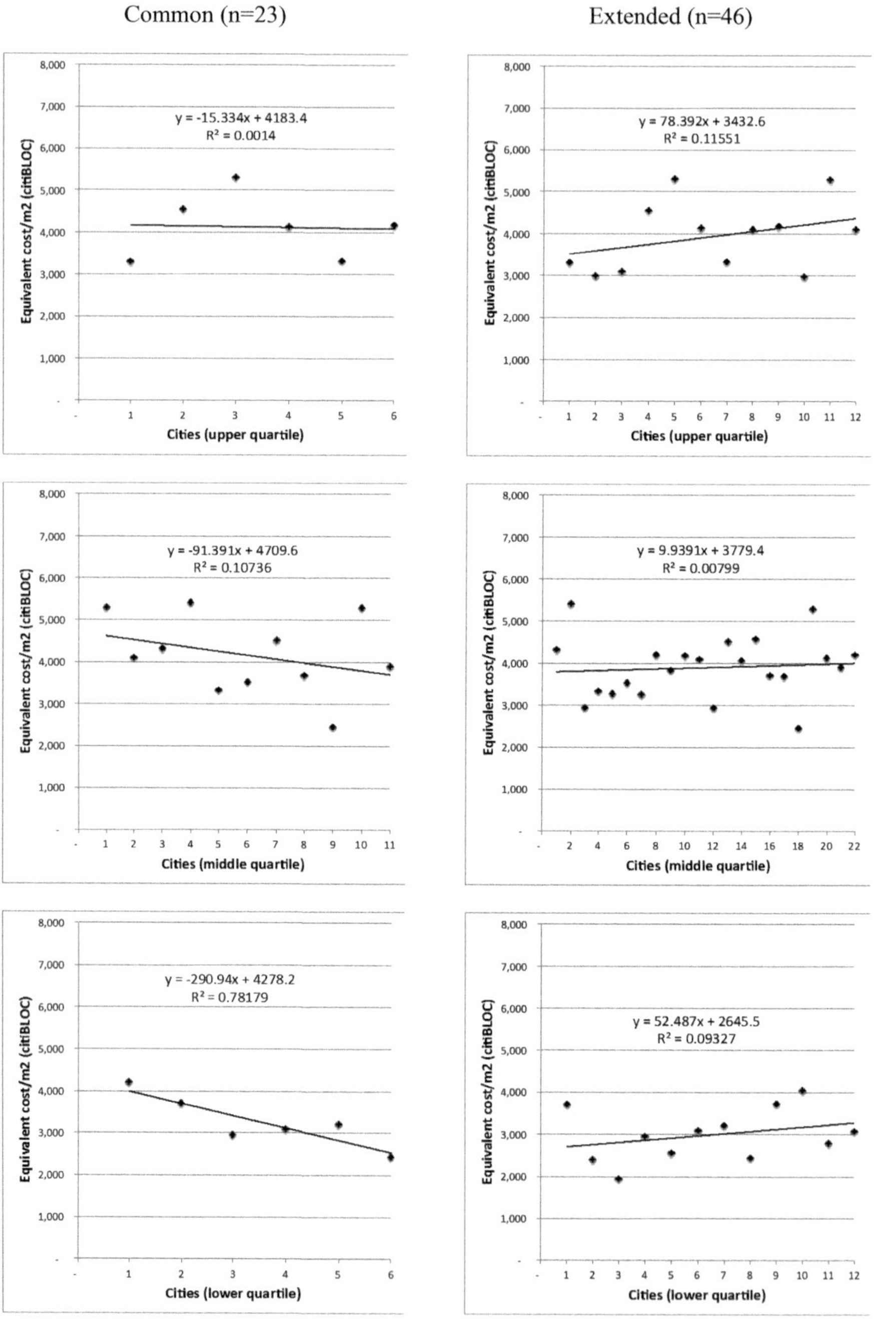

Figure 3.1 Regression analysis of equivalent cost/m^2 (by quartile)

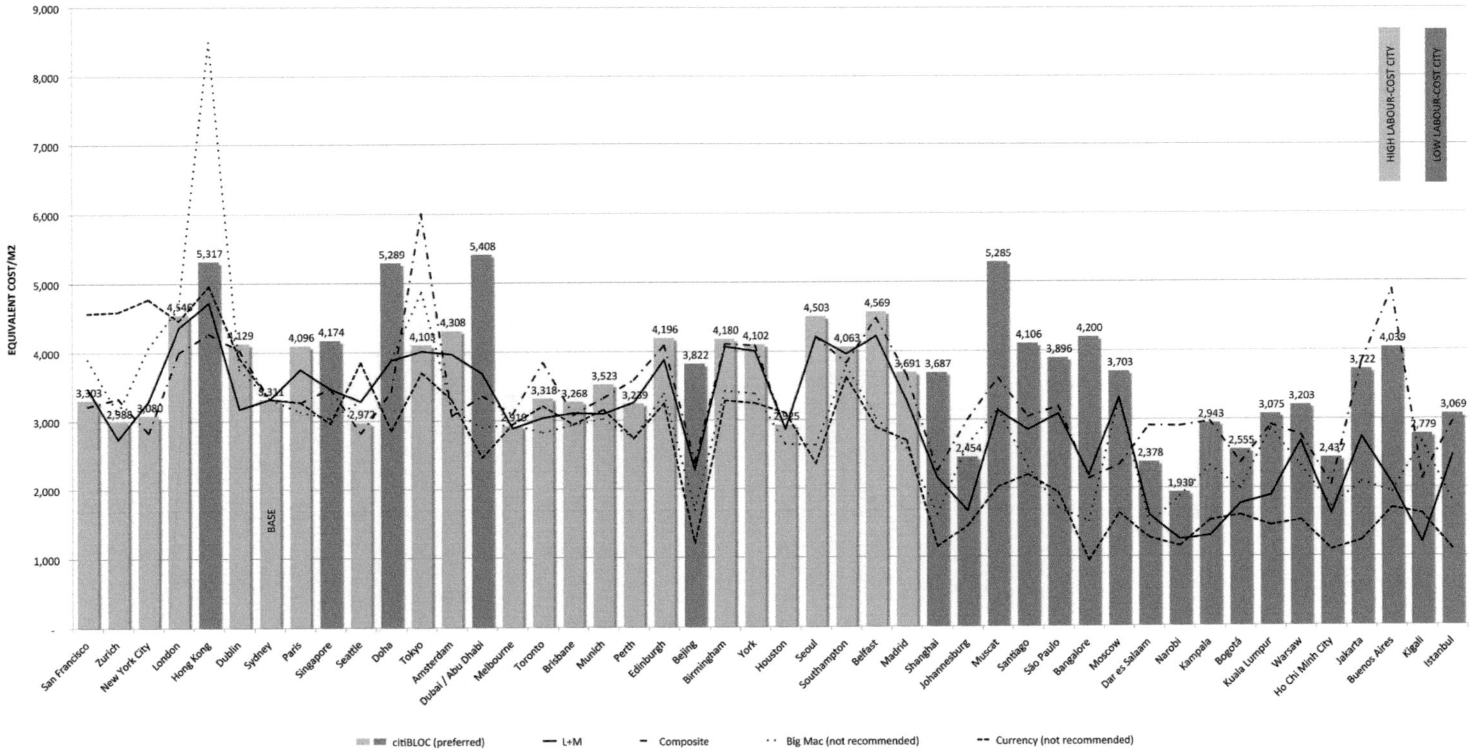

Figure 3.2 International cost benchmarking (various conversion methods, n=46)

generally decline in keeping with the cost of living, and the reason *citiBLOC* has the lowest CoV is probably because this method is the best at smoothing out the data. This is because mean cost/m^2 (in local currency) divided by a balanced cost/basket of local commodities (also in local currency) produces a more stable ratio (i.e. basket/m^2). Cost effectively cancels out, as does currency conversion. Resultant variations are therefore reflecting other differences between locations, such as productivity levels, contractor margins, standards of construction, statutory requirements, local practices and concern for worker health and safety.

One of the big differences between cities in this study is the cost of labour. Using the data in Table 3.4, the ratio of labour to material in the L+M PPP can be computed. This varies from 55:45 (Zurich) to 8:92 (Bogatá). The mean ratio across all cities is 27:73 (n=23) and 30:70 (n=46). High labour-cost and low labour-cost cities have been shaded differently in Figure 3.2 earlier. Not all low labour-cost cities have lower values for cost of living, with Hong Kong, Singapore, Doha and Dubai/Abu Dhabi being notable examples. However, all cities in the lower quartile (n=23 and n=46) deploy cheap labour in construction (mean ratio is 15:85 in both cases).

Finally, it should be noted that any city can be selected as the base. Turner and Townsend (2013) used Sydney, as does this study, but later surveys changed the base to London. The choice of base has no effect on the conclusions reached herein.

Conclusion

The conclusion from Langston (2016: 74) stated that:

> Construction project costs between countries cannot be compared reliably using currency exchange rates, as this fails to take account of the local cost of living. The citiBLOC PPP uses a standard basket of 10 construction items, comprising notional 50% material, 40% labour and 10% plant, to calculate PPP values in each city. The average price of items in the standard basket for a particular city is then divided by the average price for a base city to calculate relative PPPs. When benchmarking international project cost performance, making relative cost comparisons between cities in different countries is necessary. PPP is the correct methodology to apply.
>
> This paper demonstrates that citiBLOC PPPs have the lowest CoV of any of the five methods investigated, and using the Law of One Price as the test, certainly out-perform currency conversion in terms of lower volatility. Given that most practitioners still use USD currency conversion to draw conclusions about relative cost performance in different locations, it seems that many of their conclusions may be unreliable or erroneous. While presentation of construction project costs in terms of USD or other standard currency has its place, citiBLOC PPP is the preferred method whenever judgements about relative project cost performance are involved.

The same conclusion can now be drawn from the 2018 data presented in this chapter. This study has added further confidence in the earlier work, and the findings are most likely to be repeatable in future years.

References

Baffes, J. (1991). Some further evidence on the law of one price: The law of one price still holds, *American Journal of Agricultural Economics*, 73(4), 1264–1273.

Best, R. (2008). *The Development and Testing of a Purchasing Power Parity Method for Comparing Construction Costs Internationally* (PhD thesis), University of Technology, Sydney.

Best, R. and Meikle, J. eds. (2015). *Measuring Construction: Prices, Output and Productivity*, London and New York, Routledge.

Gustav, C. (1918). Abnormal deviations in international exchanges, *The Economic Journal*, 28(112), 413–415.

Krugman, P., Obstfeld, M. and Meiltz, M. (2010). *International Economics* (9th Edition), Pearson Higher Ed, Boston.

Langston, C. (2014). Construction efficiency: A tale of two developed countries, *Engineering, Construction and Architectural Management*, 21(3), 320–355.

Langston, C. (2016). The reliability of currency and purchasing power parity conversion for international project cost benchmarking, *Benchmarking: An International Journal*, 23(1), 61–77.

Langston, C. and Best, R. (2005). Using the big mac index for comparing construction costs internationally, in proceedings of *QUT Research Week*, July, Brisbane.

Pakko, M. R. and Pollard, P. S. (2003). Burgernomics: A Big Mac™ guide to purchasing power parity, *Federal Reserve Bank of St. Louis Review*, 85(6), 9–28.

Rogoff, K. (1996). The purchasing power puzzle, *Journal of Economic Literature*, XXXIV(2), 647–668.

Turner and Townsend (2013). *International Construction Cost Survey 2013*. Available at: www.turnerandtownsend.com/en/insights/international-construction-cost-survey-2013/ [Accessed 05.12.13]

Turner and Townsend (2018). *International Construction Market Survey 2018*. Available at: www.turnerandtownsend.com/en/insights/international-construction-market-survey-2018/ [Accessed.02.06.18]

UBS (2003). *Prices and Earnings: A Comparison of Purchasing Power Parity Around the Globe* (2003 Edition), Union Bank of Switzerland, Zurich.

Part II

Measuring residential construction activity and subsequent environmental issues

4 Measuring high rise building stock

Survival and redevelopment, the case of Hong Kong

Wai Kin Lau and Yung Yau

Introduction

The ageing of building stock is becoming an increasingly urgent issue in several more developed regions. It is like an ageing population in which buildings last a long time, reducing the rate at which they need to be replaced and calling for more retrofitting and rehabilitation. In Europe and the US, ageing building stock has caught the attention of policy makers and researchers, who want to improve the energy efficiency of existing, old building stock. Aksözen et al. (2015), for instance, investigated the energy consumption pattern of buildings in the city of Basel and argued that building age is a non-linear indicator of energy consumption with potential for saving on energy costs. In Hong Kong and similar Asian high-rise, high density cities that developed rapidly over the past few decades, finding ways to manage the building stock to tackle building dilapidation are high on the policy agenda.

So, what is the pace of ageing of the building stock and more fundamentally how long do buildings last? As things stand, there is little discussion about the first question while some have tried to answer the second. In Johnstone (1993, 1994), it was found that housing in New Zealand on average survived 90 years. Komatsu et al. (1994) studied the survival of different types of buildings in Japan. For example, reinforced concrete (RC) apartment houses and RC office buildings were found to survive 35 years and 51 years, respectively. In Aksözen et al. (2017), the median survival time of domestic and non-domestic buildings in the city of Zurich was found to be 130 years. Apart from academic papers, it was reported that buildings in China only survived 25 to 30 years (China Daily, 2010). Without uniform measures, nevertheless, the above figures provide inconsistent information, and it is not possible to find reliable answers to the questions. Furthermore, the figures tended to vary leaving questions unanswered, such as whether buildings in high-rise, high density cities can be expected to have longer or shorter useful lives and what the causes of premature demolition may be.

There is a popular saying that "you can't manage it, if you can't measure it." This describes the management of building stock. There are many advantages in knowing the expected survival of buildings. At the micro level, home and building owners find it difficult to decide whether to maintain or renovate a building, if they cannot even predict how long their homes or buildings will last. At the macro level, government officials, policy makers, developers, property and facilities managers, property investors and others invariably have difficulties managing the existing and future building stock and property portfolios, if they do not understand the critical factors that determine the life span of buildings. The information about how long buildings survive and the pace of ageing is particularly important in high-rise, high density cities, where policy intervention is necessary to ensure timely maintenance and rehabilitation in multi-storey, multi-owner buildings. Otherwise, the public may be put at risk as buildings age and become dilapidated and unsafe.

When a building approaches the end of its useful life, demolition and redevelopment are inevitable. Unlike redevelopment, only recently has demolition as a research subject been given greater attention. Thomsen and van der Flier (2011) conceptualised obsolescence and stated clearly that demolition was not always preceded by obsolescence. Further research is needed to find factors causing demolition. In Thomsen et al. (2011: 331), a few research issues and questions have been posited, such as "What is the average life span and demolition rate in similar countries?" To find determinants of the life span of buildings, Liu et al. (2014) investigated demolished buildings in Chongqing, China and found that external factors such as location and neighbourhood characteristics played an important role in determining life span. In contrast to the socio-economic impact of redevelopment, the *performance* of redevelopment projects has been under-researched, including the time it takes to complete a redevelopment and the factors that affect the durability of redevelopments.

Why Hong Kong?

Given this background, it would be important to study and measure survival and redevelopment of buildings in high-rise, high density cities. Hong Kong, which is a typical city of this kind, (see Figure 4.1), is worthy of in-depth study for a number of reasons. The ageing of buildings and the lack of proper building maintenance in the city have long been overlooked. Hong Kong society in general was not alarmed until the collapse of a building at 45J Ma Tau Wai Road in January 2010 claimed four lives (Buildings Department, 2010). Since then, several measures such as Mandatory Building and Window Inspection have been taken to enhance building safety and combat the problems of ageing building stock. Even so, accidents still happen as in a balcony collapse and falling windows that killed one tourist in June 2017 and another in January 2019 respectively (South China Morning Post, 2017, 2019).

Old and dilapidated buildings are urban time bombs, especially those in high-density built environments. The density of Hong Kong's high-rise buildings and built environment is well illustrated in Table 4.1 in which the profile of the ten major housing estates is presented. Comprising 495 private residential blocks, the ten major housing estates housed more than 0.27 million people, i.e. around 550 residents per block. In such a multi-owner setting, collective action is difficult

Figure 4.1 *(a)(left) and (b)(right)*: High-rise, high density cityscape of Hong Kong

Table 4.1 Profile of the ten major housing estates in Hong Kong

Region			*No. of Blocks/Storeys/Units*	*Floor Area (in sq ft)*	*Date Occupation Permit Issued*	*Building Age (in years, as of mid 2019)*	*No. of Residents^*
Ten Major Housing Estates	Hong Kong Island	Taikoo Shing	61 Blocks/ 23–30 Storeys/ 12,698 Units	563–1,237	12/1976–05/1987	32.1–42.5	35,509
		Kornhill	32 Blocks/ 18–31 Storeys/ 6,648 Units	582–1,064	12/1985–06/1987	32–33.5	18,737
		South Horizons	34 Blocks/ 25–42 Storeys/ 9,812 Units	632–1,100	11/1991–03/1995	24.3–27.6	30,886
	Kowloon	Mei Foo Sun Chuen	99 Blocks/ 15–21 Storeys/about 13,200 Units	616–1,849	10/1968–05/1978	41.1–50.7	37,303
		Whampoa Garden	88 Blocks/14–16 Storeys/about 15,000 Units	351–1,107	12/1985-01/1991	28.4–33.5	30,198
		Laguna City	38 Blocks/25–28 Storeys/8,072 Units	517–1,608	12/1990–12/1991	27.5–28.5	25,281
	New Territories	City One Shatin	52 Blocks/27–34 Storeys/10,643 Units	389–1,018	06/1981–10/1987	31.7–38	25,524
		Kingswood Villas	58 Blocks/27–39 Storeys/about 15,800 Units	573–824	12/1991–12/1997	21.5–27.5	39,964
		Discovery Park	12 Blocks/45 Storeys/3,360 Units	593–848	04/1997–03/1998	21.3–22.2	8,893
		Metro City	21 Blocks/38–43 Storeys/6,768 Units	487–1,026	12/1996–04/2000	19.2–22.5	18,714
Total			495 Blocks/102,000 Units	–	–	–	271,009

^ Source: Census and Statistics Department, Hong Kong (2016).

to achieve making maintenance, rehabilitation and redevelopment of high-rise buildings extremely difficult. Studying and measuring survival and redevelopment of buildings will not provide immediate solutions, but the findings will help to manage existing and future building stock and help solve the problems in the long term. The findings from Hong Kong are also indicative of potential problems affecting other similar high-rise, high density Asian cities, where the ageing of buildings and building dilapidation will occur sooner or later.

While a database of private buildings in Hong Kong is still under construction for the purpose of studying survival, demolition and redevelopment, a study of the survival of public rental housing (PRH)[1] blocks and the redevelopments of the Urban Renewal Authority (URA) in Hong Kong is also being undertaken. This chapter therefore focuses on these two aspects separately and discusses how survival and redevelopment can be measured.

Measuring survival of public rental housing blocks (PRH) in Hong Kong

Not only famous for being the most expensive city to buy a home for in the last decade, Hong Kong also has a large proportion of its population living in public housing, (see Figure 4.2). In 2017, about 3.3 million, or 44.7% of Hong Kong's population lived in public housing. Among them, about 2.14 million, or 29% of the territory's population lived in 850,000 PRH units developed and managed by the Hong Kong Housing Authority (HKHA) and the Hong Kong Housing Society (HKHS), the two major public housing agencies in the city (Transport and Housing Bureau, 2018). In view of the large PRH stock in the portfolios of HKHA and HKHS, studying age distribution and survival of PRH provides essential information for improving the management of the stock and helps to depict the state of Hong Kong's ageing building stock.

The indicators for measuring the survival of buildings

To find how long buildings will last is essentially a survival analysis of buildings. Although seemingly straightforward, the age of a building at a given time and the actual life span of a building must be clarified. One method of calculating the age of a building at a given time is by subtracting the month and year its occupation permit was issued from the month and year at a given time. The actual life span of a building can be found by subtracting the month and year its occupation permit was issued from the month and year its demolition consent was issued:

> Building age at a given time = Month and year of given time – month and year the occupation permit was issued (in years)
>
> Actual life span of a building = Month and year demolition consent was issued – month and year its occupation permit was issued (in years)

Let us now recall the building age shown in Table 4.1. As no residential buildings in the ten major housing estates had been demolished, the apparent building age

Figure 4.2 A typical public rental housing estate in Hong Kong

at a given time is used. When the above two fundamental measures are clarified, building age at a given time will be one of the input data for survival analysis using the Kaplan-Meier (KM) method. (See Appendix 1 of this chapter for The Kaplan-Meier method.) The following indicators that enable measurement and comparison of survival of buildings within and across cities are also used in the analysis:

- Median survival time (in years)
- Age-specific mortality
- Life expectancy (in years)

To express the survival rate of buildings, the median survival time is used or the length of time when half of the buildings under study are expected to survive. Because it is difficult to estimate means from heavily right-censored data without strong parametric assumptions, the median, not the mean, survival time is more commonly used (Brookmeyer, 2014). By comparing the median survival time of a stock of buildings, estimated over periods of time, the pace of ageing can be determined. The median survival time can also be used to describe the characteristics of building stock in a city.

The frequency of demolition of an age group or cohort, the age-specific mortality rate, M_x, can be used. It is calculated by dividing the number of demolitions of that age group by the number of buildings in that age group. With this indicator, one can determine whether there are premature demolitions and at what age most buildings are demolished.

To find how long buildings last is equivalent to finding the life expectancy of buildings. The life expectancy of buildings, $\dot{e}_x$, is found by dividing the total useful life, T_x, by the survivorship function, l_x. The details of its calculation are provided below. Not only is this indicator of interest to many, but it also facilitates comparison between cities.

Apart from building age at a given time and the actual life span of a building can be found by simple calculation. Median survival time may be found by the KM method. Age-specific mortality and life expectancy can be found by the life table method. In addition to referring to the appendix, readers may wish to refer to Kleinbaum and Klein (2005) for details of the KM method, Aksözen et al. (2017) for its application in survival analysis of buildings and Johnstone (1993: 24–37), who derived and explained the life table method.

Collecting data for survival analysis of PRH blocks

Government records of occupation permits and demolition consents, which are respectively the birth and death records of buildings, are needed to extract the date of issue and hence to find the age and actual life span of a building. The Monthly Digest published by the Buildings Department of Hong Kong is a useful source of data that gives information on occupation permits and demolition consents issued to private buildings on a monthly basis. Other information about buildings, such as the number of storeys and the total gross floor area (GFA) that are useful for further statistical analysis to find mortality factors, can also be collected from the two documents. The birth and death of PRH blocks, however, cannot be obtained from occupation permits and demolition consents as they are issued to private buildings only. For surviving and recently demolished PRH blocks, their year of completion and demolition can be obtained from the websites and annual reports of HKHA (using the "Estate Locator") and HKHS. For PRH blocks that were demolished a long time ago, a website called "Hong Kong Place" is a credible source and contains relevant information. Survival analysis of PRH blocks using the KM method and the life table method can then be conducted.

Existence and disappearance of short building life syndrome

The PRH blocks constructed by HKHA and HKHS and their predecessors between 1951 and 2016 were studied and analysed. This observation period is long enough to cover all surviving and demolished PRH blocks and left censoring is not needed. As of the end of 2016, a total of 2,467 PRH blocks had been constructed, of which 1,702 blocks were still surviving and 765 blocks had been demolished.

The survival curves of PRH blocks built in different periods are shown in Figures 4.3(a) to (f). From Figure 4.2(a), the survival curve dropped significantly between buildings that were 25 years old and 35 years old, indicating that many demolitions occurred during this period. Short building life syndrome, a term proposed by Professor Tomonari Yashiro (Yashiro, 2009), was identified. The survival curve then headed downward gradually and stayed above 0.2 at age 50 and older. This pattern is also observed in Figures 4.3(b) to (e), i.e. PRH blocks constructed between 1951 through 1970, indicating that demolition occurred early at around age 15 and persisted until age 30 in these cohorts. Demolition then dropped and became rare beyond age 30. In Figures 4.3(g) and (h), the survival functions of 1976–1980 and 1996–2000 cohorts were at or close to 1.0 showing that demolition of PRH blocks built after 1975 was limited. Short building life syndrome was not found in these two groups of PRH blocks, nor in the younger cohorts built after 1975. Whether the survival functions of different PRH cohorts are significantly different can be further tested by the log-rank test. Besides the survival curve patterns, the median survival time of all PRH blocks is found to be 37 years, ranging between 29 years and 34 years in PRH blocks built between 1951 and 1975 (Table 4.2).

Determined by the life table method, the age-specific mortality rates do not increase with age (Table 4.3). If PRH blocks survived for 0 to 24 years, there was no demolition and thus a zero or close to zero mortality rate can be observed. When PRH blocks survive for 25 to 53 years, the mortality rates become higher indicating that more demolitions took place. The highest four age-specific mortality rates were 8% at ages 29 and 46, 11% at age 35, 16% at age 53 and 20% at age 51. Among the oldest old PRH blocks, which here refer to those that survived for more than 53 years, there was again no demolition and thus mortality rates beyond age 53 were all zero. In Tables 4.4 and 4.5, the number of PRH blocks demolished in different periods and the number of PRH blocks by age of demolition are summarised.

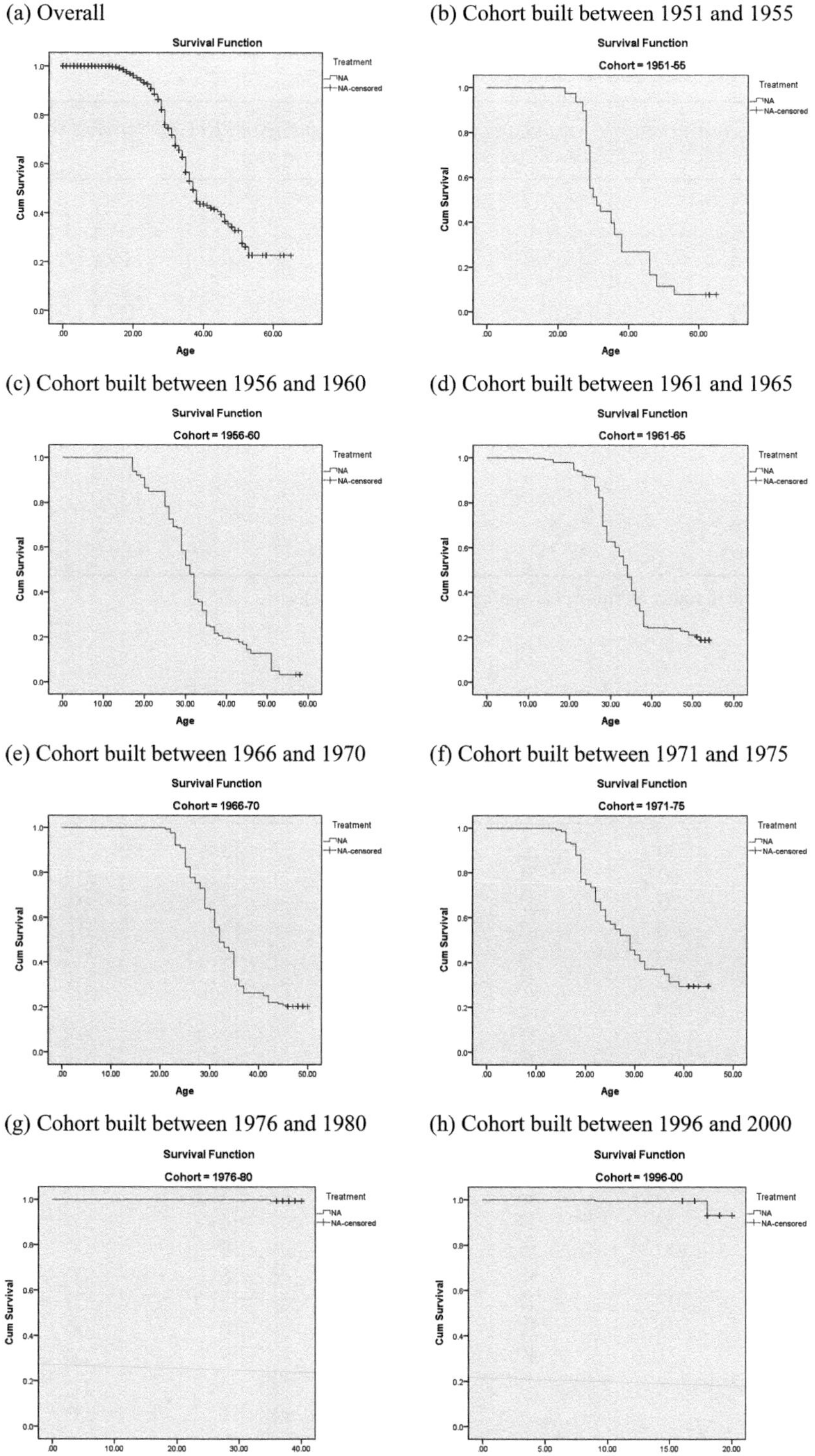

Figure 4.3 Survival curves of PRH blocks built in different periods produced by the KM method

Table 4.2 Mean age, median age and survival rate of PRH blocks built in different periods (as of the end of 2016)

Period of Construction	*Mean Age of PRH Blocks (in years)*	*Median Age of PRH Blocks (in years)*	*Survival Rate (%)*
1951–1955	36.4	31.0	7.7
1956–1960	32.6	31.0	3.4
1961–1965	36.0	34.0	19.4
1966–1970	34.7	32.0	20.4
1971–1975	30.6	29.0	29.3
1976–1980	40.0	-	99.4
1981–1985	33.0*	33.0*	100.0
1986–1990	27.7*	28.0*	100.0
1991–1995	23.1*	23.0*	100.0
1996–2000	19.8	-	96.0
2001–2005	13.6*	14.0*	100.0
2006–2010	7.7*	8.0*	100.0
2011–2016	2.4*	3.0*	100.0
All Cohorts	42.2	37.0	69.0

* Mean/median found by simple calculation in the absence of event.

Table 4.3 Age-specific demolition rate of the PRH blocks

Interval Start Time (Age of buildings at)	*Hazard (Demolition) Rate*	*Interval Start Time (Age of buildings at)*	*Hazard (Demolition) Rate*	*Interval Start Time (Age of buildings at)*	*Hazard (Demolition) Rate*
0	.00	20	.01	40	.00
1	.00	21	.01	41	.01
2	.00	22	.01	42	.03
3	.00	23	.01	43	.01
4	.00	24	.01	44	.02
5	.00	25	.02	45	.03
6	.00	26	.03	46	.08
7	.00	27	.02	47	.03
8	.00	28	.05	48	.04
9	.00	29	.08	49	.04
10	.00	30	.02	50	.00
11	.00	31	.04	51	.20
12	.00	32	.06	52	.06
13	.00	33	.03	53	.16
14	.00	34	.05	54	.00
15	.00	35	.11	55	.00
16	.01	36	.07	56	.00
17	.01	37	.07	57	.00
18	.01	38	.10	58	.00
19	.01	39	.03	59	.00
				60	.00
				61	.00
				62	.00
				63	.00
				64	.00
				65	.00

Table 4.4 Number of PRH blocks built and demolished in different periods

Period of Construction	*No. of PRH Blocks Constructed*	*No. of PRH Blocks Demolished/Cohort Mortality Rate*						*No. of PRH Blocks Surviving/Cohort Survival Rate*
		1971–1980	*1981–1990*	*1991–2000*	*2001–2010*	*2011–2016*	*Total*	
1951–1955	78	5 (6.4%)	46 (59.0%)	13 (16.7%)	8 (10.3%)	-	72 (92.3%)	6 (7.7%)
1956–1960	179	27 (15.1%)	77 (43.0%)	45 (25.1%)	21 (11.7%)	3 (1.7%)	173 (96.6%)	6 (3.4%)
1961–1965	346	7 (2.0%)	44 (12.7%)	174 (50.3%)	48 (13.9%)	6 (1.7%)	279 (80.6%)	67 (19.4%)
1966–1970	167	-	12 (7.2%)	74 (44.3%)	39 (23.4%)	8 (4.8%)	133 (79.6%)	34 (20.4%)
1971–1975	140	-	21 (15.0%)	46 (32.9%)	29 (20.7%)	3 (2.1%)	99 (70.7%)	41 (29.3%)
1976–1980	168	-	-	-	-	1 (0.6%)	1 (0.6%)	167 (99.4%)
1981–1985	238		-	-	-	-	-	238 (100.0%)
1986–1990	330		-	-	-	-	-	330 (100.0%)
1991–1995	191			-	-	-	-	191 (100.0%)
1996–2000	200			-	1 (0.5%)	7 (3.5%)	8 (4.0%)	192 (96.0%)
2001–2005	239				-	-	-	239 (100.0%)
2006–2010	77				-	-	-	77 (100.0%)
2011–2016	114					-	-	114 (100.0%)
Total	2,467	39	200	352	146	28	765	1,792 (69.0%)

Table 4.5 Number of PRH blocks by period of construction and by age of demolition

Period of Construction	*No. of PRH Blocks Constructed*	*No. of PRH Blocks by Age at Demolition/Percentage of Cohort*						*No. of PRH Blocks Surviving*
		≤20	*21–30*	*31–40*	*41–50*	*>50*	*Total*	
1951–1955	78	-	38 (48.7%)	19 (24.4%)	12 (15.4%)	3 (3.8%)	72 (92.3%)	6
1956–1960	179	24 (13.4%)	62 (34.6%)	58 (32.4%)	12 (6.7%)	17 (9.5%)	173 (96.6%)	6
1961–1965	346	8 (2.3%)	121 (35.0%)	133 (38.4%)	11 (3.2%)	6 (1.7%)	279 (80.6%)	67
1966–1970	167	-	61 (36.5%)	62 (37.1%)	10 (6.0%)		133 (79.6%)	34
1971–1975	140	35 (25.0%)	44 (31.4%)	20 (14.3%)	-		99 (70.7%)	41
1976–1980	168	-	-	1 (0.6%)			1 (0.6%)	167
1981–1985	238	-	-	-			-	238
1986–1990	330	-	-				-	330
1991–1995	191	-	-				-	191
1996–2000	200	8 (4.0%)					8 (4.0%)	192
2001–2005	239	-					-	239
2006–2010	77	-					-	77
2011–2016	114	-					-	114
Total	2,467	75	326	293	45	26	765	1,702

Why short building life syndrome and what happened to PRH blocks?

It is clear from Figures 4.3(b) to (f) that half of the PRH blocks built between 1951 and 1975 survived up to 25 to 35 years. Such a short lifespan is definitely abnormal but explicable. These PRH blocks were demolished as they had become physically, functionally and economically obsolete. In the 1960s, Hong Kong faced severe water shortages on the one hand but also experienced a building boom to cope with the rising population on the other. In the meantime, corruption and malpractices in construction projects were not uncommon. Problems of the jerry-built PRH blocks gradually came to light in the early 1980s and as many as 577 PRH blocks were found to have structural problems of varying degrees. Among them, 26 blocks were far below standard and were in imminent danger of collapse. As a result, they had to be demolished within a very short time. Being beyond economic repair, some of the remaining blocks were demolished later. Functionally, the pre-1970 PRH blocks provided no self-contained accommodation and shared bathrooms and toilets. They had obviously failed to keep up with rising living standards in Hong Kong and therefore became obsolete. Famous for its expensive housing market and the limited land and space, Hong Kong had to utilise scarce land effectively to house an increasing population. As a result, there was a need to build taller, more densely and intensely. The older PRH blocks were redeveloped to give way to new PRH blocks to realise development potential.

Redevelopment projects of the Urban Renewal Authority (URA) of Hong Kong

The URA has a key role to play in the urban regeneration of Hong Kong as it is the statutory body having the power to acquire private land to implement redevelopment. The work of URA should align with the government's policy set out in the Urban Renewal Strategy (URS), which is to carry out urban renewal, specifically redevelopment and rehabilitation, to tackle urban decay. That said, many criticised the economic-driven nature of URA redevelopments and URA has been the largest "bulldozer" that demolished many buildings in the urban area of Hong Kong.

The indicators for measuring the redevelopment of buildings

Right from the start finding reasons why buildings are demolished and detecting what buildings are at risk of demolition were two prioritised issues. It was later noticed that some indicators would potentially be useful to measure different aspects of redevelopment projects which are largely overlooked and understudied. The indicators proposed and used below include the project scale, degree of intensification and duration. These enable further studies to be made, such as investigating the factors that affect the duration of redevelopments. Unlike those for measuring the survival of buildings, these indicators take measurements at project and micro level. They include:

Project scale indicators

- Site area (in m^2)
- Existing GFA (i.e. total GFA before redevelopment) (in m^2)
- New GFA (i.e. total GFA after redevelopment) (in m^2)
- Number of buildings affected (demolished) (in number of blocks)
- Number of flats/units affected
- Number of population affected

Intensification indicators

- Existing plot ratio (PR) = Existing GFA/Site area
- New PR = New GFA/Site area
- PR or GFA gain (in %) = (New PR – existing PR)/Existing PR x 100% or (New GFA – existing GFA)/Existing GFA x 100%

Project duration indicators

- (Planned/actual) project duration = Date of project completion – date of project commencement (in years or days)

Others

- Median/mean age of affected buildings (Age of affected buildings = Date demolition consent issued – date of occupation permit issued)
- Composition of different existing/new uses (in %)
- Changes in the composition (in %)

The measurement of the scale of redevelopment projects can be done directly by considering the site area, the existing and new GFA and the number of affected buildings, flats/units and population. Despite that, urban intensification has attracted some discussion, the degree of intensification, which can be determined by (the percentage of) gross floor area (GFA) or plot ratio (PR), gain in a redevelopment has seldom been measured. In construction project management research, measuring construction duration and identifying project delay factors are well-studied topics. Apparently, this is not the case when it comes to measuring and shortening the duration of redevelopments. Using URA's redevelopment project as an example, the duration of a redevelopment project is the time between URA gazetted and announced project commencement moving on to acquisition and the Lands Department issuing a Certificate of Compliance (CC) after all construction works have been completed and the lease conditions are all fulfilled. For others, the median or mean age of affected buildings can tell how old (or young) buildings are, when they are demolished, and the composition indicators can detect the changes in use.

Collecting data for measuring URA redevelopments

The research rested on several sources of information. In order to measure developments, it is crucial to have access to government and private data and records, specifically on project information from the initiators, who are private developers, government or government agencies. To measure URA redevelopments, several sources of information are available. They include: (1) URA press releases; (2) project information of URA redevelopments; (3) annual reports of the URA; and (4) Hong Kong Legislative Council papers on the work of URA. These were all retrieved, reviewed and analysed. Following the review of documents and an internet search, 68 URA redevelopment projects were studied and the findings below were generated.

Diminishing scale of URA redevelopments

In terms of the scale of URA redevelopments, more than 922 blocks of buildings were knocked down, (most but not all were residential buildings), and more than 40,000 people were affected in the past 18 years, since the year 2001. The number of demolished buildings and the size of the population directly affected are reasonable indicators of the scale of redevelopment. In earlier projects, greater numbers of buildings and people had been demolished and relocated, implying that these projects had been larger in scale. In recent years, a decreasing trend in the size of projects has been noted, as fewer buildings and population were affected by individual projects. For the development potential and intensification of land use, the median plot ratio (PR) or the gross floor area over site area, before redevelopment was 4.5, increasing to 8.4 after redevelopment. The average median site area, existing GFA and new GFA were 1,695m^2, 6,934m^2 and 13,134m^2 respectively. Class C sites dominated in URA redevelopments, and a few originally Class A or Class B sites were assembled to form Class B or Class C sites. To explain in a simple way, Class C sites are sites that abut on three specified streets and have the highest PR. Among the completed redevelopments, it took on average 9.6 years to complete projects and the duration of each project ranged from 6.3 to 15.9 years. For on-going projects, the average planned duration was 9.5 years, with a few demand-led projects taking 6.4 years and a large-scale project taking as much as 19 years to complete.

Because owners of commercial and industrial buildings are more sensitive and interested in the return on investment, they will tend to carry out, on their own initiative, repair and maintenance and even redevelopment. Residential buildings were primarily targeted in URA redevelopments. After redevelopment, residential use dominated and accounted for more than 80% to 85% of total GFA, while the rest mostly went to commercial use. Although one of the main urban renewal objectives as set out in URS was "to provide more open space and community/welfare facilities" (Development Bureau, 2011: 4), two-thirds of the redevelopments provided no open space and three-fourths had no space for government, institution or community (G/IC) use. For readers' ease of reference, Table 4.6 presents the details of the redevelopments using the indicators suggested above. In Table 4.7, the redevelopments are grouped by year of commencement into former Land Development Corporation (ex-LDC) projects (i.e. commenced before 2001), projects commenced before 2010 and projects commenced in or after 2010.

Looking back, looking forward: the future trend of redevelopments

Table 4.7 shows that ex-LDC projects are the largest in scale and have the highest PR/GFA gain. They appear to be economically more viable and attractive. When completed, however, they added significant density to an already dense built environment. In recent redevelopments, both the scale and PR/GFA gain have been declining. If there is no reform of the current economic-driven model of redevelopment, it will be very difficult to justify and commence future redevelopment as the residual development potential of relatively young existing buildings appears to be declining, further reducing PR/GFA gain. Although conditions may be varied, most buildings tend to be long-lived and only relatively few old buildings will be redeveloped in any one year in the future. To manage the existing building stock in a sustainable way implies that it may not be a question of redevelopment but more a matter of refurbishment, retrofitting and rehabilitating existing buildings. Although the URA has the statutory power to acquire land for redevelopment, on average it took ten years to complete a redevelopment. Without such statutory power, it would have taken even longer to complete private-led redevelopments. At this point, studies about the measures needed to shorten the redevelopment period are limited. Even though fewer redevelopments are anticipated, the subject of shortening the redevelopment period warrants further investigation.

Conclusions

The ageing of building stock is taking place naturally and can be expected to increase and spread eventually to currently developing regions and cities. The challenges brought to individual cities vary. In high-rise, high density cities, such as Hong Kong, there is a pressing need to find sustainable ways of managing the existing, ageing building stock to tackle urban dilapidation and foster building safety. As failing to measure is failing to manage, it is important to know how long buildings are likely to survive and the pace of building stock ageing are fundamental to the long-term management of the existing and future building stock. The two cases from Hong Kong illustrate how survival and the redevelopment of buildings can be measured with the indicators suggested. If we do not measure building stock, "syndromes" and trends in the survival of PRH blocks and URA redevelopments cannot be identified and diagnosed. The older cohorts of PRH blocks built before the mid-1970s have frequently been found to be short-lived, while

Table 4.6 Summary of URA redevelopments presented using suggested indicators by year of commencement

Project	*Project scale indicators*					*Intensification indicators*			*Project duration indicators*	*Others (Composition of new uses, in %)*					*Year of Commencement*
	Site Area	*EXIST GFA*	*New GFA*	*No. of buildings demolished*	*No. of population affected*	*EXIST PR*	*NEW PR*	*PR gain*	*Planned[T]/ actual duration*	*RESI*	*COM*	*G/IC GFA*	*Open space*	*Others*	
1 H1	7964	25792	66233	50	648	3.2	8.3	159%	NA	91.5	0.6	7.9	1.8	0.0	ex-DLC
2 H9	6793	12555	62310	31	975	1.8	9.2	411%	NA	84.3	5.5	10.1	0.0	0.0	ex-LDC
3 H12	6075	24808	62904	15	1683	4.1	10.4	154%	NA	99.8	0.0	0.2	3.7	0.0	ex-DLC
4 K2	11976	40810	167414	58	2603	3.4	14.0	312%	NA	96.1	3.9	0.7	0.0	0	ex-LDC
5 K8	1607	4190	15160	10	178	2.6	9.4	262%	NA	84.1	15.9	0.0	0.0	0.0	ex-LDC
6 K10	3869	6610	32012	19	444	1.7	8.3	388%	NA	100.0	0.0	0.0	5.2	0.0	ex-LDC
7 K11	8299	27309	102625	20	220	3.3	12.4	276%	NA	44.4	55.6	0.0	1.2	0.0	ex-LDC
8 K13	20300	56851	134185	22	7119	2.8	6.6	136%	NA	80.4	17.3	2.3	2.8	0.0	ex-LDC
9 H16	1970	7640	20567	21	333	3.9	10.4	167%	6.7	87.4	12.6	0.0	0.0	0.0	01/02
10 K3	4510	14416	43231	33	1020	3.2	9.6	200%	12.7	84.4	11.4	4.3	0.0	0.0	01/02
11 K26	1384	5129	12453	8	246	3.7	9.0	143%	8.7	83.3	16.7	0.0	2.0	0.0	01/02
12 K19	1394	4898	12534	8	327	3.5	9.0	157%	8.2	83.4	16.6	0.0	2.0	0.0	07/02
13 K27	535	2411	4921	4	122	4.5	9.2	104%	6.9	83.7	16.3	0.0	0.0	0.0	10/02
14 H20	3536	15690	38178	30	777	4.4	10.8	145%	7.6	89.7	4.5	5.8	1.8	0.0	11/02
15 H17	378	1806	3984	5	25	4.8	10.5	119%	7.3	88.9	11.1	0.0	0.0	0.0	03/03
16 H19	1997	3049	6117	16	98	1.5	3.1	107%	NA	85.8	14.2	0.0	7.7	0.0	03/03
17 K25	2592	9923	21214	19	528	3.8	8.2	116%	10.4	83.3	4.5	12.1	0.0	0.0	07/03
18 K30	1229	6313	10363	7	280	5.1	8.4	65%	7.2	88.9	11.1	0.0	0.0	0.0	07/03
19 K33	277	834	2338	2	9	3.0	8.4	180%	8.2	88.8	11.2	0.0	0.0	0.0	07/03
20 H15	8236	36534	77348	52	1613	4.4	9.4	114%	12.1	84.5	12.2	3.3	5.1	0.0	10/03
21 H21	1871	9834	19555	17	400	5.3	10.5	98%	11.3	83.5	16.5	0.0	0.0	0.0	11/03
22 K20	1003	5935	9030	10	158	5.9	9.0	53%	11.4	83.3	16.7	0.0	0.0	0.0	04/04

(*Continued*)

Table 4.6 (Continued)

Project	Project scale indicators					Intensification indicators			Project duration indicators	Others (Composition of new uses, in %)					Year of Commencement
	Site Area	EXIST GFA	New GFA	No. of buildings demolished	No. of population affected	EXIST PR	NEW PR	PR gain	Planned^T/ actual duration	RESI	COM	G/IC GFA	Open space	Others	
23 K21	2614	14193	23526	24	496	5.4	9.0	67%	12.7	83.3	16.7	0.0	0.6	0.0	04/04
24 K22	2134	10114	19170	22	362	4.7	9.0	91%	12.9	83.3	5.2	11.5	0.8	0.0	04/04
25 K23	1399	8286	12858	11	344	5.9	9.0	53%	11.8	83.3	16.7	0.0	0.0	0.0	04/04
26 K31	2195	10332	19735	12	594	4.7	9.0	91%	6.9	83.2	16.8	0.0	0.0	0.0	12/04
27 K32	2328	11802	20952	12	518	5.1	9.0	76%	8.0	83.3	16.7	0.0	2.1	0.0	12/04
28 SSP/1/001–002	3339	13197	29721	17	551	4.0	8.9	123%	10.5	83.4	16.6	0.0	2.0	0.0	03/05
29 H14	710	3796	5680	2	21	5.3	8.0	51%	14.8	88.9	11.1	0.0	0.0	0.0	09/05
30 SYP/1/001	2150	4140	16469	14	213	1.9	7.7	305%	10.4	98.5	1.5	0.0	7.9	0.0	12/05
31 TKT/2/001	560	4071	4843	3	273	7.3	8.6	18%	9.8	82.7	17.3	0.0	0.0	0.0	12/05
32 SSP/1/003–005	7507	25344	57339	37	1277	3.4	7.6	124%	13.6^T	87.1	9.3	3.6	2.6	0.0	02/06
33 K7	53500	96104	401250	24	313	1.8	7.5	317%	7.3, 14^T, 19^T	40.0	52.2	3.6	2.3	4.0	03/07
34 H18	5230	20219	67528	37	740	3.9	12.9	231%	11–15^T	33.8	64.3	1.9	3.1	0.0	07/07
35 K1	4637	2051	37097	36	109	0.4	8.0	1900%	15.9	93.7	6.3	0.0	3.8	0.0	10/07
36 K28	2478	14434	22301	14	431	5.8	9.0	55%	9.3	77.8	22.2	0.0	0.0	0.0	12/07
37 TKW/1/001	931	5226	8376	5	302	5.6	9.0	61%	9.3	83.3	16.7	0.0	0.0	0.0	02/08
38 MTK/1/001	772	3772	6944	5	229	4.9	9.0	84%	8.0	83.3	16.7	0.0	0.0	0.0	02/08
39 TKT/2/002	726	3348	6529	6	245	4.6	9.0	96%	10.5	0.0	100.0	0.0	0.0	0.0	03/08
40 MTK/1/002	1170	6046	10346	7	290	5.2	8.8	69%	9.1^T	84.8	15.2	0.0	0.0	0.0	05/09
41 SSP/3/001	827	3820	7159	5	159	4.6	8.7	89%	9.0	83.2	16.8	0.0	0.0	0.0	06/09
42 TKW/1/002	3377	11104	24397	16	660	3.3	7.2	118%	9.3^T	83.3	12.6	4.1	2.0	0.0	02/10
43 KC-006	1277	6389	9780	12	296	5.0	7.7	54%	8.5^T	83.4	16.6	0.0	0.0	0.0	03/11
44 SSP-014	649	2456	5030	6	194	3.8	7.8	105%	7.5^T	88.9	11.1	0.0	0.0	0.0	03/11
45 KC-007	1622	7258	12456	8	475	4.5	7.7	71%	8.8^T	83.3	16.7	0.0	0.0	0.0	11/11
46 YTM-010	1640	10024	12510	5	682	6.1	7.6	25%	8.6	83.3	16.7	0.0	0.0	0.0	02/12

47 DL-2:SSP	470	2952	3597	1	239	6.3	7.7	22%	7.4[T]	87.1	12.9	0.0	0.0	0.0	04/12
48 DL-1:SSP	483	2547	3639	1	172	5.3	7.5	42%	6.4[T]	88.9	11.1	0.0	0.0	0.0	04/12
49 DL-3:YTM	865	5105	6520	11	330	5.9	7.5	27%	8.4	85.3	14.7	0.0	0.0	0.0	04/12
50 IB-2:SSP	1393	12145	16716	1	0	8.7	12.0	38%	7.7[T]	100.0	0.0	0.0	0.0	0	01/13
51 SSP-015	1268	4964	9513	6	232	3.9	7.5	92%	10.5[T]	83.3	16.7	0.0	0.0	0.0	03/13
52 DL-4:SSP	599	3817	4884	1	229	6.4	8.2	28%	6.4[T]	83.3	16.7	0.0	0.0	0.0	04/13
53 DL-5:SSP	1640	10313	13410	1	552	6.3	8.2	30%	10.4	67.8	32.2	0.0	0.0	0.0	04/13
54 DL-6:YTM	769	3461	5741	2	171	4.5	7.5	67%	8.3	88.9	11.1	0.0	0.0	0.0	06/13
55 DL-8: KC	553	2467	4546	3	142	4.5	8.2	82%	11.8[T]	83.3	6.8	9.9	0.0	0.0	12/13
56 SSP-016	1900	7335	14841	8	402	3.9	7.8	100%	8.6[T]	83.3	16.7	0.0	0.0	0.0	02/14
57 DL-10:KT	865	5304	6663	1	393	6.1	7.7	26%	6.8[T]	88.9	3.6	7.5	0.0	0.0	11/14
58 DL-11:YTM	474	3228	3527	1	234	6.8	7.4	9%	6.3	88.9	11.1	0.0	0.0	0.0	05/15
59 KC-009	8042	39644	66600	27	2640	4.9	8.3	69%	9.5[T]	83.3	16.7	0.0	0.0	0.0	03/16
60 KC-008(A)	2475	3738	14724	7	200	1.5	5.9	293%	9.3[T]	83.3	16.7	0.0	0.0	0.0	05/16
61 KC-010	4951	21495	41058	19	1462	4.3	8.3	93%	9.5[T]	83.3	16.7	0.0	0.0	0.0	06/16
62 KC-011	2635	12628	21960	12	821	4.8	8.3	73%	9.3[T]	83.3	16.7	0.0	0.0	0.0	06/16
63 KC-012	1258	5023	10530	7	343	4.0	8.4	110%	9.3[T]	83.3	16.7	0.0	0.0	0.0	06/16
64 KC-013	1749	7458	11797	2	463	4.3	6.7	56%	9.5[T]	83.3	16.7	0.0	0.0	0.0	03/17
65 C&W-005	1120	NA	8270	14	235	NA	7.9	NA	9.2[T]	95.2	4.8	0.0	0.0	0.0	07/17
66 C&W-006	2460	NA	11290	NA	NA	NA	4.6	NA	10.5[T]	85.8	6.6	0.0	4.8	8.0	03/18
67 YTM-011	820	NA	5985	NA	186	NA	7.3	NA	9.5	83.3	16.7	0.0	0.0	0.0	03/18
68 KC-014	3016	NA	25720	NA	1060	NA	8.5	NA	NA	83.3	16.7	0.0	0.0	0.0	06/18

Table 4.7 Comparison of URA redevelopments using suggested indicators by year of commencement

Median and mean of:	*Ex-LDC*	*Before 2010*	*In or after 2010*
Overall			
	8 projects Completed – 8 (100%) Class C sites – 8 (100%)	33 projects Completed – 25 (75.8%) On-going – 8 (24.2%) Class A sites – 5 (12.8%) Class B sites – 11 (28.2%) Class C sites – 23 (59.0%)	27 projects On-going – 27 (100%) Class A sites – 7 (25.9%) Class B sites – 10 (37.0%) Class C sites – 10 (37.0%)
Project scale indicators			
Site area (in m^2)	7,379/8,360	1,970/3,822	1,277/1,791
EXIST GFA (in m^2)	25,300/24,866	6,313/11,658	5,304/8,298
NEW GFA (in m^2)	64,569/80,355	16,469/32,111	10,530/13,915
No. of buildings demolished (in blocks)	21/28	12/15	5/6
No. of population affected	812/1,734	313/406	296/475
Intensification indicators			
EXIST PR	3/2.9	4.6/4.3	4.8/5.0
NEW PR	9.3/9.8	9/8.9	7.7/7.8
PR/GFA gain (in %)	269/262	104/184	71/67
Project duration indicator			
Planned/actual duration (in years)	NA/NA	10.1/10.3	9/8.7

the more recent cohorts may be expected to last much longer than their design life of 50 years. Redevelopments led by URA, on the other hand, are diminishing in scale suggesting that the opportunities for redevelopment become fewer amid ageing building stock. This is a start, not an end, of the measures discussed in this chapter, as their indicative power has not yet been fully utilised. They have ample scope of application in built environment research. With them, the dynamics and changes in the building stock over time and the differences between cities can be traced and compared for further studies and policy planning.

Acknowledgement

The work described in this chapter was partially supported by a grant from the Research Grants Council of the Hong Kong Special Administrative Region, China (Project No. UGC/FDS25/E13/16).

Note

1 The term public rental housing is used in Hong Kong. See Available at www.housingauthority.gov.hk/en/flat-application/application-guide/index.html

References

Aksözen, M., Magdalena, D., Hassler, U. and Kohler, N. (2015). Building age as an indicator for energy consumption, *Energy & Buildings*, 87(1), 74–86.

Aksözen, M., Hassler, U., Rivallain, M. and Kohler, N. (2017). Mortality analysis of an urban building stock, *Building Research & Information*, 45(3), 249–277.

Anson, J. (2002). The life table: A sociological review, in Wunsch, G., Mouchart, M. and Duchene, J. (eds.) *The Life Table: Modelling Survival and Death*, Kluwer Academic, Kluwer, pp. 283–305.

Brookmeyer, R. (2014). *Median survival time*. Available at: https://onlinelibrary.wiley.com/doi/abs/10.1002/9781118445112.stat06043 [Accessed 14.06.2019]

Buildings Department (2010). *Report on the Collapse of the Buildings at 45J Ma Tau Wai Road*. Available at: www.bd.gov.hk/english/BuildingCollapseReport_e.pdf [Accessed 11.02.2019]

Census and Statistics Department (2016). *2016 Population by-Census: The "district council district/constituency area (DC/CA) system"*. Available at: www.bycensus2016.gov.hk/en/bc-dp.html [Accessed 13.02.2019]

China Daily (2010). *'Most homes' to be Demolished in 20 Years*. Available at: www.chinadaily.com.cn/china/2010-08/07/content_11113982.htm [Accessed 11.02.2019]

Development Bureau (2011). *Urban Renewal Strategy*. Available at: www.devb.gov.hk/filemanager/en/Content_3/URS_eng_2011.pdf [Accessed 17.12.2018]

Johnstone, I. M. (1993). *The Mortality of New Zealand Housing Stock* (Unpublished PhD Thesis), Department of Architecture, The University of Auckland.

Johnstone, I. M. (1994). The mortality of New Zealand housing stock, *Architectural Science Review*, 37(4), 181–188.

Kleinbaum, D. G. and Klein, M. (2005). *Survival Analysis: A Self-learning Text* (Second Edition). Springer, New York.

Komatsu, Y., Kato, Y. and Yashiro, T. (1994). Survey on the life of buildings in Japan, *Proceedings of Strategies and Technologies for Maintenance and Modernisation of Buildings*, CIB W070 Tokyo Symposium, 1, 111–118.

Liu, G., Xu, K., Zhang, X. and Zhang, G. (2014). Factors influencing the service lifespan of buildings: An improved hedonic model, *Habitat International*, 43, 274–282.

South China Morning Post (2017). *Another Balcony to be Demolished after Collapse at Old Hong Kong Tenement Block*. Available at: www.scmp.com/news/hong-kong/law-crime/article/2099274/lucky-escape-hung-hom-flat-residents-floor-collapses-under [Accessed 11.02.2019]

South China Morning Post (2019). Hotel Cleaner Arrested after Pedestrian Killed by Falling Window on Busy Hong Kong Street. Available at: www.scmp.com/news/hong-kong/health-environment/article/2182965/pedestrian-killed-busy-hong-kong-street-after [Accessed 11.02.2019]

Thomsen, A. and van der Flier, K. (2011). Understanding obsolescence a conceptual model for buildings, *Building Research & Information*, 39(4), 352–362.

Thomsen, A., Schultamnn, F. and Kohler, N. (2011). Deconstruction, demolition and destruction, *Building Research & Information*, 39(4), 327–332.

Transport and Housing Bureau (2018). *Housing in Figures 2018*. Available at: www.thb.gov.hk/eng/psp/publications/housing/HIF2018.pdf [Accessed 13.02.2019]

Yashiro, T. (2009). Overview of building stock management in Japan, in Fujino, Y. and Noguchi, T. (eds.) *Stock Management for Sustainable Urban Regeneration*, Springer-Verlag, Tokyo, pp. 15–32.

Appendix

The Kaplan-Meier method and the life table method

The Kaplan-Meier method

This method can be used to find the median survival time of buildings. By using it, the survival function $S(t)$ which is the probability that the lifetime of a building T exceeds the specified time t can be calculated and the median survival age can be obtained then:

$$S(t) = \Pr\ (T > t) \tag{1}$$

The survival curve that illustrates the survival function is a stepped curve beginning at $S(t) = 1$ at $t = 0$ and heads downward towards zero as t increases towards infinity, as time is counted in years. In the absence of censoring, the survival function is a sum of probability at the time, t_k, with k observed failure times:

$$S(t) = \Pr(T > t) = \sum_{t_k > t} pr(t_k) \text{ with } k = 1, 2, 3, \ldots \tag{2}$$

Where undemolished buildings are right censored, either the age when buildings are demolished or the age standing buildings remain are used to calculate the Kaplan-Meier estimate (KME). The lifetime of demolished or undemolished buildings up to is L and the practical lifetime of buildings from the year of completion to the end of observation is C. The observed lifetime of buildings is defined as:

$$T = \min\{L, C\} \tag{3}$$

If buildings under study have a lifetime, L, greater than or beyond the observation period, only the practical lifetime C within the observation period is considered. The hazard function is opposite to the survival function, as it measures failure. Considering them together, the survival function $S(t)$ and hazard rate $h(t)$ at each time, t_k and its product until time t is given by:

$$\hat{S}(t) = \prod_{t_k \le t} \left[1 - h(t_k)\right] \tag{4}$$

And the survival function for building stock estimated by the KM method is:

$$(t) = \prod_{t_k \le t} (1 - \frac{D_k}{B_k + D_k}) \tag{5}$$

where D_k is the number of demolished buildings (i.e. the event concerned) that have survived t_k; and B_k is the number of buildings that have survived longer than t_k.

And finally, the mean survival time is estimated by:

If $T_L = t_k$

$$\hat{\mu} = \begin{cases} \sum_{i=0}^{k-1} \hat{S}(t_i^+) \times (t_{i+1} - t_i) \\ \sum_{i=0}^{k-1} \hat{S}(t_i^+) \times (t_{i+1} - t_i) + \hat{S}(t_i^+) \times (T_L - t_k) \end{cases} \tag{6}$$

otherwise

with T_L being the largest observation time,

$T_L = t_k$, if T_L is uncensored;

t_a^+ is a right censored observation at time t_k; and

$t_0 = 0$ and $\hat{S}(t_0^+) = 1$

The status of buildings at *T*, either demolished (=1) or no event (=0), must be known. Besides, buildings aged between x and x + z can be grouped into different z-year cohorts to conduct the log-rank test to determine whether survival curves of two cohorts are statistically different.

The life table method

When analysing survival, a life table may be constructed to find the age-specific mortality rates and life expectancy of buildings. The construction of a table is based on the manipulation of mortality rates, ${}_nM_x$ and their translation into mortality probabilities, ${}_nq_x$, a survivorship curve I_x and life expectancies $(\dot{e}_x)$ (Anson, 2002: 289). This method was derived and explained in Johnstone (1993: 24–37):

The crude loss rate (M) and the age-specific loss rate (M_x) of buildings from a building stock is given by:

$$M = \frac{D}{P} \tag{7}$$

where

P = Average total building stock exposed to building losses over one calendar year.

D = Total building losses, or the sum of total building losses of all ages over the year. And

$$M_x = \frac{D_x}{P_x} \tag{8}$$

where

P_x = Cohort of buildings aged between x and x + 1 standing at the middle of the calendar year.

D_x = Age-specific building losses from the same cohort over the calendar year.

The annual probability of loss (q_x) and the annual probability of survival (p_x) is expressed by:

$$q_x = \frac{D_x}{P_x + \frac{1}{2}D_x} = \frac{M_x}{1 + \frac{1}{2}M_x} \tag{9}$$

and

$$p_x = (1 - q_x) \tag{10}$$

The probability of survival, ${}_np_x$, of a building aged x surviving through n years is the product of survival over successive years:

$${}_np_x = (p_x)(p_{x+1}) \ldots (p_{x+n-1}) \tag{11}$$

Similarly, the probability of loss (${}_nq_x$) is the complement of the probability of survival (${}_np_x$):

$${}_nq_x = (1 - {}_np_x) \tag{12}$$

In a typical building stock life table, the following information is provided:

- Age interval: the interval between two exact ages.
- Probability of loss (${}_nq_x$): the probability of building loss is given by:

$${}_nq_x = \frac{I_x - I_{x+n}}{I_x} \tag{13}$$

where I_x and I_{x+n} are the expected surviving stock which survive to the exact age x and x + n marking the beginning of each respective age interval.

- Surviving stock (I_x): the number of buildings of exact age x which are still standing at the beginning of each age interval.
- Stock losses (${}_nd_x$): the losses over successive age intervals x to x + n, is given by:

$${}_nd_x = I_x - I_{x+n} \tag{14}$$

- Stock in age interval (${}_nL_x$): the number of stationary stock buildings in the indicated age interval, is given by:

$$ {}_nL_x = {}_nI_{x+n} + {}_nd_{xn}\, a_x \text{ or } {}_nL_x = {}_nI_x - {}_nd_{xn}\, a_x \tag{15} $$

or

$$ {}_nL_x = {}_n(I_x - \frac{{}_nd_x}{2}) \tag{16} $$

If ${}_na_x$ (the average number of years provided by the stock lost in the interval) is assumed to be uniform.

- Total useful life (T_x): the number of stationary stock buildings in the indicated age interval and all subsequent age intervals, is given by:

$$ T_x = {}_nL_x + {}_nL_{x+n} + \cdots = \sum_{i=0}^{\infty} {}_nL_{x+in} \tag{17} $$

- Life expectancy at age x ($\dot{e}_x$) : the average number of service-years remaining to be provided by those buildings which are still standing at the beginning of an age interval x and x + n, is given by:

$$ \dot{e}_x = \frac{T_x}{I_x} \tag{18} $$

5 Deep renovation in different business environments

Terttu Vainio and Eero Nippala

Introduction

Energy efficiency has become a key priority of the Europe 2020 strategy for smart, sustainable and inclusive growth, as well as resource efficiency (EU, 2010a). Through efficiency, security of the energy supply can be improved. Emissions can also be reduced, and energy reserves that would otherwise be wasted due to inefficiency can be recovered.

The EU's updated strategy, which will extend up to 2030, has the aim of reducing greenhouse gases by 40 per cent compared to the 1990 level. In addition, a binding target has been set for the use of renewable energy (EU, 2014). The Paris climate agreement, signed in the autumn of 2015, is still expected to further tighten requirements set for the energy efficiency of buildings and the adoption of renewable energy (UN, 2015).

The first step in implementing the strategy with regard to the existing building stock was the requirement to improve energy efficiency during renovations (EU, 2010b). In addition, the public sector has been tasked with setting an example by entering into energy efficiency agreements, improving the energy efficiency of public buildings, making energy efficiency a criterion for awarding public contracts and obliging energy companies to help consumers cut energy consumption.

The energy efficiency of buildings is regulated by a specific 'Energy Performance of Buildings Directive (EPBD)'. However, the generally applicable Energy Efficiency Directive (EED) requires measures that go further. It requires EU member states to incentivise investment in the deep renovation of buildings (EU, 2012). Construction is also subject to the Renewable Energy Directive (EU, 2009) on the use of renewable energy and the Eco Design Directive on the energy efficiency of products (EU, 2010c). Energy performance certificates (EPC) are a result of regulations such as these.

Definition of deep renovation

Horizon 2020 Energy Efficiency Call 2015 defines 'deep renovation' in accordance within the Energy Efficiency Directive (EU, 2012) as a cost-effective renovation which leads to a refurbishment that reduces both the delivered and final energy consumption of a building by a significant percentage compared with the pre-renovation levels, leading to a very high energy performance. It also states that such deep renovations could also be carried out in stages. The European Commission Staff Working Document (EU, 2013) indicates that energy savings should be more than 60 per cent, if they are to be viewed as significant efficiency improvements resulting from deep renovation According to Economidou et al. (2011), a 'deep renovation' typically adopts an holistic approach, viewing the renovation as a package of measures working together and resulting in final energy savings of 60 per cent to 90 per cent.

The recast of the directive of energy performance of buildings (EU, 2010b) does not mention 'deep renovation' at all. Instead, it states that Member States should be able to choose to define a 'major renovation' either in terms of a percentage of the surface of the building envelope or in terms of the value of the building. If the value is chosen, the value of the land upon which the building is situated should be excluded. In Article 2, the recast gives two alternative definitions (Sajn, 2016; Artola et al., 2016) of 'major renovation' for Member States to choose. 'Major renovation' is done if either a) the total cost of the renovation relating to the building envelope or the technical building systems is higher than 25% of the value of the building, excluding the value of the land upon which the building is situated, or (b) more than 25% of the surface of the building envelope undergoes renovation.

In their analysis of the renovation of the EU building stock for the period to 2050, Boermans et al. (2012) do not define 'deep renovation' properly. The 'deep renovation and high use of renewable energy' is defined to include a renovation rate of 2.3% for a high level of energy efficiency improvement, (namely about an 80% reduction in energy use for space heating), high focus on energy efficiency of the building envelope and advanced systems (high use of renewable energy and heat recovery ventilation).

Fabbri et al. (2016) highlight that there is currently no common definition of 'deep renovation'. But they provide an overview of the main definitions of deep renovation used in the EU. According to Fabbri et al., deep renovation is a process enabling the full potential of a building to reduce its theoretical energy-demand by careful planning of the renovation to avoid the installation of lock-in measures. Deep renovation can be approached with the following methods: (1) Percentage of energy-savings realised; (2) Maximum energy performance; and (3) A selection of energy-saving measures to be executed.

After a series of webinars and a questionnaire, Shnapp et al. (2013) argue that 'Deep Renovation' or 'Deep Energy Renovation' in the EU captures the full economic energy efficiency potential of improvement works, with a main focus on the building shell, of existing buildings and leads to a very high-energy performance. Renovated buildings energy reductions are 75% or more compared to the status of existing buildings before renovation. The primary energy consumption after renovation, which includes, among other things, energy used for heating, cooling, ventilation, hot water and lighting after the deep renovation of an existing building is less than 60 kWh/m2/yr.

In terms of the EU directive, instead of a definition for deep renovation, a long-term efficiency objective is used (Fabbri et al., 2016): existing buildings must achieve the E60 level by 2050 corresponding to a primary energy demand of 100 kWh/m^2 for gross surface, combined with a series of mandatory requirements (measures and installations). New buildings today must achieve an efficiency level of E60, while nZEB level is defined as E30.

The objective of this study is to compare the challenges of deep renovation in different economic environments. The comparison is made from an economic point of view and only concerns residential buildings. The functionality and living standards are excluded even though they may be important positive or negative factors.

Methodology

The method used in this country by country comparison is based on the payback period criterion. This means the time that a project requires to recover the investment. In a deep renovation project, the investment is a set of measures, which cut energy use by 60 %. The saving target is the minimum quoted in the definition paragraph. Investment is covered by energy savings. The payback period of a project is expressed in years and is computed using the following, applied formula:

$$\text{Payback period} = \frac{\text{Investment required for a project}}{\text{Net annual cash flow}} \sim \frac{\text{Deep renovation}}{\text{Energy saving}}$$

According to this method, the project that promises a quick recovery of initial investment is considered desirable. If the payback period of a project computed by the above formula is shorter than or equal to the management's maximum desired payback period, the project is accepted, otherwise it is rejected. For example, if a company wants to recoup the cost of an investment within 5 years of purchase, the maximum desired payback period of the company would be 5 years.

Advantages of payback period are:

1. Payback period is very simple to calculate.
2. It can be a measure of risk inherent in a project. Since cash flows that occur later in a project's life are considered more uncertain, payback period provides an indication of how certain the project cash inflows are.
3. For companies facing liquidity problems, it provides a good ranking of projects that would return money early. In this case saving energy after the payback period is good for housing companies, who benefit from lower energy costs.

Disadvantages of payback period are:

1. Payback period does not take into account the time value of money, which is a serious drawback since it can lead to wrong decisions. One variation of

the payback method that attempts to remove this drawback is called the discounted payback period method.

2 The payback period does not take into account, the cash flows that occur after the payback period.

Variables by country

In Table 5.1, the variables are country specific and adopted either from Eurostat or other EU data sources to ensure the consistency and comparability of the input data. This review is based on the price levels in 2015–2016.

Heating degree days, (D in Table 5.1): Consumption of energy depends strongly on weather conditions. If the temperature decreases below a certain value, "heating threshold", more energy is consumed due to the increased need for space heating (Eurostat, Heating degree-days).

Specific energy consumption of residential buildings per m^2 at normal climate, **(X in Table 5.1),** is based on formula: X=A/(1-(B*0,9)*(1-C/D))/E where A is energy consumption of a residential building; B is the share of space heating; C is degree-days; D is normal degree-days (1980–2004); E is the total floor area of permanently occupied-dwelling (EU, Building Stock Observatory).

Residential construction price level index, (Y in Table 5.1): The index expresses the residential construction price levels in the EU28. If the price level index of a country is higher than 100, the country concerned is relatively expensive., while if the price level index is lower than 100, then the country is relatively cheap. (Eurostat, Comparative price levels for investments, year 2015).

Value added tax rate (V in Table 5.1): The value added tax (VAT), is a general, broadly based consumption tax assessed on the value added to goods and services. VAT is charged as a percentage of prices, meaning that the actual tax burden is visible at each stage in the production and distribution chain (European Union VAT rates, year 2014).

Electricity price (Z in Table 5.1): The price of energy depends on a range of different supply and demand conditions, including the geopolitical situation, import diversification, network costs, environmental protection costs, severe weather conditions and levels of excise and taxation. Prices presented in the table include taxes, levies and VAT for household consumers (Eurostat, Energy price statistics, year 2016).

Deep renovation: The deep renovation concept is common to all countries and it is formed on the basis of the EU GUGLE project (Morishita, 2016). The concept includes renovation of facades and windows and installation of heat recovery and photo voltaic panels. The total cost of reparation concept (I) is 190 euro per m^2 (price level EU27 excluding VAT and subsidies). The total cost is tailored to each country by considering the construction price level and VAT rate.

Table 5.1 Variables by country

	Heating degree days (D)	*Residential buildings, specific energy consumption kWh/m2; a (X)*	*Residential construction price level index EU27 = 100 (Y)*	*Value added tax rate % (V)*	*Electricity price euro/kWh (Z)*
Belgium	2696	263	99	21	0.25
Bulgaria	2403	121	35	20	0.10
Czech Republic	3327	234	59	15	0.14
Denmark	3235	169	150	25	0.31
Germany	3063	200	136	19	0.30
Estonia	4302	290	67	20	0.12
Ireland	2841	166	91	14	0.23
Greece	1449	121	62	24	0.18
Spain	1686	103	69	10	0.22
France	2340	190	116	20	0.17
Croatia	2316	250	44	25	0.13
Italy	1829	175	74	10	0.24
Cyprus	600	69	64	5	0.15
Latvia	4161	292	61	21	0.16
Lithuania	3931	204	59	21	0.12
Luxembourg	2967	205	106	17	0.17
Hungary	2594	150	46	27	0.11
Malta	499	47	64	18	0.13
Netherlands	2727	152	114	21	0.16
Austria	3301	198	116	20	0.20
Poland	3439	238	53	23	0.13
Portugal	1166	70	51	6	0.24
Romania	2773	308	35	19	0.13
Slovenia	2774	228	53	10	0.16
Slovakia	3160	173	55	20	0.14
Finland	5596	248	131	24	0.15
Sweden	5291	215	166	25	0.19
United Kingdom	2990	184	96	5	0.20
Norway	4963	215*	169	25	0.15
Switzerland	2996	198*	188	8	0.23

*Norway: same as in Sweden; Switzerland: same as in Austria

Results and discussion

Figure 5.1 includes payback periods of deep renovations in European countries. Periods are calculated by using variables from Table 5.1.

The longest payback period (20 years) is in Norway, where the construction price level is high, and energy is relatively cheap. The fact that more than 99% of the electricity production in mainland Norway is covered by hydropower plants and the motivation for deep renovation is understandably very weak.

Example Netherlands

Payback period = ((I*Y/100)*((100+V)/100) / (60 % * X * Z)

= (190 € * 114/100)*(121/100) / (60 % * 152 kWh *0.16 €/kWh;a) ~ 17.7 years.

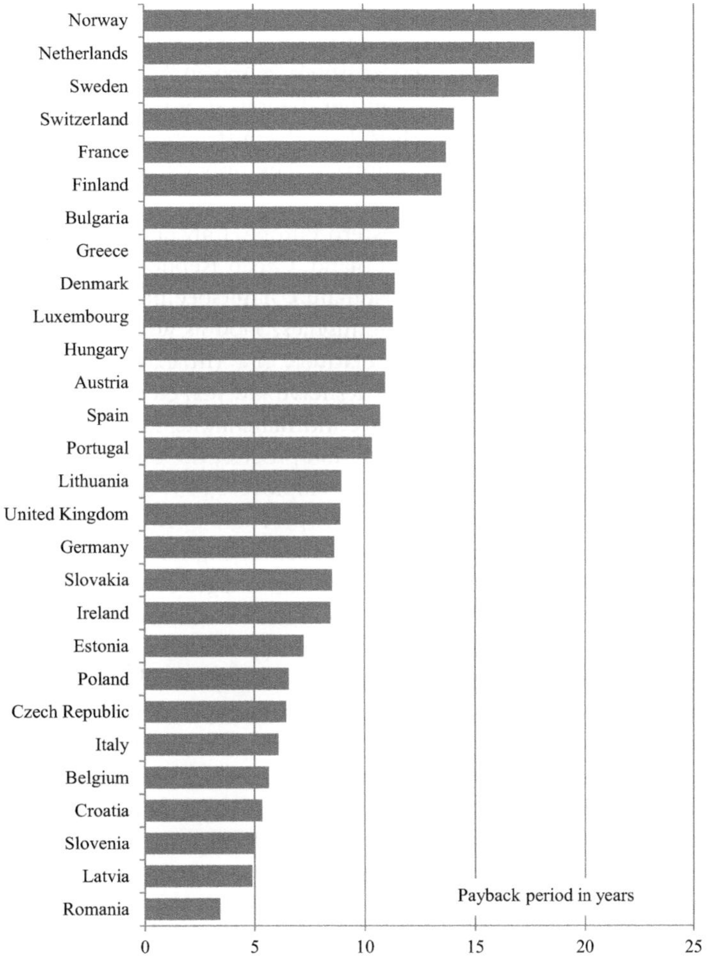

Figure 5.1 Payback periods

The shortest payback period is in Romania, where the electricity price is nearly as low as it is in Norway. But because the construction cost level is also low, the payback time is very short, only four years. If we take account of the purchasing power parity, the relative affordability of energy improvement is understandable.

Payback period 13–21 years (Northern and Central Europe)

This includes Norway, Netherlands, Sweden, Switzerland, France and Finland. All these countries have relatively high residential construction price levels (114–188 index EU27) compared to the other countries in the study. They also have relatively low electricity prices (0.15–0.19 euro/kWh); except for Switzerland with 0.23 euro/kWh). Together these cause a long payback period for deep renovation construction packages.

Payback period 9–12 years (Central and Southern Europe)

Most Central European and Southern European countries are in this category. These countries have either the lowest or the highest electricity price (0.10–0.30 euro/kWh). Residential construction price levels are either low or average in these countries. The only exceptions are Denmark and Germany.

Payback period 3–8 years (Eastern Europe, Italy and Belgium)

In this category are: Estonia, Poland, Czech Republic, Italy, Belgium, Croatia, Slovenia, Latvia and Romania. The specific energy consumption of residential buildings is rather high, 175–308 kWh/m2,a. The construction price level is nevertheless relatively low (index= 35–74; except for Belgium, 99). Also, these countries have low real electricity prices (0.12–0.16 euro per kWh, except for Italy and Belgium, which have higher electricity prices).

Conclusion

Energy Efficiency Directive (EED) Article 4 obliges countries to undertake deep renovations or staged deep renovations of their existing buildings, even if there is no common definition and content for "deep renovation". Unofficial definitions estimate that deep renovations should save around 60–75 per cent on energy costs (heating energy, cooling, ventilation, hot water, electricity for building services).

Deep renovation payback periods are generally long in Northern European countries and some middle European countries because of relatively low energy and relatively high construction costs. The payback periods tend to be short in Eastern European countries and in Italy and Belgium. The reasons for this are high energy consumption (kWh/m2, a), low construction price levels and low energy price levels.

Financial costs are excluded from the payback period analysis. If a loan (interest) is included in the investment cost to be covered by energy savings, the payback period would be a little longer. Even though interest rates are above the average European level in Eastern Europe (approximately 3.5%), payback periods will remain reasonable allowing renovations to be carried out immediately.

A structural renovations target is difficult and costly to achieve in most European countries. The goal is almost achievable in cases where the initial energy consumption is very high. The second question is whether it is worth repairing such weak buildings. This question is justified both in depopulation areas and in growing cities.

The goal can more easily be achieved if savings are generated by replacing bought energy with native energy production or by replacing fossil fuels by Renewable Energy Supplies, (RES), namely geothermal energy, wind power, solar power and biofuels. In these cases, energy needs and structural performance of building remains the same. The only difference is the energy procurement system.

Most European countries have efficient centralized energy production (district heating, hydro power, nuclear power networks) and distribution systems. Local RES production challenges this system but also secures energy supply. Parallel systems can be a positive development, even if they are also overlapping investments from the viewpoint of the national economy. Also, too big a distributed photovoltaic (PV) and geothermal energy production may cause problems in the form of sharp electricity demand peaks. Germany and Denmark are already planning to limit intensive use of PV production.

References

Artola, I., Rademaekers, K., Williams, R. and Yearwood, J. (2016). Boosting building renovation: What potential and value for Europe? *European Parliament: Directorate General for Internal Policies*. DOI: doi.org/10.2861/331360.

Boermans, T., Bettgenhäuser, K., Offermann, M. and Schimschar, S. (2012). *Renovation Tracks for Europe up to 2050. Building Renovation in Europe – What Are the Choices?* Available at: www.eurima.org/uploads/ModuleXtender/Publications/90/Ecofys_X_leaflet_05_10_2012_web_Final.pdf

Economidou, M., Laustsen, J., Ruyssevelt, P., Staniaszek, D., Strong, D. and Zinetti, S. (2011). *Europe' s Buildings under the Microscope*, Buildings Performance Institute Europe (BPIE), Brussels.

EU (2009). *Directive 2009/28/EC – The use of Energy from Renewable Sources*. Available at: http://eur-lex.europa.eu/legal-content/EN/TXT/PDF/?uri=CELEX:32009L0028&rid=1 [Accessed 28.11.2016]

EU (2010a). *Europe 2020 – A European Strategy for Smart, Sustainable and Inclusive Growth*. Available at: https://ec.europa.eu/info/european-semester/framework/europe-2020-strategy_en [Accessed 28.11.2016]

EU (2010b). *Directive 2010/30/EU – The Indication by Labelling and Standard Product Information of the Consumption of Energy and other Resources by Energy-Related Products*. Available at: http://eur-lex.europa.eu/legal-content/EN/TXT/PDF/?uri=CELEX:32009L0028&rid=1 [Accessed 28.11.2016]

EU (2010c). *Directive 2010/31/EU – The Energy Performance of Buildings*. Available at: http://eur-lex.europa.eu/legal-content/EN/TXT/PDF/?uri=CELEX:32010L0031&rid=1 [Accessed 28.11.2016]

EU (2012). *Directive 2012/27/EU – The Energy Efficiency*. Available at: http://eur-lex.europa.eu/legal-content/EN/TXT/PDF/?uri=CELEX:32012L0027&rid=1 [Accessed 28.11.2016]

EU (2013). *Commission Staff Working Document – Financial Support for Energy Efficiency in Buildings*. Available at: https://ec.europa.eu/energy/sites/ener/files/documents/swd_2013_143_accomp_report_financing_ee_buildings.pdf [Accessed 11.12.2016]

EU (2014). *A Policy Framework for Climate and Energy in the Period from 2020 to 2030*. Available at: https://ec.europa.eu/energy/en/topics/energy-strategy/2030-energy-strategy [Accessed 28.11.2016]
Fabbri, M., De Groote, M. and Rapf, O. (2016). *Building Renovation Passports: Customised Roadmaps Towards Deep Renovation and Better Homes*. Available at: http://bpie.eu/wp-content/uploads/2017/01/Building-Passport-Report_2nd-edition.pdf.
Morishita, N., Heidenreich, M., Hemmers, R., Vankann, M., Sahakari, T., Vainio, T., Treberspurg, M. and Öterreicher, D. (2016). *EU-GUGLE: A Sustainable Renovation for Smarter Cities from a Pilot Project*, Smart and Sustainable Planning for Cities and Regions, Cham, Switzerland, pp. 353–382.
Sajn, N. (2016). *Energy Efficiency of Buildings: A Nearly Zero-Energy Future?* Available at: www.csa.com/partners/viewrecord.php?requester=gs&collection=TRD&recid=20080322014046EA
Shnapp, S., Sitjà, R. and Laustsen, J. (2013). *What Is a Deep Renovation Definition?* Available at: www.gbpn.org/sites/default/files/08.DR_TechRep.low_.pdf
UN (2015). *Paris Agreement*. Available at: http://unfccc.int/files/essential_background/convention/application/pdf/english_paris_agreement.pdf [Accessed 28.11.2016]

Data sources

EU, EU, Building Stock Observatory. Available at: https://ec.europa.eu/energy/en/eubuildings
Eurostat, Comparative price levels for investments. Available at: http://ec.europa.eu/eurostat/statistics-explained/index.php/Comparative_price_levels_for_investment
Eurostat, Energy price statistics. Available at: http://ec.europa.eu/eurostat/statistics-explained/index.php/Energy_price_statistics
Eurostat, Heating degree-days. Available at: http://appsso.eurostat.ec.europa.eu/nui/show.do?dataset=nrg_esdgr_a&lang=en
European Union VAT rates. Available at: www.vatlive.com/vat-rates/european-vat-rates/

Part III

Accounting for construction processes from design to construction management in different countries

6 Activities causing cost overruns on construction projects in South Africa

Abimbola Windapo and Alireza Moghayedi

Introduction

The construction industry has been used universally to boost the economy and help economies recover from recession. While in developed countries the construction industry is not considered to be capital intensive, the perception of construction may be as a highly capital-intensive industry compared to other sectors of the economy in an African context. Consequently, it can be argued that there is a need to closely monitor the performance of construction projects (Baloyi and Bekker, 2011) in terms of construction activities such as excavation work, brickwork, finishes, roofing and external works. Cost and time overruns have been a persistent problem on construction projects, especially in developing countries (Gaetsewe et al., 2015; Kaming et al., 1997; Le-Hoai et al., 2008; Memon et al., 2011; Mukuka, 2015; Ramabodu and Verster, 2010).

In Australia, infrastructure projects were found to incur cost overruns ranging from 12% to 35% depending on the projects' procurement methods. Procurement methods determine the contractual relationship between the client and other parties in the construction of a project (Windapo and Rotimi, 2012). Other causes of cost overruns established in the literature are unpredictable weather, material cost inflation, inaccurate material estimates, poor site management, price fluctuations, poor contract management and changes in the scope of the work (Kaming et al., 1997; Omoregie and Radford, 2006; Le-Hoai et al., 2008; Baloyi and Bekker, 2011). Memon et al. (2011) found that time overrun has a strong linear relationship with cost overruns due to the increase in a project's fixed overhead costs.

Drawing on the review of time and cost overruns on projects globally, it is evident that although the causes and consequences are not entirely the same for all countries, there are similarities. Due to the persistence of the challenges faced on construction projects, according to Memon et al., 2011, various procurement strategies have been adopted to help manage and control projects. Common procurement strategies used include traditional, management oriented, integrated (design and build) and in-house teams. Nevertheless, Memon et al. (2011) argue that despite the implementation of the strategies mentioned, many construction projects are still faced with the problems of delays and cost overruns. To date, much of the research that has been undertaken focuses on identifying the factors that cause overruns at a macro level. There has been limited research that examines the factors causing overruns in projects at the activity level. This chapter focuses on the impact of the factors causing overruns on individual construction activities to identify those activities that are highly impacted. This will give construction managers a more insightful view of activities that need to be monitored closely in a South African context that may also be of use to managers in other countries.

This chapter therefore evaluates activities that cause cost overruns and whether there are significant differences in the activities causing cost overruns based on project parameters,(such as client type, procurement system and building structural form). To do this, an overview of project activities is presented, followed by an outline of the research methodology, results and discussion of findings of the research and thereafter, the conclusions of the study.

Overview of activities causing cost overruns on construction projects

Multiple factors are known to influence the cost performance of construction projects (Odediran and Windapo, 2014). Table 6.1 outlines the construction activities causing cost overruns distributed by level of impact and the literature source.

Table 6.1 Activities causing cost overrun distributed by level of impact and literature source

Level of Impact	*Literature Source*
High Impact Activities	
Foundations	Apipattanavis et al. (2010); Kaming et al. (1997); Stasiak-Betlejewska and Potkány (2015)
Roof construction	Lowe et al. (2007); Stasiak-Betlejewska and Potkány (2015); Oliphant et al. (2016)
Earthworks	Apipattanavis et al. (2010); Kaming et al. (1997)
Electrical installation	Oliphant et al. (2016)
Formwork	Oliphant et al. (2016)
Plumbing installation	Oliphant et al. (2016)
Low Impact Activities	
Painting	Oliphant et al. (2016); Stasiak-Betlejewska and Potkány (2015)
Carpentry and joinery	Oliphant et al. (2016); Stasiak-Betlejewska and Potkány (2015)
Ceilings and partitions	Oliphant et al. (2016); Stasiak-Betlejewska and Potkány (2015)
Plastering	Stasiak-Betlejewska and Potkány (2015)
Mechanical installation	Oliphant et al. (2016)
Waterproofing	Oliphant et al. (2016)

Apipattanavis et al. (2010), Kaming et al. (1997) studying cost overruns on projects in Chile and Indonesia respectively found that construction activities causing significant cost overruns on projects are earthworks and foundations. These tended to be because of rain, which increases soil humidity. In the United Kingdom, 286 case studies reviewed by Lowe et al. (2007) established that the critical activity causing the highest level of cost overrun is roof construction. Lowe et al. (2007) found that roof construction had an 80% chance of causing a cost overrun on a construction project. This finding was corroborated by Oliphant et al. (2016) and Stasiak-Betlejewska and Potkány (2015).

Furthermore, Oliphant et al. (2016) found that electrical installation, formwork and plumbing installation caused the most significant changes to construction costs in South Africa. While other activities causing relatively lower or less significant cost overruns included painting, carpentry and joinery, ceiling and partitions (Oliphant, 2016). Activities such as plastering and painting were found to cause relatively low-cost overruns on construction projects (Oliphant et al., 2016; Stasiak-Betlejewska and Potkány, 2015).

Methodology

A mixed methods research approach was used to collect data. Initially, a survey was undertaken to determine the extent to which construction activities impacted cost overruns in South Africa. The population of the study was comprised of 131 quantity surveying companies, 56 contractors, 281 consulting engineering and 15 project management companies (N=483) listed in the Professions and Projects Register (Times Media, 2015). The scope of the research was limited to cost overruns at the project level, a requirement met by all the entities listed. Probability sampling technique was used to select half of the entities on the sample frame to obtain a sample size of 242 organisations. Findings from two case studies were used in provide context to the questionnaire findings. While Case Study 1 is a high-rise commercial facility, Case Study 2 is a six-floor residential building for student accommodation. Both projects are in Cape Town, South Africa. The project clients were private sector clients. The FIDIC form of contract was used in project procurement, and the procurement system used on both projects was Design and Build. For the research findings to be valid, the case studies used should be consistent with the sampling criteria, based on the study parameters of type of client, (public or private), location of project, building type (use of building), building structure (framed/solid/surface) and procurement method.

An online survey was sent to the targeted organisations. For the purpose of this research some related construction activities were grouped together under a main activity umbrella because an activity consists of many inputs which are interrelated and jointly influence or contribute to it. For example, foundation construction activity involves the placing of formwork, reinforcing steel and the pouring of concrete. Excavation activity focuses on the earthworks, while the brickwork includes all structural masonry used in the construction process. Finishes involves different types of floor covering such as tiling, carpeting and epoxy flooring. Roof construction takes into account roof covering and its structural support, waterproofing and rainwater disposal. Plumbing installation activity includes all plumbing and drainage requirements, while the electrical installation activity focusses on the electrical fittings and cabling of the construction process. Carpentry and joinery involve all wooden fittings, wardrobes, ceilings and partitions. Painting and decorating activities are comprised of decorative plastering and painting. External works include paving and landscaping.

The data collected from the study was analysed using descriptive and inferential statistics. A five-point Likert scale was used to assess the influence of construction activities on cost overruns from the perception of respondents with values on the scale as follows: 1 was "very low", 2 was "low", 3 was "average", 4 was "high" and 5 was "very high". The Mean Item Score (MIS) was used to determine the level of impact of the construction activity on cost overruns within the set parameters. Factors with MIS values between 4 and 5 were considered to have high impact on cost overrun.

The Kruskal Wallis test was used to test whether there was a significant difference in the level of impact of activities causing cost overruns based on the project parameters of type of client, type of structure and method of procurement. Cronbach Alpha was used to measure the internal consistency of the study instrument, providing evidence that the findings were reliable. The resulting Cronbach Alpha numerical coefficient ranges from 0 to 1, where a coefficient less than 0.3 indicates low reliability and a coefficient greater than 0.7 indicates high reliability of the assessment tool used. The Cronbach Alpha for the 18 variables measured in the survey was 0.851, indicating a very high level of reliability of the assessment tool used.

Data findings and discussion

The online survey gathered 85 responses, representing a response rate of 35%. A significant number of the respondents (58.8%) were quantity surveyors, more than 84% held a bachelor's degree or higher; 77% had more than 16 years of experience hence it was assumed they would have been exposed to various projects with different parameters, reducing the chances of bias; 83% were from the director cadre or management category and hence from the higher echelons of management. These suggest that the respondents were in a position to provide valuable, relevant and meaningful information useful for this study, because a significant number of those surveyed were employed to manage costs on projects and are likely to have been tasked with management roles on projects due to their qualification, years of experience and position.

Project information

The study sought to find the parameters of the recent projects on which the survey respondents were involved. While 53% of the respondents were recently involved with the procurement of framed building structures, 44% and 3% were engaged on solid and surface structures respectively, and 69% were working on projects identified as five floors and below. The building uses identified included shopping malls, residential, schools, hospitals and office buildings. It also emerged that while 70% of the respondents used the Joint Building Contracts Committee (JBCC) contract on recently completed projects, 8% used the New Engineering Contract (NEC), 6% used the International Federation of Consulting Engineers or Fédération Internationale des Ingénieurs-Conseil (FIDIC) contracts, and 16% used other forms of contract notably the General Conditions of Contract (GCC) used in South Africa. The data also showed that 78% of the projects were procured using the traditional approach, while 12% of the projects were procured using a management procurement approach through, for example, project managers and 10 per cent of projects adopted an integrated approach. The clients on 55% of the projects were in the private sector, 40% were public sector clients, while 5% worked on projects where the clients were in a public-private partnership.

Level of cost overruns

The cost overrun from each project was calculated and expressed as a percentage. It emerged that almost half of all respondents reported cost overruns of zero to ten per cent, and a further 23 per cent of respondents experienced cost overruns of 11 per cent to 20 per cent. As many as 9 per cent of respondents had worked on projects where the cost overrun reached over 50% of the budget.

Activities that cause cost overrun

Table 6.2 presents the Mean Item Score of the rating of the respondents on construction activities causing cost overruns on projects, where 5 is very high and 1 is very low impact. It can be seen from Table 6.2 that the activities perceived to impact cost overruns are the foundations, external works and excavations in ranking order and the factor considered to be the least impacting factor is the finishes.

Activities that cause cost overrun by project parameters of client, structure and procurement methods

Are cost overruns a greater problem in the public sector compared to the private sector? This might imply that one or other sector is more capable of managing delivery and costs than the other or alternatively, one or other sector requires more complex structures to be built. A cross case analysis of the study data between type of client and cost overrun shows that private and public sector clients' projects tend to incur greater cost overruns – 16% and 15% respectively, compared to projects procured using public private partnership agreements (PPP). Respondents reported that clients using PPP had experienced cost savings of 6%. Table 6.3 shows the perception of the respondents on the on-site causes of cost overruns due to construction activities by project client type.

Table 6.2 Respondents' perceptions of activities causing cost overruns on projects

Rank	*Activities*	*Mean item score*
1	Foundations	3.30
2	External works	3.26
3	Excavations	3.24
4	Carpentry and joinery	3.05
5	Electrical installations	2.86
6	Brickwork	2.71
7	Painting and decorating	2.62
8	Roof construction	2.50
9	Plumbing	2.47
10	Finishes	2.13

Table 6.3 Activities causing cost overrun on projects distributed by client type

Activities	*Private*		*Public*		*PPP*		*Overall score*
	MIS	*Rank*	*MIS*	*Rank*	*MIS*	*Rank*	
Foundation	3.00	6	3.50	1	3.50	3	1
External works	3.06	5	3.45	3	5.00	1	2
Excavations	3.41	2	3.47	2	2.50	6	3
Carpentry and joinery	3.25	3	2.67	7	3.00	4	4
Electrical installations	3.10	4	2.55	8	0.00	9	5
Brickwork	2.14	10	3.33	4	3.00	5	6
Painting and decorating	2.64	8	2.33	9	4.00	2	7
Roof construction	2.58	9	2.75	6	1.00	8	8
Plumbing	2.70	7	2.25	10	0.00	10	9
Finishes	3.55	1	2.91	5	2.00	7	10
Kruskal Wallis Test	K-Value = -0.61 x^2 = 5.99						

Table 6.3 shows that while the respondents working on projects procured by private clients, they perceived that finishing activities had the highest impact on cost overruns. The respondents on projects procured by the public sector and public-private partnership clients ranked the foundation and external works as activities that had the highest impact on cost overruns from a ranking perspective. The Kruskal Wallis test was used to determine whether there was a difference in perception of the respondents on the activities that caused cost overruns on construction projects, based on the type of client. The K-value obtained was – 0.61, which is less than the tabulated x^2 value of 5.99. Hence, it can be deduced that there is a significant difference in the construction activities that cause cost overruns on projects depending on client type. However, public sector clients may have to provide more complex structures such as bridges, hospitals and power stations (unless procured entirely at the private sector's risk), and this complexity adds to the risk of cost overruns in the public sector. Nevertheless, this is a significant finding.

Activities that cause cost overruns distributed by type of structure

Is there any significant difference between the perception of respondents and the perception of the construction activities impacting cost overruns by type of structure? A cross case analysis of the study data between type of structure and cost overruns shows that framed structures experienced the highest cost overruns, with costs going over budget by up to an average of 92.3 per cent, while solid and surface structures experience cost overruns averaging 70% and 14.2% respectively. Table 6.4 shows the ranking of the respondents' perception on construction activities causing cost overruns by type of structure.

We see from Table 6.4 that while the respondents working on framed structures, perceived that finishes had the highest impact on cost overruns, the respondents on solid and framed structures ranked excavation and carpentry and joinery as activities that had the highest impact on cost overruns. The Kruskal Wallis test was used to determine whether there was a difference in perception of the respondents on the activities causing cost overruns on construction projects, based on the structure that was built. The K-value was – 0.95, which is less than the tabulated x^2 value of 5.99. Hence, the study found that there was a significant difference in the construction activities causing cost overruns on projects according to y type of structure.

Activities that cause cost overrun distributed by procurement method

To observe the extent to which the procurement method selected may impact on cost overruns, a cross case analysis was used to compare cost overruns by the procurement method. This shows that the highest cost overrun of 92% was observed in the traditional procurement approach, followed by the integrated procurement method and management approach with cost overruns of 36% and

Table 6.4 Activities causing cost overruns on projects by type of building structure element

Activities	*Type of structure*						
	Framed Structure		*Solid Structure*		*Surface Structure*		*Overall Rank*
	MIS Score	*Rank*	*MIS Score*	*Rank*	*MIS Score*	*Rank*	
Foundations	3.15	3	3.54	2	2.00	7	1
External works	3.25	2	3.00	4	4.33	2	2
Excavation	3.12	4	3.80	1	2.50	5	3
Carpentry and Joinery	2.86	7	2.56	7	5.00	1	4
Electrical installation	2.77	8	2.91	6	2.00	7	5
Brickwork	3.00	5	3.00	4	1.00	10	6
Painting and decorating	2.50	10	2.50	8	3.00	3	7
Roof construction	2.91	6	1.88	10	2.50	5	8
Plumbing installation	2.67	9	2.22	9	3.00	3	9
Finishes	3.54	1	3.11	3	2.00	7	10
Kruskal Wallis Test	K-Value = -0.61 x^2 = 5.99						

20% respectively. Table 6.5 shows the ranking of the respondents' perception on construction activities causing cost overruns by procurement method.

Table 6.5 shows that while respondents, whose projects were procured using the traditional approach, perceived that external works have the highest impact on cost overruns, the respondents whose projects were procured using the management approach and integrated design and build/Public Private Partnership approach identified excavation and foundations as construction activities that have the highest impact on cost overruns. The Kruskal Wallis test was used to determine whether there is a difference in perception of the respondents on the activities causing cost overruns on construction projects, by method of procurement. The K-value obtained was −5.49, which is less than the tabulated x^2 value of 5.99. Hence, the study found that there was a significant difference in the construction activities causing cost overruns on projects depending on the procurement method used.

Case study results

Case Study 1 consisted of a 10,088m^2 commercial warehouse facility located in Cape Town, South Africa. Due to the client's planned use of the warehouse for electronic sales, storage and distribution of valuable merchandise; fire risk and disaster prevention were key considerations. Hence, the client's professional team was comprised of civil and structural engineers, fire and heating, ventilation and air conditioning engineers (HVAC), electrical consultants and architects who also served as project managers. The construction of Case Study 1 commenced on 21 November 2014 and was completed in 12 months. The design and build method of project procurement was used, with a 10% construction guarantee and ZAR10,000 penalties imposed per day.

Table 6.5 Activities causing cost overrun on projects by procurement method

Activities	*Procurement Method*						
	Traditional		*Management*		*Integrated design and Build/PPP*		*Overall Rank*
	MIS Score	*Rank*	*MIS Score*	*Rank*	*MIS Score*	*Rank*	
Foundations	3,22	2	3,60	2	3,25	4	1
External works	3,26	1	3,20	3	3,50	2	2
Excavation	3,22	2	4,20	1	3,50	2	3
Carpentry and Joinery	3,06	5	3,00	4	3,00	5	4
Electrical installation	2,94	6	1,00	10	2,75	6	5
Brickwork	2,73	8	3,00	4	2,50	7	6
Painting and decorating	2,75	7	2,25	8	1,00	10	7
Roof construction	2,58	9	3,00	4	1,50	9	8
Plumbing installation	2,57	10	2,00	9	2,33	8	9
Finishes	3,11	4	3,00	4	4,33	1	10
Kruskal Wallis Test	K-Value = -5.49 x^2 = 5.99						

The client of Case Study 2 had an existing relationship with the contractor from past projects. The project was a six-floor student housing block consisting of 295 bedrooms, 21 kitchens, 17 ablutions, 8 study areas and 3 common rooms, with a gross building floor area of 8000m^2 is in Cape Town, South Africa. A Design and Build contract was used to procure the project and a negotiated pricing method was implemented. The project had a 10% variable construction guarantee and ZAR10,000 per day worth of penalties, if the contractor failed to deliver the project on the agreed date of completion.

The budgeted and actual net contract values, cost per m2 and level of cost performance are shown in Table 6.6.

Table 6.6 shows that the actual cost of the first case study exceeded the budgeted costs by 8.04%. In Case Study 2, the overrun was 4.78%. Further interrogation of the data presented in Table 6.7 reveals that in case study 1 carpentry

Table 6.6 Case studies 1 and 2 – Net contract values and costs per m^2

	Contract Values	
	Case Study 1	*Case Study 2*
Budgeted (ZAR)	77,953,327.00	46,991,624.00
Actual (ZAR)	84,216,603.00	49,235,598.00
Cost Overrun (ZAR)	6,263,276.00	2,243,974.00
Cost Overrun (%)	8.04%	4.78%
Cost per m^2 (Budgeted)	7,727.33	5,873.95
Cost per m^2 (Actual)	8,348.20	6,189.00

Table 6.7 Construction activities causing cost overruns on case study projects

Construction Activities	*Level of Cost Overruns*			
	Case Study 1		*Case Study 2*	
	ZAR	%	ZAR	%
Foundations	44,429	7.26%	97,241	3.05
External works	1,381,481	38.82%	0	0.00
Excavation	34,640	11.19%	*-31,120*	-0.63
Carpentry and Joinery	*-257,460*	*-12.93*	355,226	10.08
Electrical installation	540,409	5.80	8,588	0.17
Brickwork	0	0.00	*-1,162,605*	*-32.97*
Painting and decorating	*-220,407*	*-8.72*	-432,689	-22.67
Roof construction	*-156,808*	*-5.19*	-62,352	-3.93
Plumbing installation	5,075	0.22	-35,553	-0.96
Finishes	1,597,259	32.06	103,265	5.82

Note: ZAR – Difference on allocated costs/cost overrun amount in South African Rands (1 USD = 14.38 ZAR; 1 GBP = 18.31 ZAR as at 01/01/2019)
% – Percentage difference between allocated cost and final cost of the construction activity
The italics indicates the amount by which the actual cost of the construction activity exceeds the budgeted cost

and joinery, painting and decorating and roof construction activities were the three joint causes of the cost overrun with a difference on allocated costs of 12.93%, 8.72% and 5.19% respectively. Meanwhile in Case Study 2, the top three causes of its cost overrun were brickwork (32.97%), painting and decorating (22.67%) and roof construction (3.93%). Savings of 38.82% were made on external works in Case Study 1, and 10.08% were made on carpentry and joinery in Case Study 2.

Discussion

The findings of the survey and case studies confirm that there is a tendency for costs to overrun on construction projects in South Africa. The findings are aligned with previous studies by Ramabodu and Verster (2010), Mukuka (2015) and Gaetsewe et al. (2015). The survey is indicative that the activities causing cost overruns are, in order of significance, foundation, external and excavation works, while finishes are the lowest source of cost overrun. However, this finding is not entirely corroborated by the case study findings where brickwork, painting and decoration are found to be the highest sources of cost overruns on construction projects.

The findings of the survey are aligned to earlier research by Apipattanavis et al. (2010); Kaming et al. (1997) and Stasiak-Betlejewska and Potkány (2015) who found that foundation work has the highest impact on cost overruns. The case studies are not aligned to these findings because the design and build method which allowed for the involvement of the contractor from the design phase and carrying out the foundation activity in-house as opposed to subcontracting it, allowed for the construction organisations to have more control over the cost of this activity. It also emerged from the study that there are significant differences in the causes of cost overruns on construction projects based on the type of client, structure and the type of procurement method used. While finishes are the primary source of cost overruns for construction projects procured by private clients, for framed structures and the integrated procurement method, external works are the greatest source of cost overruns for projects procured by PPP clients, surface structures and the traditional procurement method. This suggests that in South Africa the project context is an important factor in causing cost overruns and that projects acquired through a combination of public sector clients, surface structures and the traditional method of procurement tend to have higher cost overruns.

Conclusions and recommendations

The research examined the activities that cause cost overrun on construction projects and whether there are significant differences in the activities causing cost overruns based on the contextual factors of client, project and procurement type. There is very limited research about actual activities that cause cost overruns on projects in the South African context. It emerged that 52% of the construction projects surveyed experienced cost overruns above 10% of budgeted costs, while the case study projects experienced cost overruns of between 4% and 8%. Also, it was found that the activities causing cost overrun on construction projects tended to be in the area of foundations, external works and excavations. There was a significant difference in the perceptions of respondents on construction activities causing cost overruns depending on the project parameters of type of client, structure and procurement method. Based on these findings, the study concludes that cost overrun is a reality in the South African construction industry and that there are activities such as foundations, external works and excavations that are most likely to experience higher levels of cost overrun than other activities depending on the client, the structure and the procurement method used.

Construction activities such as foundations, external works and excavations should be carefully managed and monitored during construction as these activities experience the greatest number of cost overruns when traditional methods of procurement (which is the most common approach to project acquisition) is used. It is also recommended that construction companies subcontract activities, which experience the least cost overrun and carefully monitor activities likely to experience the highest cost overrun in-house.

Further research is needed to confirm the findings by sourcing and evaluating the cost information on more historic projects and evaluating the methods various contractors use to group items in order to form activities. There is a need to analyse construction cost overrun by activity, by procurement system, by different structure and different client types to allow a comparison to be made between the findings on the perceptions of activities causing cost overruns and that sourced from actual projects. The survey reported here does not consider the probability of bias or untruthfulness of the participants due to past experiences or unethical conduct in tendering and estimating. For this reason, the survey was carried out in a manner that preserved the anonymity of the participants to protect the sensitive nature of the data that was collected. This must be acknowledged as a limitation and thus the results should only be viewed as indicative.

Acknowledgements

The financial assistance of the National Research Foundation (NRF) (Grant Number: 105301) towards this research is hereby acknowledged. Opinions expressed and conclusions arrived at, are those of the authors and are not to be attributed to the NRF.

References

Apipattanavis, S., Sabol, K., Molenaaar, K. R., Rajagopalan, B., Xi, Y., Blackyard, B. and Patil, S. (2010). Integrated framework of quantifying and predicting weather-related highway construction delays, *Journal of Construction Engineering and Management*, 136, 1160–1168.

Baloyi, L. and Bekker, M. (2011). Causes of construction cost and time overruns: The 2010 FIFA world cup stadia in South Africa, *Acta Structilia*, 18(1), 51–67.

Gaetsewe, R., Monyane, T. and Emuze, F. (2015). Overruns again in public projects: Perspective from Northern cape, South Africa. In *Proceedings of the 6th International Conference on Engineering, Project and Production Management*, 2–4 September, Surfers Paradise Marriott Resort & Spa, pp. 37–46.

Kaming, P., Olomolaiye, P., Holt, G. and Harris, F. (1997). Factors influencing construction time and cost overruns on high-rise projects in Indonesia, *Construction Management and Economics*, 15(1), 83–94.

Le-Hoai, L., Dai Lee, Y. and Yong Lee, J. (2008). Delay and cost overruns in Vietnam large construction projects: A comparison with other selected countries, *KSCE Journal of Civil Engineering*, 12(6), 367–377.

Lowe, D., Emsley, M. and Harding, A. (2007). Relationships between total construction cost and design related variables, *Journal of Financial Management of Property and Construction*, 12(1), 11–24.

Memon, A., Rahman, I. and Azis, A. (2011). Preliminary study on causative factors leading to construction cost overrun, *International Journal of Sustainable Construction Engineering & Technology*, 2(1), 57–71.

Mukuka, M. J. (2015). *Cost and Schedule Overruns on Construction Projects in South Africa* (Doctoral Dissertation), University of Johannesburg.

Odediran, S. J. and Windapo, A. O. (2014). Systematic review of factors influencing the cost performance of building projects. *Proceedings of the 8th Construction Industry Development Board (cidb) Postgraduate Conference.*

Oliphant, D., Windapo, A. and Moghayedi, A. (2016). Establishing the relationship of cost changes to construction work groups and the estimated construction cost to improve overall project control. *Proceedings of the DII-2016 Conference on Infrastructure Development and Investment Strategies for Africa: Achieving Solutions for Renewable Energy and Sustainable Development*, pp. 189–197.

Omoregie, A. and Radford, D. (2006). Infrastructure delays and cost escalation: Causes and effects in Nigeria. Paper presented at the *Proceedings of the 6th International Postgraduate Research Conference in the Built and Human Environment.*

Ramabodu, M. and Verster, J. (2010). Factors contributing to cost overruns of construction projects. In *Proceeding of the 5th Built Environment Conference*, 18–20 July, Durban, South Africa, pp. 131–143.

Stasiak-Betlejewska, R. and Potkány, M. (2015). Construction cost analysis and importance to the economy, *Procedia Economics and Finance*, 34, 35–42.

Times Media (2015). *Professions and Projects Register: The Directory for the Built and Construction Industry in South Africa.* Times Media Ltd., Pretoria, South Africa.

Windapo, A. O. and Rotimi, J. O. B. (2012). Determining project performance criteria and key procurement methods in Nigeria: Client's perspectives. *Proceedings of the Joint CIBW070, W092 and TG72 International Conference on Facilities Management*, Procurement Systems and Public Private Partnership – Delivering Value to the Community, pp. 250–259.

7 The adoption of building information modelling as a measure of international construction innovation

David Greenwood

Introduction

Building Information Modelling (BIM) first emerged as a 'sustaining technology': a 3D tool that produced construction designs more efficiently. It later became a potentially 'disruptive technology', that is, one that can result in the reconfiguration of the whole construction process (Tobin, 2013). From its first emergence from CAD in the 1960s, through the early software developments of the 1970s and 1980s, BIM has been an international affair with parallel contributory development work carried out in the USA and in Northern and Central Europe. It is now a globally-recognised phenomenon, though its adoption remains inconsistent and variable between and within different national markets. However, measuring these differences is problematic, partly due to the complexity of what is meant by BIM.

Definitions of BIM

An early definition from the USA refers to BIM as a 'digital representation of physical and functional characteristics of a facility' (National Institute of Building Sciences, 2007). This definition has two informative components: first, that models can contain not only 3-D geometry, but also non-geometric *functional characteristics*; second, that such models relate to *facilities* (and not just to buildings). But while this description may be adequate for the *models* themselves; it does not consider the activities involved in producing them. In this respect a more helpful definition is that by the UK-based National Building Specification (NBS, 2016a) which describes BIM as 'a process for creating and managing information on a construction project across the project lifecycle'.

Two questions arise from these definitions. The first concerns *what* these 'physical and functional characteristics' are; the second relates to *how* the information is created and managed. The answers to both questions are best revealed by the following summary of the range of uses to which BIM can be applied.

BIM applications

The information is held digitally in sets of databases that comprise the model itself and which can be accessed through the project's life for a wide range of functions, some of which have been described as 'dimensions'. For example, based upon the initial 3D geometric model, there could be: 4D, for time planning and control of construction activities (e.g. Gledson and Greenwood, 2017); 5D, for estimating and cost management (e.g. Lu et al., 2016), 6D, for energy use, resource efficiency and other aspects of sustainability (e.g. Alwan et al., 2015); and 7D for management of facilities or assets (e.g. Parn et al., 2017).

The digital nature of model information also offers the potential for interfaces with other digitally-driven systems. These can provide inputs to the model, as in the case of the retrospective modelling of existing facilities through point cloud capture using laser scanning (e.g. Taneja et al., 2011), or benefit from a model's outputs, for example for the automated manufacture of building components (e.g. Ezcan et al., 2013).

BIM technology

Much of the technology driving BIM comes in the form of a variety of software products that have been developed commercially to meet the needs of specialist designers, (e.g. architects, structural engineers and building services engineers) or contractors. A problem arises with the need to combine these individual models with their distinct formats into a single coordinated project version – a so-called 'federated' project model. A solution to this problem of interoperability is an intermediary format called *Industry Foundation Classes* (IFC). Most producers of BIM software now aim to ensure that their products can import and export information using the IFC standard.

Not all stakeholders require *all* the information, in *all* its detail, that could potentially exist within the project model. An example would be the asset's owners, users, maintainers and operators, who may ultimately require little or none of its geometric information, but whose interest lies in the technical data, warranties, spares, maintenance schedules etc. of the asset and its parts. Construction Operation Building information exchange (COBie), is an IFC subset that satisfies these requirements. It is commonly delivered in the form of a spreadsheet and is an important example of the many forms that BIM outputs can take.

BIM processes

In the foreword to their 'BIM handbook', Eastman and his co-authors note that BIM adoption requires a 'process change' (Eastman et al., 2011). There is thus a link between BIM maturity and the adoption of optimal processes. It is commonly accepted that to fully exploit the potential of BIM requires early and extensive collaboration of project participants (see, for example: Grilo and Jardim-Goncalves, 2010; Singh et al., 2011) to enable them to share information digitally in what the British Standards Institute, (BSI), describes as a 'Common Data Environment' or simply a CDE (BSI, 2013). Establishing optimal processes, especially where their adoption requires major change, requires the 'buy-in' of people. Studies, such as that of Dossick and Neff (2011) have shown that 'human factors' (such as leadership, capability, education, organisational culture, team working) play a leading part in the successful adoption of BIM.

BIM and policy

The rate of innovation adoption and diffusion can be significantly influenced by policy measures. Many countries (e.g. Singapore, in 2014; the UK and South Korea, in 2016; France, in 2017) have mandated the use of BIM for public sector projects; some (such as the United States and Germany) are precluded from national mandates because of their federal systems. Perhaps more important is the way policies are driven. Among the earliest adopters of BIM were in Scandinavian countries. Public mandates have been less centralised, though public policy standards towards interoperability and other guides have been in place since around 2007. In the UK, the government followed its 2011 'BIM mandate' (Cabinet Office, 2011) by taking a lead in creating standardised solutions, conventions and guides for working in BIM. Their production drew initially upon similar documents in the USA, such as the American Institute of Architects' 'Digital Practice Documents' (AIA, 2013). Some are designated as 'British Standard' (BS) while others are 'Publicly Available Specifications' (PAS). An example is PAS 1192–2:2013 (BSI, 2013) 'Specification for information management for the capital/delivery phase of assets using building information modelling' which specifies a process for delivering projects in Level 2 BIM. Further standards (BIM Level 2, 2016) include:

- PAS 1192–3 (for information management in the operational phase)
- BS 1192–4 (employers information exchange requirements using COBie)
- PAS 1192–5:2015 (for digital security)
- PAS 1192–6:2015 (sharing and use of structured hazard and risk information for health and safety)
- the CIC BIM Protocol (a BIM supplement to standard forms of contract)
- Government Soft Landings (a protocol that specifies asset handover to owners)
- BIM Toolkit and Digital Plan of Work (to specify and verify data delivery)
- A Unified BIM Classification System (a logical underpinning for information creation, search, and retrieval)

BIM and procurement

It has already been noted that a key component of the BIM process is the collaboration of project participants. The way projects are traditionally procured could arguably compromise the ability to collaborate right from the start. The American Institute of Architects (AIA) has advocated a project delivery approach called 'Integrated Project Delivery' (IPD) that 'integrates people, systems, business structures and practices . . . through all phases of design, fabrication and construction' (AIA California Council, 2007). Similarly, in an initiative that runs parallel to its commitment to BIM, the UK Government Cabinet Office has recommended new approaches to procurement that would produce 'high levels of supply chain integration, innovation and good working relationships' (Cabinet Office, 2014: 7).

BIM education and training

One of the perceived barriers to BIM implementation is the shortage of knowledge and skills to support the digital transformation of traditional construction activities and processes. The successful adoption of any innovation requires a commitment to acquiring new skills and knowledge, and even in so-called developed countries these are often in short supply (e.g. House of Commons, 2017). According to McKinsey's 'industry digitisation index' for 2015 the construction sector is a digital under-achiever and was the worst-performing (other than agriculture and hunting) of the 22 different sectors assessed (McKinsey, 2015: 5). Such challenges can be met from a variety of sources and a range of study modes, including course-based education by universities or colleges; vocational training offered by a range of providers including software distributers; and professional development activities.

Attempts to measure BIM maturity

From its earliest introduction there has been a desire to measure how much and how well BIM is being used. Within the UK Government's 2011 announcement that 'collaborative 3D BIM' was to be required by 2016, there is a concept of 'levels' of BIM, associated with the BIM Maturity Diagram devised in 2008 by Bew and Richards (BSI, 2013). The aim of the UK BIM mandate was for public sector projects to achieve 'Level 2' BIM: the question then arose as to what exactly was meant by this, as the Bew-Richards model had little accompanying detail and relied on subsequent interpretations (e.g. the PAS 1192 documents, see above).

What is 'Level 2 BIM'?

According to the guidance developed jointly by NBS and BSI, a project that has attained BIM Level 2 is characterised by 'a series of domain and collaborative federated models . . . consisting of both 3D geometrical and non-graphical data' where information can be exchanged 'within the context of a common data environment' and 'project participants will have the means necessary to provide defined and validated outputs via digital transactions in a structured and reusable form' (BIM Level 2, 2016). Regarding this 'structured and reusable form' the NBS website adds that the 'minimum target' is that the 'software . . . [used] . . . must be capable of exporting to one of the common file formats such as IFC or COBie' (NBS, 2014).

BIM maturity assessments

Previous BIM maturity assessments at national market levels can be broadly categorised as either market surveys or academic research. In the former category are the 'Business Value of BIM' series of reports initiated by the publisher McGraw Hill Construction (Young et al., 2009, McGraw-Hill, 2014) originally covering North America and then extending to other countries and regions, including Europe, China, the Middle East, Australia and New Zealand and South Korea (Jones and Bernstein, 2014). In the UK, the NBS has produced a National BIM Report each year since 2011 (e.g. NBS, 2018) and an occasional 'International' Report, the last of which (NBS, 2016b) compared BIM adoption across the UK, Czech Republic, Canada, Japan and Denmark.

Most academic investigations have focused on the market within a single country. These include studies in Australia (Gu and London, 2010), China (Cao et al., 2017), Finland (Tulenheimo, 2015), Iceland (Kjartansdóttir, 2011), India (Shah et al., 2018), Jordan (Matarneh and Hamed, 2017), Malaysia (Chin et al., 2018), South Africa (Shakantu and Froise, 2014), South Korea (Lee and Yu, 2015), Sweden (Hooper, 2015), Taiwan (Mom et al., 2011), United Kingdom (Khosrowshahi and Arayici, 2012) and the United States (Azhar et al., 2015). Some authors have adopted cross-country or even occasionally world-wide comparisons (e.g. Cheng and Lu, 2015; Jung and Lee, 2015). The references here are examples and are not intended to be exhaustive.

What emerges is a picture of inconsistency. To assess BIM maturity the industry surveys typically adopt a single criterion, such as access to the relevant software. The academic studies tend to be more systematic and based upon multiple criteria though the choice of criteria can appear arbitrary and limited. Most academic investigations have adopted what Kassem et al. (2016) call the 'traditional approach' of a survey of industry stakeholders.

A new method of BIM maturity analysis

In their 2015 paper entitled 'Macro-BIM adoption: Conceptual structures', Succar and Kassem describe an 'alternative methodology' for investigating and measuring BIM adoption at the 'macro level'. The authors' use of the term 'adoption' to cover both *implementation* and *diffusion* (while recognising their semantic differences) and the term 'macro' to focus on defined national boundaries. The approach was designed, tested and refined over several years (see Succar, 2009, 2010; Kassem et al., 2013; Succar and Kassem, 2015; Kassem et al., 2016; Kassem and Succar, 2017). The result, as explained in their 2015 paper is a set of five complementary adoption models shown in Table 7.1. The models offer functions that are both normative (i.e. as guides for developing BIM adoption policies) and descriptive (i.e. allowing multi-criteria measurement of relative levels of BIM adoption).

For the present purposes, the model of interest is *Model B: Macro-Maturity Components* as its purpose is to assess BIM maturity at the national level.

Table 7.1 Macro-BIM adoption models and intended uses

Adoption model title	*Intended use*
A Diffusion Areas	Establish the diffusion areas to be assessed
B Macro-Maturity Components	Assess the BIM maturity of countries
C Macro-Diffusion Dynamics	Assess and compare diffusion pressures and mechanisms
D Policy Actions	Identify, assess and compare actions to facilitate adoption
E Macro-Diffusion Responsi-bilities	Assess and compare roles played of stakeholder groups

Source: Adapted from Succar and Kassem, 2015.

The Macro-Maturity Components model (model B) contains eight components for measuring Macro-BIM adoption of a country (or at a similar macro-level). These are:

I. Objectives, stages and milestones;
II. Champions and drivers;
III. Regulatory framework;
IV. Noteworthy publications;
V. Learning and education;
VI. Measurements and benchmarks;
VII. Standardised parts and deliverables; and
VIII. Technology infrastructure

In the resulting BIM Maturity Index (BIMMI) these eight components are assessed using five standard levels of maturity:

a) Ad-hoc or low maturity;
b) Defined or medium – low maturity;
c) Managed or medium maturity;
d) Integrated or medium – high maturity; and
e) Optimised or high maturity.

The resulting BIMMI framework is shown in Table 7.2. The table here has been adapted from the more complex Table 11 in Succar and Kassem (2015: 74). Alongside each BIM maturity component is a summary of its rationale (for which more detail is available at www.bimthinkspace.com), and, in the third column, an example of what the 'optimised or high maturity' rating would be for this component (for finer grained definitions, see Succar and Kassem, 2015, Table 11).

Results of applying the macro-maturity components model

The maturity model was populated with survey data gathered between 2015 and 2016. These data were obtained from 21 countries whose selection was based

Table 7.2 The Macro-Maturity Components model (Model B)

BIM maturity components	*Rationale for each component*	*Description of optimised/highest maturity level [e]*
I Objectives, stages and milestones	Clear BIM-specific policy objectives, intermediate capability stages, and measurable maturity milestones with a quantifiable future target.	BIM objectives & stages are continuously refined to reflect advancements in technology, facilitate process innovation, and benefit from international best practices.
II Champions and drivers	The individuals, groups, organizations or authorities that demonstrate the efficacy of an innovative software solution, process, or standard.	Driver(s) coordinate all macro-adoption activities, minimise activity overlaps, & address diffusion gaps
III Regulatory framework	The contractual environment, intellectual property rights, and insurance context surrounding collaborative BIM projects.	Regulatory framework is continuously refined to reflect technological advancement & optimised collaborative workflows.
IV Noteworthy publications	Publicly-available documents of relevance (guides, protocols, mandates) developed by influential stakeholders.	Noteworthy publications are continuously optimised to reflect international best practices.
V Learning and education	Educational activities covering BIM concepts, tools & workflows via tertiary education, vocational training or professional development.	BIM learning topics are infused into education, training & professional development programmes.
VI Measurements and benchmarks	Market-wide metrics for benchmarking project outcomes & assessing the capabilities of individuals, organizations & teams.	Standardised metrics are continuously revised to reflect evolving accreditation requirements & international best practices.
VII Standardised parts and deliverables	Standardised, data-rich model parts to populate object-based models. O&M data requirements (e.g., COBie)	Standardised object libraries, model uses & operational data requirements are continuously optimised to improve usage, accessibility, interoperability & connectivity.
VIII Technology infrastructure	Availability, accessibility & affordability of hardware, software and network systems.	Technology infrastructure is intuitive & accessible allowing seamless interchange between all users, virtual systems & physical objects across the whole lifecycle.

Source: Adapted from Succar and Kassem, 2015.

Table 7.3 Countries surveyed by region using the Macro-Maturity Components model (Model B)

Region	*Countries surveyed*
Europe	Finland, Ireland, Italy, Netherlands, Portugal, Russia, Spain, Switzerland, United Kingdom
North America	Canada, United States
South America	Brazil, Mexico
East Asia	China, Hong Kong, Malaysia, South Korea
Middle East	Qatar, United Arab Emirates
Australasia	Australia, New Zealand

upon three initial criteria: first, that each must have shown evidence of BIM policy discussion; second, that the country had a sufficient number, a minimum of three, well-informed participating contractors or organisations (i.e. actively and publicly involved in high-level BIM discussions within their respective countries) and responsive individuals; and third, that the resulting sample of countries produced a reasonable geographical distribution. More detail on the study can be found in the original article (Kassem and Succar, 2017) but the results have been summarised here. Table 7.3 shows the countries from which data were gathered, by region.

Expert respondents in each country were asked to rate each of the eight macro-maturity components for their respective countries using the same five-level maturity index (*ad-hoc or low maturity* to *optimised or high maturity*). Respondents were provided with standard detailed descriptions of the metrics they should use for each component.

From the returns for each country, a weighted average score was calculated over the eight macro-maturity components and these are shown in Figure 7.1, which is arranged in increasing order of the cumulative weighted average score for all eight components. Each component is colour-coded for visual effect alone.

The highest achievable aggregate score would have been 32 points (i.e. 4 points each of the eight components). Overall, the United Kingdom had the highest cumulative maturity score (17.6), followed by China (15.24), South Korea (12.92), Netherlands (12.04), Finland (11.4), Spain (10.48) and the United States (10.4).

For further inspection, the point-based indices shown in Figure 7.1 can be converted into percentages (where 100% would represent the full score of 4). The results of this are shown in Table 7.4, where the shading of cells shows bands of the assessed level of maturity (the darker shading the higher the aggregated level of maturity).

Discussion

The work presented offers a greater sophistication than other survey approaches that have been used to-date in academia and practice and as a result reveals

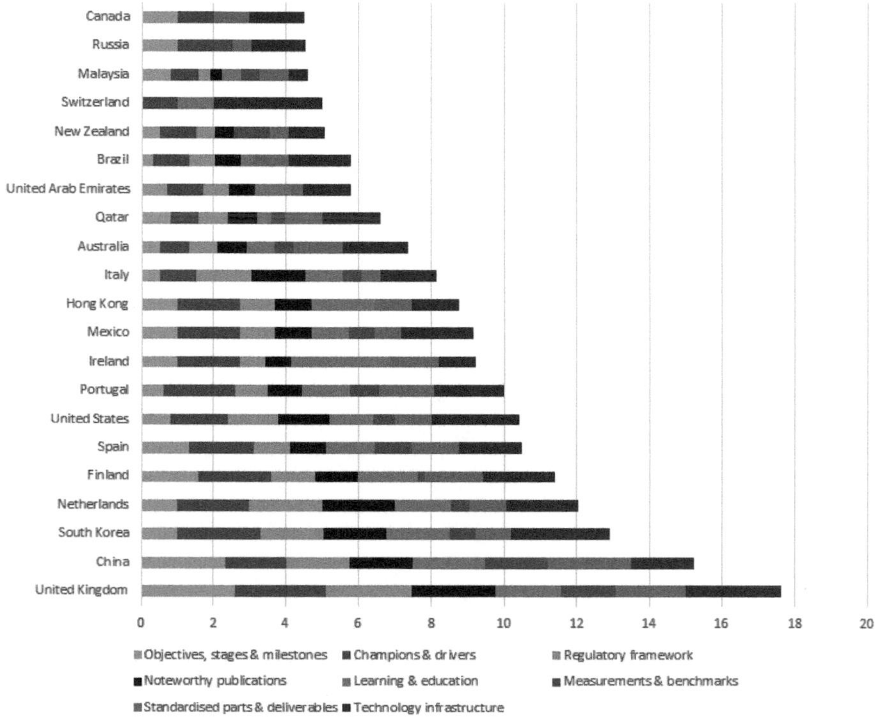

Figure 7.1 Aggregate ratings for countries surveyed using the Macro-Maturity Components model

Source: Adapted from Kassem and Succar, 2017.

several issues on comparative national BIM maturity and policies towards BIM adoption that are worthy of discussion and speculation. These are itemised below and refer predominantly to Table 7.4, with occasional reference to Figure 7.1.

1 *High-maturity adoption is not evident and remains a longer-term aspiration.* No country achieved a 100% rating across all eight components. Relatively, the UK achieved the highest rating across the greatest number of components (5 out of 8) but did not exceed 65% (Medium to high maturity) on any single component. Over 90% of the 168 (8 x 21) individual component ratings (156 out of a total of 168) were at 50% or less (equivalent to *medium to low* or *low* maturity).
2 *There is no single superior policy approach.* No individual country has a higher maturity rating than the other countries in more than three of the eight macro adoption topics.

Table 7.4 Comparison of the ratings (%) of each macro component across the 21 countries

	Objectives, stages and milestones	*Champions and drivers*	*Regulatory framework*	*Noteworthy publications*	*Learning and education*	*Measurements and benchmarks*	*Standardised parts & deliverables*	*Technology infrastructure*
Australia	13	20	20	20	20	13	33	45
Brazil	8	25	18	18	8	0	25	43
Canada	25	25	0	0	0	0	25	38
China	58	43	43	43	50	43	58	43
Finland	40	50	30	30	40	5	40	50
Hong Kong	25	43	25	25	43	0	25	33
Ireland	25	43	18	18	68	0	33	25
Italy	13	25	38	38	25	13	13	38
Malaysia	20	20	8	8	13	13	20	13
Mexico	25	43	25	25	25	18	18	50
Netherlands	25	50	50	50	38	13	25	50
New Zealand	13	25	13	13	0	25	13	25
Portugal	15	50	23	23	33	20	38	48
Qatar	20	20	20	20	10	10	25	40
Russia	25	25	0	0	0	13	13	38
South Korea	25	58	43	43	43	18	25	68
Spain	33	45	25	25	33	25	33	43
Switzerland	0	25	0	0	25	0	0	75
United Arab Emirates	18	25	18	18	25	0	8	33
United Kingdom	65	63	58	58	45	38	48	65
United States	20	40	35	35	30	15	25	60

Note: The shading shows bands of the assessed level of maturity (the darker the shading the higher the aggregated level of maturity), as follows: 0% = low maturity; 1–25% = medium to low maturity; 26–50% = medium maturity; 51–75% = medium to high maturity; 76–100% = optimised, high maturity.
Source: Adapted from Kassem and Succar, 2017.

3 *There is considerable diversity between countries*. Eight of the countries had a zero rating in at least one component of their BIM maturity: in Switzerland five of the eight components showed a zero rating; Canada had a zero rating in four; Russia in three; and Hong Kong, New Zealand, Brazil, Ireland and UAE each had a zero rating in one component.

4 *However, there is consistency over the component range for each country*. By and large, the eight component results for each country were consistent. For example, results for the UK were regularly at *medium* to *medium – high* maturity and those for Malaysia were consistently at *medium – low* maturity.

5 *There were several anomalies*. Some results, however, did not show the same consistency. The clearest example was Switzerland, which registered the highest score for the *Technology Infrastructure* component but 5 *low maturity* (0%) and 2 *medium – low maturity* (1–25%) scores in every other component. This places Switzerland towards the bottom (see Figure 7.1) of the aggregate component ratings. It could be speculated that the federal structure of Switzerland (and others) may be a relevant factor. The result cannot, however, be taken to imply that the country is digitally backward!

Summary and conclusions

BIM is widely recognised as an opportunity to revolutionise the way the construction and property sectors around the world do business, offering the potential for improved efficiency and effectiveness throughout. For many countries it has assumed a matter of economic importance to their industrial policies (e.g. in the UK, the Department for Business, Energy and Industrial Strategy, 2018) and governments have therefore encouraged, or promoted BIM adoption. There is an accompanying need to measure the extent to which these interventions have succeeded, how current positions can be benchmarked internationally and where further effort is needed.

In doing this, the research presented here has constructed a systematic, reliable and replicable system of metrics that produced a comparison across 21 countries that shows their similarities and differences in components that are critical to advancing BIM adoption. These results are both restricted in number and time-bound (see the following section on limitations) but they, and, more importantly, the tools developed to obtain them go some way to support policy makers as well as contributing to the body of knowledge about macro-BIM policy development.

As noted earlier, for the purposes of data collection and analysis for their Macro-Maturity Components model, Succar and Kassem (2015: 65) use the generic term 'adoption' to cover both implementation and diffusion. However, using a different model within the research (Model C – Macro Diffusion Dynamics) the authors have investigated (and continue to do so in the ongoing study) how and from-where diffusion takes place. Further information on the concepts behind and the results of that work can be found in Succar and Kassem (2015), Kassem and Succar (2017), respectively.

Limitations and future work

The work presented necessarily has limitations. The first concerns what it *does and does not* purport to do. The results presented here do not indicate the presence or absence of BIM expertise in any country, but rather the relative coherence of national approaches to BIM adoption. This is illustrated by the nature of the eight components: three (components I to III), of which measure the extent of a systematic 'top down' and interventionist approach to national BIM adoption; two (components IV and V) substantially (though not entirely) relate to the involvement of academia; leaving three (components VI to VIII) that concern the creators and users of the technologies themselves.

The positions of relative maturity derived from the aggregated component totals must be seen in this context. As noted above and as shown in Table 7.4, it is perfectly possible, as in the example of Switzerland, for a country to have the highest score for the *technology infrastructure* component and to score poorly (including 5 zero scores) against the others. It appears likely that the political structure of a country is an issue, and further research would be required to determine whether this, or indeed a country's dominant political philosophy (e.g. free-market or interventionist) is a limiting factor in terms of national BIM policy and maturity (as measured here).

The second major limitation is in the volume of data obtained. Relatively speaking this study is probably the most comprehensive to-date but it is still limited. The 21-country sample is tolerable, but the relative sample sizes from each country (set at a minimum of three expert respondents per country) are informative and yet insufficient for significant inferential conclusions. However, the current results, representing replies up to early 2016, will be amplified as the project continues online at *http://bimexcellence.org/projects/macro-adoption/*. This will allow periodic updates with better sample sizes and more contemporary information.

References

AIA (2013). *Guide, Instructions, and Commentary to the 2013 AIA Digital Practice Documents*. Available at: www.aiacontracts.org/resources/69541-guide-instructions-and-commentary-to-the-2013-aia-digital-practice-documents. [Accessed 31.12.2018]

AIA California Council (2007). *Integrated Project Delivery: A Working Definition* (Version 2). McGraw-Hill Construction and American Institute of Architects, California Council, Sacramento, CA.

Alwan, Z., Greenwood, D. and Gledson, B. (2015). Rapid LEED evaluation performed with BIM based sustainability analysis on a virtual construction project, *Construction Innovation*, 15(2), 134–150.

Azhar, S., Khalfan, M. and Maqsood, T. (2015). Building information modelling (BIM): Now and beyond, *Construction Economics and Building*, 12(4), 15–28.

BIM Level 2 (2016). *Webpage. BSI and the Department of Business, Energy & Industrial Strategy*. Available at: https://bim-level2.org/en/about/ [Accessed 29.12.2018]

BSI (2013). *PAS 1192–2: Specification for Information Management for the Capital/Delivery Phase of Construction Projects Using Building Information Modelling*, BSI Standards Limited, London, UK.

Cabinet Office (2011). *Government Construction Strategy*. Available at: www.gov.uk/government/uploads/system/uploads/attachment_data/file/61152/Government-Construction-Strategy_0.pdf [Accessed 24.03.2017]

Cabinet Office (2014). *New Models of Construction Procurement*. Available at: www.gov.uk/government/publications/new-models-of-construction-procurement-introduction [Accessed 24.03.2017]

Cao, D., Li, H., Wang, G. and Huang, T. (2017). Identifying and contextualising the motivations for BIM implementation in construction projects: An empirical study in China, *International Journal of Project Management*, 35(4), 658–669.

Cheng, J. C. and Lu, Q. (2015). A review of the efforts and roles of the public sector for BIM adoption worldwide, *Journal of Information Technology in Construction* (ITcon), 20(27), 442–478.

Chin, L., Chai, C., Chong, H., Yusof, A. M. and bt Azmi, N. (2018). The potential cost implications and benefits from Building Information Modeling (BIM) in Malaysian construction industry. In *Proceedings of the 21st International Symposium on Advancement of Construction Management and Real Estate*, Springer, Singapore, pp. 1439–1454.

Department for Business, Energy & Industrial Strategy (2018). *Construction Sector Deal*. Policy Paper. Available at: www.gov.uk/government/publications/construction-sector-deal [Accessed 04.01.2019]

Dossick, C. S. and Neff, G. (2011). Messy talk and clean technology: Communication, problem-solving and collaboration using Building Information Modelling, *The Engineering Project Organization Journal*, 1(2), 83–93.

Eastman, C., Teicholz, P., Sacks, R. and Liston, K. (2011). *BIM Handbook: A Guide to Building Information Modeling for Owners, Managers, Designers, Engineers and Contractors* (2nd Edition). John Wiley & Sons, Hoboken, NJ.

Ezcan, V., Isikdag, U. and Goulding, J. (2013). BIM and off-site manufacturing: Recent research and opportunities. *Proceedings of the 19th CIB World Building Congress*, Brisbane, Australia. Available at: www.irbnet.de/daten/iconda/CIB_DC27218.pdf [Accessed 19.12.2017]

Gledson, B. J. and Greenwood, D. J. (2017). The adoption of 4D BIM in the UK construction industry: An innovation diffusion approach, *Engineering, Construction and Architectural Management*, 24(6), 950–967.

Grilo, A. and Jardim-Goncalves, R. (2010). Value proposition on interoperability of BIM and collaborative working environments, *Automation in Construction*, 19(5), 522–530.

Gu, N. and London, K. (2010). Understanding and facilitating BIM adoption in the AEC industry, *Automation in Construction*, 19(8), 988–999.

Hooper, M. (2015). BIM standardisation efforts-the case of Sweden, *Journal of Information Technology in Construction* (ITcon), 20(21), 332–346.

House of Commons (2017). *'Digital skills crisis'. House of Commons Science and Technology Committee Fourth Special Report of Session 2016–17 HC270*. Available at: https://publications.parliament.uk/pa/cm201617/cmselect/cmsctech/936/936.pdf. [Accessed 31.12.2018]

Jones, S.A. and Bernstein, H.M. (2014). *Business Value of BIM in Australia and New Zealand*, SmartMarket Report. Available at: http://www.consultaustralia.com.au/docs/default-source/bim/the-business-value-of-bim-in-australia-new-zealand.pdf. [Accessed 10.06.2019]

Jung, W. and Lee, G. (2015). The status of BIM adoption on six continents, *International Journal of Civil, Environmental, Structural, Construction and Architectural Engineering*, 9(5), 444–448.

Kassem, M. and Succar, B. (2017). Macro BIM adoption: Comparative market analysis, *Automation in Construction*, 81, 286–299.

Kassem, M., Succar, B. and Dawood, N. (2013). *A Proposed Approach to Comparing the BIM Maturity of Countries*, Teesside University Research Repository. Available at: http://tees.openrepository.com/tees/handle/10149/323596 [Accessed 24.12.2018]

Kassem, M., Vukovic, V., Dawood, N. N., Hafeez, A., Chahrour, R. and Naji, K. (2016). *Approaches for Assessing BIM Adoption in Countries: A Comparative Study within Qatar*. Available at: http://tees.openrepository.com/tees/handle/10149/621046. [Accessed 01.01.2019]

Khosrowshahi, F. and Arayici, Y. (2012). Roadmap for implementation of BIM in the UK construction industry, *Engineering Construction and Architectural Management*, 19(6), 610–635.

Kjartansdóttir, I. B. (2011). *BIM Adoption in Iceland and Its Relation to Lean Construction*, Master of Science in Construction Management, Reykjavík University, Reykjavík.

Lee, S. and Yu, J. (2015). Comparative study of BIM acceptance between Korea and the United States, *Journal of Construction Engineering and Management*, 142(3).

Lu, Q., Won, J. and Cheng, J. C. (2016). A financial decision-making framework for construction projects based on 5D Building Information Modeling (BIM), *International Journal of Project Management*, 34(1), 3–21.

Matarneh, R. T. and Hamed, S. A. (2017). Exploring the adoption of Building Information Modeling (BIM) in the Jordanian construction industry, *Journal of Architectural Engineering Technology*, 6(1), 189.

McKinsey (2015). *Digital America: A Tale of the Haves and Have-Mores*. Available at: www.mckinsey.com/~/media/McKinsey/Industries/High%20Tech/Our%20Insights/Digital%20America%20A%20tale%20of%20the%20haves%20and%20have%20mores/MGI%20Digital%20America_Executive%20Summary_December%202015.ashx [Accessed 01.01.2019]

Mom, M., Tsai, M. H. and Hsieh, S-H. (2011). On decision-making and technology-implementing factors for BIM adoption. *International Conference on Construction Applications of Virtual Reality* (CONVR2011), Weimar, Germany.

National Institute of Building Sciences (2007). *National BIM Standard-United States™*. Available at: www.nationalbimstandard.org/files/NBIMS-US_FactSheet_2015.pdf [Accessed 31.12.2018]

NBS (2011–2016). *NBS National BIM Report 2011–2016*. Available at: www.thenbs.com/topics/bim/reports/index.asp [Accessed 24.03.2017]

NBS (2014). *BIM Levels Explained*. Available at: www.thenbs.com/knowledge/bim-levels-explained [Accessed 31.12.2018]

NBS (2016a). *What Is Building Information Modelling (BIM)?* Available at: www.thenbs.com/knowledge/what-is-building-information-modelling-bim [Accessed 31.12.2018]

NBS (2016b). *International BIM Report 2016*. Available at: www.thenbs.com/knowledge/nbs-international-bim-report-2016 [Accessed 31.12.2018]

NBS (2018). *NBS National BIM Report 2018*. Available at: www.thenbs.com/knowledge/the-national-bim-report-2018 [Accessed 28.12.2018]

Parn, E. A., Edwards, D. J. and Sing, M. C. P. (2017). The building information modelling trajectory in facilities management: A review, *Automation in Construction*, 75, 45–55.

Shah, D., Shaikh, M. Z., Anand, K. and Kawale, V. (2018). Increasing adoption of BIM in Indian construction industry, *International Journal of Engineering Science*, 16855.

Shakantu, W. and Froise, T. (2014). Diffusion of innovations: An assessment of building information modelling uptake trends in South Africa, *Journal of Construction Project Management and Innovation*, 4(2), 895–911.

Singh, V., Gu, N. and Wang, X. (2011). A theoretical framework of a BIM-based multi-disciplinary collaboration platform, *Automation in Construction*, 20(2), 134–144.

Succar, B. (2009). Building information modelling framework: A research and delivery foundation for industry stakeholders, *Automation in Construction*, 18(3), 357–375.

Succar, B. (2010). The five components of BIM performance measurement, *CIB World Congress*, United Kingdom, Salford.

Succar, B. and Kassem, M. (2015). Macro-BIM adoption: Conceptual structures, *Automation in Construction*, 57, 64–79.

Taneja, S., Akinci, B., Garrett, J. H., P. E., Soibelman, L., Ergen, E., Pradhan, A., Tang, P., Berges, M., Atasoy, G., Liu, X., Shahandashti, M. S. and Anil, E. B. (2011). Sensing and field data capture for construction and facility operations, *ASCE Journal of Construction Engineering and Management*, October, 870–881.

Tobin, J. (2013). BIM becomes VDC: A case study in disruption, *Building Design and Construction Network*. Available at: www.bdcnetwork.com/bim-becomes-vdc [Accessed 31.12.2018]

Tulenheimo, R. (2015). Challenges of implementing new technologies in the world of BIM – Case study from construction engineering industry in Finland, *Procedia Economics and Finance*, 21, 469–477.

Young, N. W., Jones, S. A., Bernstein, H. M. and Gudgel, J. (2009). *The business value of BIM-getting building information modeling to the bottom line*. Available at: http://images.autodesk.com/adsk/files/final_2009_bim_smartmarket_report.pdf [Accessed 10.06.2019]

8 The contribution of architectural services

Peter Raisbeck

Introduction

Architects exist and compete in a global system. Within this system, architects can be regarded as knowledge producers who compete to gain revenues and create profit in order to survive and prosper. This chapter will begin to develop a comprehensive picture of this system using publicly available historical data and information pertaining to this global system. In doing so, the chapter will identify and illuminate the various markets for architectural services that exist across the globe. This is important because the practice of architecture is intimately linked to the design and construction cycle. However, data, statistics and information about the economic activity of the architectural profession across the globe is by and large scant. IBISWorld, the business information and market research provider, claims that in the five years after the Global Financial Crisis (GFC), revenue in this global market for architectural services in 2017 was $USD223 billion. Yet, across the globe, business and research data concerning the market for architectural design services is sporadic, fragmented and partitioned into various silos. This situation reflects the different data gathering capabilities and professional regimes existing between different nations, regional states and firms.

To compound the above situation, very little data has been collected or analysed regarding international architectural practices and their cross-border activities. In addition, little information abounds regarding architectural markets in the global south. In contrast, the global construction, engineering and infrastructure sectors appear to be better covered via various stock indices, disclosures to stock exchanges and information aggregated by supranational, national and regional bodies. In order to begin to address these issues, this chapter will survey the available global data, highlighting any gaps and in doing so create a variegated picture of the global market for architectural services. For the purpose of definition global architectural data is that data that is connected to globalised architectural practice. This data may be related to various geographic markets, individual firms or national economic, trade and census data. The data discussed here includes statistical data aggregated at both a global and national level of the firm in order to give an overview of global architectural practice. In other words, it is any data that is related to the global market for architectural services.

One way to address the issues of sporadic and fragmented global data regarding architects would be to understand this data based on geography, regions or project type. Inevitably this approach leads to an overall picture or mosaic of information built up from the data used in various market segments. The overall mosaic then provides knowledge about what is both included and what is missing; revealing a landscape about the global market for architectural services across different nations, jurisdictions and economies. While this approach is necessary and valuable, the aim here is to explore the interaction between the data and the global socio-technical context in which it has been produced. This methodology is relevant given that architects are producers of knowledge who seek to sell this knowledge and associated technical expertise. Architects are selling a knowledge-based service and not the delivered time and cost outcomes associated with a physical project.

Global data about architects is not a fixed quantitative entity. All data has an information agency, which is embodied and entangled in various social-material practices. Data is a material entity and while debates might abound about its status as a virtual, and seemingly ethereal entity, only existing as digital bytes it still has a material presence. Granting data the status of materiality highlights the interlinking of data with the social entities and various practices of architecture. Therefore, in creating a global picture of data, around architectural service markets, it is essential to bear in mind that data in these global markets has a socio-technical agency. The use to which this data is put, and the information that is conferred upon it, is critical in developing a picture of the global landscape of architect orientated service markets. Hence, the chapter will explore the social, political and cultural dimensions of data as it relates to architects and the global market for architectural services. In this chapter, the focus is on the narratives of the information that architectural data – data about architects – has been given across the global market for architectural services. This chapter explores three main narratives of Data Agency in this context. This approach is more revealing of the ways that data is created, mobilised and given agency within architecture (Raisbeck and Adams, 2018).

Data with three different types of socio-technical agency can be seen to emerge from the global market for architectural services. First, there is that data that has a normative agency since the data is referential, iterative and historical and used to benchmark. Often this data arises out of regulatory contexts. Second, there is data exhibiting a dynamic agency. This data illustrates the various processes, dynamics and systems inherent to certain markets. For example, this data might describe labour force figures and gender issues. However, this data might also, and perhaps more commonly, be related to economic outputs in order to explain trends related to financial or economic dynamics of architectural service markets. Finally, there is that data that is conferred with a future orientated strategic agency where the data is used to forecast and make predictions about future trends and issues. Data with a strategic agency is often given a narrative that has the appearance of being high-level, strategic and symbolic of future innovation. To some degree, these categories of agency overlap and co-exist, but they nevertheless serve to highlight the socio-technical agency of data associated with architects as they create and trade their knowledge across global markets.

Global data providers and architects

There are numerous data providers, who produce data about the global market for architectural services that is aggregated and then distributed in various forms. Often this data and the information and knowledge that emanates from it is monetised and sold. For example, one of the world's key private data providers is IBISWorld. IBISWorld creates reports pertaining to the global architectural services industry, and most of the IBIS data is behind a paywall. Although the group allows small snippets in order to entice paid customers such as:

> The Global Architectural Services industry has expanded over the years to 2017. Economic growth and an infusion of government-funded building projects in emerging nations fuelled industry revenue early in the period. Moreover, increased employment and corporate profit in developed economies helped revive privately funded construction activity, ultimately benefiting architecture firms (IBISWorld, 2018).

Global data on architectural services is not always monetised and supranational bodies may also occasionally present data on the global trade in architectural services. For example, the OECD is a sporadic aggregator and publisher of global data on architectural service markets. In 2007 the OECD (2007) issued a report entitled *The Global Trade in Architectural Services*. In assessing the global trade in architectural services, the report drew on several data sources including the Engineering News Record (ENR) and the national professional body, the American Institute of Architects. Global Insight, now part of IHS Markit, a London-based global information provider. The authors of this report noted the paucity and difficulties of gaining global data on architects: "To date the author has not been able to identify any surveys that document and/or rank which countries are the primary exporters of architectural services." The report employed ENR data from 2005 in order to describe the "global regional distribution of the firms engaged in international work." At that time the report noted that:

> The importing of foreign architectural services to developed architectural markets is characterized by three leading situations; a) the commissioning of recognized design architects of distinction having achieved a high public recognition and a record of award winning commissions; b) clients seeking a foreign architect with recognized experience in a particular building type; and c) architects who have entered and won an open or invitational architectural competition.
>
> (OECD, 2017, p. 8)

The Global Financial Crisis (GFC) of 2009 is another critical moment in the gathering of global data concerning architectural service markets, as well as the associated property and construction markets. The crisis in subsequent years became a kind of benchmark itself, and consequently, numerous studies have looked at various aspects of the GFC and its impact on the global property and construction industry. Few studies, however, have looked at the impact of the GFC in relation to the global market for architectural services.

Many global data providers provide information that touches on the global market for architectural services and this points to the inconsistent, disparate and fragmentary nature of information related to architects. For example, Statista is an online portal that claims to be "a leading provider of market and consumer data" and "one of the largest statistics portals worldwide." Among other things, some of the available Statista datasets, related to architects, includes the number of employed full-time architects in the United Kingdom (UK) in 2018 and annual revenue figures of architects in the United States from 2009 to 2014. Statista also includes global rankings of global architectural firms based on the number of architects employed by each company (Statista, 2018).

Global real estate and property data is also an area where global data related to architects can be gleaned. There are numerous data providers in this space across the globe. MSCI real estate, which approaches real estate as an asset class, is also a global provider of business intelligence products to investors and real estate owners and property managers. MSCI has a number of products and services including global market indexes and property market and portfolio analytics and intelligence services (MSCI, 2018). For example, SNL Real Estate (2018) is a provider that supplies property data and analytics for over "1,000 current companies in 46 different countries around the world and more than 100,000 properties." In Australia and New Zealand, Core Logic is the largest property data and analytics provider in Australia and New Zealand. Core Logic provides data to professionals in the real estate, property and property finance sectors (CoreLogic, 2018).

Supranational organisations also provide a glimpse into the global market for architectural services, and these include the World Bank, the IMF, OECD, and the European Union. UN-Habitat has produced many important reports that gather together global statistics about urbanisation and cities. These include reports on cities in different regions, the ranking of cities and or issues around urbanisation and sustainability. Architectural bodies with large memberships such as the Union of International Architects (UIA), the Architects Council of Europe, American Institute of Architects (AIA) and the Royal Institute of British Architects (RIBA) all collect various statistics.

Given this global landscape of data abundance and intelligence, it is worth noting that as knowledge-intensive firms architectural practices are different from construction and engineering companies that are directly involved in delivering physical and material outputs. Ruddock (2002) argued strongly for the need to have a globally integrated system of construction data noting the lack of information regarding global construction data. He pointed out that this was a long-standing problem citing previous studies by Bon (1990), Cannon (1994). Ruddock argued that existing data sources were limited, that relevant data was needed to assess the impact of globalisation; particularly, in developing countries. He suggested this might come about through global construction groups and transnational organisations such as CIB and Habitat. Nonetheless, he stressed the importance of national systems in this mix citing Lievesley (2001) that national data statistics should be valid, reliable, current and "transparent with respect to known limitations: and comparability."

Data with a normative agency

The first narrative of agency about architects operating in global markets can be designated as a normative narrative. The narrative is normative and iterative because it retraces, reproduces and refers to both previous and existing norms. The normative narrative is characterised by descriptive, positivist and quantitative data. Data with this normative agency is often related to professional demographics and statistics, perhaps gained at a national level or technocratic measures developed in different geographical regions or markets. In architecture data employed with a normative narrative is often related to professional regulatory pathways and accreditation processes. The norm being who has the right to be an architect or describing how many architects there might be in a given professional region. Data embedded in this narrative is often demographic and historical and then used to benchmark. Data with this normative agency may be related to descriptive and comparative statistics, aggregated at a national level and then used to compare different geographical regions or project markets.

Moreover, data may be used to build comparisons concerned with outputs and productivity over time. To adapt the words of Gluch and Bosch Sijtsema (2016), in a study of environmental expertise, normative agency "is oriented towards the past and describes actor's reactivation of past schemas of recognition agency and action in on-going actions (habit)." Architects will use this data with a normative agency to affirm professional recognition and reinforce the boundaries of professional identity.

The ambitiously titled Architectural Practice Around the World (APAW, 2005) contains a narrative of normative aAgency, which predominated in a 2005 report produced by the Architects' Institute of Catalonia (COAC) providing a global view of architects. The research was carried out by the International Relations Department of the Collegi d'Arquitectes de Catalunya (COAC – Architects' Institute of Catalonia) under the auspices of the Professional Practice Commission of the International Union of Architects (UIA) and on behalf of its Spanish section (Consejo Superior de los Collegios de Arquitectos de España – Higher Council of Architects' Institutes of Spain). The report was based on research from professional bodies that represented the architects in their individual countries within the Union of International Architects." The report remains one of the few attempts, if not the only, to describe the architectural profession across the globe. The research extended over eight years between 1998 and 2005 arising out of work done through various commissions of the UIA (2018). The report came about after the drafting of an accord on international standards in architecture. This accord, fostering mutual recognition of architectural competencies and cross-border movement of architects, was ratified by the UIA at its Beijing conference in 1999. Following this, the Professional Practice Commission of the UIA then sought to construct a database regarding "professional practice around the world" with the aim of the research to have "reliable information about the state of the profession of the architect in the world."

Gathering data from 91 countries, representing about 83% of the world's population the COAC research included statistics, education, internships, as well as data about professional practice including issues around the architect's function, regulation, liability, insurance, fees mechanisms, professional development and ethics. Notably, the report attempted to map transnational practice and document international agreements. These agreements included identifying the multi-lateral agreements under the General Agreement on Trade and Services (GATS), which at that time (January 2005) did not exist. It also reported on regional agreements including free trade areas, customs unions, single markets and economic unions. Given its global scope, the study split global architecture into five geographic regions. These were Western Europe (21 countries), the Americas (20 countries), Eastern Europe, which also includes Central Asia and the Middle East (32 countries), Asia and Oceania (21 countries, including China and India) and Africa (24 countries). The study drew on the UN World Population and the CIA World Factbook (CIA, 2018). A critical measure in the report was the number of inhabitants per architect. Thus, Japan was listed as having 416 people per architect whereas at that time India had 40,357 inhabitants per architect. Sierra Leone and Chad were the lowest two countries on this measure with 267,000 and 455,850 per architect respectively.

The report also examined, gathered and reported on fees attempting to document the different methods established for architects to calculate fees in the form of: "scales, formulas, guidelines" and the basis for these calculations such as "surface area and complexity of the building, percentage of the total cost of construction, hours required to carry out a specific task."

More interestingly the report commented on the degree to which these different regimes might or might not be either compulsory or for guidance only and reporting that between the various reports there had been "a decrease in the compulsory nature of scales or other means for calculating fees."

The UIA no longer appears to gather international data – the UIA database entitled Architecture Around the World (APAW) seems to have no updated data after 2011. Nevertheless, in the European Union (EU) the earlier COAC data appears to have had a considerable afterlife. For example, The Architects Council of Europe (ACE) 2008 sector study was based on the COAC research. The latest ACE sector study published in 2016 builds on four previous reports (2008, 2010, 2012 and 2014). The report claims to be "the most comprehensive and significant report on the state of the architectural profession in Europe."

Arguably, this claim is correct given that the report covers 27,000 respondents in 27 European Countries claiming to encompass 94% of the profession. The report offers guidance on "policy positions with statistical evidence, [and] it contributes to enhancing the credibility of ACE in its dealings with policy-makers at EU and national levels."

The 2016 ACE stated that there were 600,000 architects in Europe, 36% of whom were working full time, and 38% of all architects were women. The report ranks nations by overall numbers of architects (Italy and Germany being the top two nations) and then ranks nations by the number of architects per 1000 population; with Italy (2.6) again leading these figures and then Portugal (2.1) and Denmark (1.8). The EU report also covers architects' field of employment; years qualified as an architect, age and gender profiles and of course practice profiles. The number and size of firms is also reported with 72% of firms having one member of staff, 13% having two staff and 11% of firms having 3 to 5 staff. The remaining 4% of firms have over 11 staff with less than 1% of firms having over five staff. As a model for the collection and reporting of data, the entire ACE report serves as a model for national, transnational and supra-national organisations. As discussed later the report covers many aspects of the market for architectural services including issues around revenues, fee mechanisms, charge out rates, practice profits, individual earnings, hours worked as well as gender demographics within the profession and data on competitions.

Data is also provided by both the AIA and RIBA which covers the American and UK markets. Data collected from these markets indicate that firm size is relatively homogenous across the global system. Clearly, this data underscores architecture as a knowledge-intensive activity reliant on people for its production processes. The RIBA chartered practice benchmarking survey shows aggregate numbers of staff employed in architectural practices, as well as data on several projects worked on, profits and revenue. In the 2017 RIBA survey, 11% of practices had more than 100 staff or more, 325 practices had 10 to 20 staff, and 36% had between three and five staff members (RIBA, 2017a). By comparison in the AIA survey of 2016, highlighting the disparity between the way different professional bodies conduct measurements, 5.1% of practices had 50 or more staff, 17.6% had 10 to 49 staff, and 77.3% had one to nine staff.

Global data appears to be collected and published sporadically. Much of this data predominates in many of the various reports either at a global or national level. It relates to numbers gathered from professional associations or allied regulators. If data with a normative agency is the basic building block of understanding the dynamics and the future of the global market for architectural services, then more data still needs to be systematically gathered.

Data with a dynamic agency

The second narrative about the architecture profession is a dynamic narrative. In this narrative data is deployed to suggest, explain and describe the different mechanisms, movements or flows of labour and capital, that describe the global market for architectural services. To reiterate, dynamic data is linked to the various movements and changes in labour and active social processes – for example, gender and racial discrimination. However, the dynamic narrative is also linked to the dynamics of economic competition and firm profitability. As a result, this data is given dynamic agency through rankings, revenues and gross figures of project value. Dynamic data also helps architectural firms, in theory at least, to orientate themselves to the present and respond to various forces and contingencies of the present. This dynamic data – to adapt the terminology of Gluch and Bosch-Sijtsema (2016) in their study on institutional work – is mobilised to "contextualize past habits and future projects to select among alternative possible trajectories of actions to meet presently arising and/or changing situations."

In Australia, the Parlour Group is "a research-based advocacy organisation working for equity in architecture and the built environment." The dynamic nature of this work is evident in the fact that Parlour uses the research to foster ongoing and active advocacy in order to "expand the spaces and opportunities available to women while also revealing the many women who already contribute in diverse ways." The Parlour group has collected detailed data, through Australian census data and surveys of the profession, regarding women in the profession. Parlour has undertaken surveys in 2011 and then five years later in 2016. To achieve its aims Parlour has analysed data including the following: women as a proportion of all registered architects, numbers of women admitted to registers, women employees and numbers of women architect practice owners. This data also outlines the proportion of women in different age groups across Australia. This statistic is seen to enable a better understanding of career pathways. Hence, participation by age going forward into the profession is measured. For example, 43% of recent architectural graduates participate in architect offices whereas in the 50 to 54 age group, only 15% of architects remain and participate in the workforce. The employment data in the survey indicates that women are "more likely to be employees rather than employers or practice owners." Moreover, the report outlines issues around part-time versus full-time work, working hours and how these differ between men and women. More importantly, the Parlour data also reports on the gender pay gap that exists between men and women in the Australian profession (Parlour, 2016; Matthewson, 2012, 2015).

Compared to the work of Parlour, few statistics have been collected in as much depth across the globe concerning gender issues. As Matthewson (2015) notes in her PhD thesis, which underpins much of the Parlour advocacy work, gender studies on the status of women in architecture is not a new phenomenon. A great deal of data collecting and research has been conducted in relation to women across the global profession and this work has not been given a voice in the profession. In other jurisdictions gender statistics are either non-existent or not as comprehensive in relation to documenting female career paths, hours worked and wages in the profession. The COAC study reports on the overall number of architects in different countries but does not break this data down by gender. The 2014 EU ACE study reports on the percentage of the number of women in each country in Europe, working as architects. This percentage ranges from Estonia

(15%) and Austria (18%) to Greece (58%) and Croatia (53%). The overall numbers of women across Europe are 61% male architects and 39% female architects. The report is at pains to note that 61% is the "lowest proportion of males recorded in the four surveys' (2012: EU17: 64%, 2010: EU23: 69%, 2008: EU17: 63%). These overall figures and the above comments might suggest that statistics and dynamic data related to women in the profession globally can be easily "fixed." Developing data infrastructure leading to a better collection of gender data by accrediting bodies and professional associations may not necessarily fix the problem. While it is essential to document the status of women – and indeed other underrepresented groups – within the profession, encouraging advocacy, and fostering female leadership may not be enough to change gender imbalances.

To take these points further, it should be noted that very few global statistics have been collected to look at data regarding ethnic identity and other aspects of gender difference within the global market for architectural services. However, the AIA produced through its diversity committee and its Demographic Task Force a 2016 report (based on 2015 data) entitled, "Diversity in the Profession of Architecture." Even so, as the 2015 AIA president noted "There is plenty of anecdotal information that suggests there has been progress in building a more diverse and inclusive profession. Yet, the information is just that – anecdotal." Interestingly the survey, with 7,522 respondents, is not a survey with quantitative data and demographic data sourced from individual firms. Rather the survey reports on perceptions of the representation for both women and "people of colour." Employing "the field of architecture" as its context the survey thus reports on perceptions of career opportunities, perceived factors leading to underrepresentation, retention in the profession and reasons for leaving architecture for both women and people of colour. As the survey notes women of colour are more likely to lose their jobs, for whatever reason and more likely to leave the profession as a result of not being recognised for their work.

Revenue and profit data

Both the AIA and RIBA report on and publish data related to revenues, profit and the value of international work. This data provides a picture of firm competition and how the market for architectural services is connected to both local and global economic conditions. RIBA reports on the types of work this revenue is derived from, the overall number of projects and indications of how much revenue is generated from outside of the UK. In the 2017 RIBA benchmarking study revenue earned by firms outside of the UK was recorded as $GBP 498 million. The RIBA survey includes data on revenue and total profits, which are estimated overall at 17 per cent of revenue but the report states the profit as a percentage of revenue "varies widely between practices of different sizes" (RIBA, 2017a). The survey also looks at types of clients, success at winning work and the use of BIM on projects. Interestingly, in the 2017 report, the RIBA decided to change its categories of firms, splitting the 50 staff or plus category, to distinguish larger practices with over 100 staff. In the words of the report: "this provides more meaningful data for the largest practices – who generate more than half of the profession's total revenue" (RIBA, 2017a). The RIBA survey data is given Dynamic Agency; being easily accessed by members through a website; and gives insight into revenue, profits, projects worked on, success at winning work (project bids vs. projects won), salaries, workforce statistics and revenue earned from work outside of the UK.

In contrast, the AIA firm survey includes aggregate economic data on national spending on non-residential buildings over time. The AIA compares year on year changes in residential spending volumes to corresponding aggregate revenues for architects. The AIA survey also maps gross revenues to the number of staff in firms. For example, in the 2016 survey it concluded that the "profession continues to see increased concentration in revenue at larger firms, but still not back to pre-downturn levels." The survey also asked respondents to gauge their profitability based on the measure of pre-tax profits allowing for bonuses and other firm compensatory schemes. The EU data does not report on profits although Euromonitor a private data provider does provide reports on architectural and engineering services across Europe behind a paywall (Euromonitor, 2018).

The rankings game

Gensler is one of the largest, if not the largest architectural firms in the world. Gensler was ranked number one in the Architectural Record Top 300 Architecture Firms and fourth largest global firm in the Building Design 2014 World Architecture 100, number one in the ENR Top 500 Design Firms. Gensler's 2014 annual report claimed overall revenues of $915 million (USD). In 2017, Gensler was cited, in the Architectural Record rankings as having revenues of $1192.37 Gensler's ranking points to the way that so-called ranking informs firm competition, strategy and marketing (Architectural Record, 2017). There are at present, and in the recent past, various published rankings systems related to the global market for architectural services. Each of these ranking systems employs different methodologies for the way in which firms are ranked. However, the main global ranking systems for global architectural services include Building Design with its World Architecture 100, The Architectural Record and the Engineering News Record rankings of professional service firms.

In 2017, the Architectural Record (AR) produced what it called the '2017 Top 300 Architecture Firms.' US domiciled companies were ranked by revenue and this also included multi-disciplinary firms. Unlike other ranking systems, the AR list ranked firms into different categories according to their specialised expertise and then noted the degree to which firms derived revenue from architectural services as compared to other services. In other words, the list also described the percentage of revenues that each firm gained through architecture. Using a percentage figure this metric involved stating if the labour force in the firm was simply architects or a combination of architects, engineers, planners, landscape architects or contractors. For example, some firms with more of an engineering bias may have earned less than 100% of the revenues from architecture. In addition, each firm's total revenue was split into domestic and international revenues. If Gensler was cited as having revenues of $1192.37 million (USD), as noted above, the bottom-ranked firm had revenues of $7.92 million (USD). The first ten firms in the 2016–2017 survey had combined architectural revenues of $23.83 billion (USD), which can be compared to what IBISWorld claims as the size of the overall market (namely $23.83 billion (USD) compared to the whole market of $223 billion).

Building Design has produced the WA 100 list each year between 2011 and 2018. The emphasis of the list is on numbers of architects employed and not on revenues, profit margins or project value. In its commentary regarding the most recent 2019 survey, based on 2018 figures, it is claimed that 37,787 architects were working in the top 100 firms a 6.45% increase over the previous year. Building Design also noted that the number of employee architects in the top 10 firms increased by 7.3% over the previous year to 13,129 notably nearly 35% of the overall number of architects accounted for in the survey. Building Design reported this number of employees in the top ten as a new record; by comparison, in 2013 the total number of employee architects in the top 10 architecture practices was 9,602 employees.

Ranking methodologies that rely on self-reporting are flawed if there is no independent verification. Anecdotal evidence would suggest that architects working in and across the global market are reluctant to release data, even if they are surveyed anonymously and then if prompted will inflate this data in order to present a better image. In response to these kinds of issues Lu (2014) analysed the data collected by Engineering News Record for its annual ranking of global contractors and engineering design firms. Lu points to the questioning of this data because it is based on self-reporting inflated revenues. Lu concluded that in fact, this method of gathering data was robust and that there was "no systemic error" in the data and the default position of some peer reviewers concerning this data was little more than bias.

The self-reporting surveys and global rankings indicate the degree to which architectural firms participate in cross-border markets. One of the few studies, written before the GFC, to examine these issues was produced by Russell V Keune, a former trustee of US/ICOMOS, who prepared the report Architectural Services in Global Trade in Professional Services for the OECD and the World Bank. The report takes a regulatory orientation and sets out the regulatory procedures needed to work in and between different countries such as China, Japan, the EU, India as well as the Asia-Pacific Economic Cooperation (APEC) economies. The report outlines some of the public policy objectives in order to ensure increased trade in cross-border architectural services. The report is U.S. centric and employed data from the 2005 ENR firm survey to indicate the percentage of firms working in the different regions and the distribution of this work in the various regions (Europe, Asia-Australia, Canada, Middle East, Latin America and Africa). Much of the report was used to produce a WTO background note on trade in architectural services in 2009.

Global data and architectural identities

In the global system, so-called star architects have come to prevail and have become embedded in a conjunction of architectural identity created from professional awards, iconic projects and both traditional and digital media fame (Sklair, 2017; Ponzini and Nastasi, 2016; Hagen, 2018). International awards are a central component of this system. However, these awards have their apparent problems. As Heynen argues, the star system, as exemplified by the Pritzker prize award, an award that began in 1979, is predominantly biased towards men. She argues that this sexist bias is because of the composition of the juries and "until 1997 no woman had ever been part of the jury." However, as recently as March 2018, Norman Foster was reported as professing "ignorance of the meaning of the word "starchitect" and the suggestion that there may be a "cult" surrounding some of the biggest names in global architecture." Some of these fault lines can be discerned in the 2005 Building Design (BD) Impact 100 ranking.

This 2005 survey related to a different and in some ways a more intellectually tantalising methodology. It indexed and ranked what was deemed as impact. To gauge impact, a methodology was used that addressed project value as well as issues concerned with media branding and symbolic capital. The methodology combined the result of a survey completed by firms, the value of projects in the firm, and a count of press articles by each firm using a newspaper and construction media database in conjunction with a scoring system for architectural awards. The methodology as it was employed gave equal weighting to construction output, media and prizes. The scoring was then normalised out of 100 for each of these three categories resulting in a score for each firm out of 100.

Occasionally, star architects and their revenues will be reported in the professional press. For instance, in March 2018 BD reported that the holding company for Zaha Hadid Architects had a 30% fall in pre-tax profit for the year to 30 April 2017. But more often than not the emphasis as the BD impact methodology suggests, peer awards and media hits are perhaps more important to architects. This approach aligns with Bos-de Vos and Volker (2017) who highlight how business strategy works and professional identity among architectural firms is interwoven. For many architects, a professional identity shaped by peer awards confers competitive advantage and has more professional standing than data with quantitative or financial attributes. Bos-de Vos and Volker (2017) point out that for architects identity is both "socially constructed and fluid", and they argue this is linked to the tensions in architectural firms between strategy work and identity. All of this suggests that concepts of professional identity, through awards and prizes, have increasingly come to dominate and may have more influence in global architectural markets. Dynamic data may, in theory at least, prompt architectural firms – as well as the profession more broadly, to develop new strategies in the face of entrenched industry structures. However, this prompt rarely happens, and perhaps this is because research indicating how architects use this data is mostly missing. As Connaughton and Meikle (2013) have concluded

Professional Service Firms (PSFs) in the construction and built environment industry were not well documented. The research areas that Connaughton and Meikle (2013) deemed as critical areas were concerned with industry structure and size and ongoing specialisation. This lack of research is despite new and emerging patterns of competition taking place in the sector. As a result, there is very little knowledge about what motivates architectural firms, to either change in strategic terms or in any way for that matter.

Data with a future agency

The third approach to the use of data relates data to a future strategic narrative and options. It is used to orientate firms to the future. This data has a strategic value that is related to future trends, predictions including changes in lifestyle, organisations or technologies. For architects this type of data is often viewed as being both strategic and symbolic of future innovation. Because the narratives surrounding this kind of data seem to accrue greater symbolic value, this kind of data is of more interest to architects than that data that has either a normative or a dynamic influence. One example of data with a strategic nature is the range of city ranking metrics and tools which are often used to suggest an innovative urbanised future. As Giffinger et al. (2010) describe, there are currently many global city ranking metrics that contribute to various campaigns for place branding, marketing as well as policy formulation and strategic decision making. In a Spanish study in 2017, Garcia et al. (2017) noted how the ranking tools, centered around the idea of global cities, have begun to include data and information about cultural services within them. They summarised and analysed ten city indexes and ranking tools including the Global Cities Index, Project Global Economic Power Index, AT Kearney Global Cities Index, World Liveable Cities, Global Power City Index, Global City Competitiveness Index, Cities of Opportunities, Global City Survey and the Wealth Report. These authors asked if global cities rankings were a "neoliberal urban planning tool" and argue that these ranking systems are being used in ways that are inappropriate. Despite architects being enmeshed in the production of global cities, and the hyperbole that surrounds them, there is scant evidence that the role of architects is accounted for in these ranking tools.

"The Future for Architects?" was another publication produced by RIBA in 2010 in the wake of the GFC (Jamieson, 2011). The report drew on global statistics from the CIA World Factbook, RICS Global Construction Forecast and numerous statistics from RIBA including the 2007 RIBA Small Practice Survey 2007 (Jamieson, 2011). The work was primarily based on qualitative information through interviews, roundtable discussions, insights from "industry leaders" and what the authors of the report called "Sightings – what we are observing around us." The report claimed to set out,

> a radical vision for the future, The Future for Architects? examines how the demands of a global economy and economic recession have transformed

> business practice, and projects the evolution of these trends into 2025 by questioning: Who will design our built environment in 2025? What role might those trained in architecture have in 2025? How might practice change by 2025.
>
> (Jamieson, 2011)

In contrast to the hyperbole of the 2011 report, the RIBA monthly Future Trends survey contains data with more practical strategic insight (RIBA, 2017). This annual survey was launched in 2009 in order to "monitor business and employment trends affecting the architecture" profession. The survey has a sectoral focus and asks architects for predictions of "their workloads" looking forward over three months. The sectors covered are "private housing, commercial, community and public sector." The results are indexed to constitute a RIBA future trends staffing index.

More pressing in terms of strategic data is the future orientated report that begins to look at global data in relation to Brexit. The RIBA sponsored report prepared by Frontier Economics is entitled: "An economic analysis of UK architecture exports and the impact of Brexit." (RIBA, 2017b). While the reports bring together data that has a clear strategic value concerning Brexit, it also relies on data in relation to trade. The report looks first at the economic contribution of UK architecture exports and then forecasts how Brexit might impact on these. The report argues that architecture contributes £4.8 billion to the UK and that revenue from international work for architects was in the order of £500 million. The report notes that one in four architects working in the UK is from the EU and that a no deal Brexit would decrease UK revenues overall by up to 15 per cent if this scenario was to take place. However, the report suggests that new trade deals for example with either the United States or even China might bring in new export income for UK architectural firms. The methodology used in this report was based on Annual Business Survey (ABS) figures used by the Office for National Statistics (ONS), and this data was then linked to national accounts data and trade data from numerous sources, including data from Eurostat, the OECD and the ABS International Trade in Services survey.

The strategic importance of the data contained in the above reports may all be overshadowed by changing conditions of relevance to architects in the reports produced by the IPCC. As Gruneberg and Folwell noted in 2013 measures of global construction is of obvious interest to policymakers assessing economic activities that are directly concerned with the Kyoto Protocol (now updated as the Paris Accord). They argue that:

> Few activities can have the impact both locally and globally that the construction sector has. The question then arises as to whether or not the global impact of construction and the international capacity of the construction industry can be measured in order to deliver environmental policies and what effect delivering sufficient buildings and infrastructure might have on global resources and the environment (Gruneberg and Folwell, 2013).

As an integral part of the construction sector for architects this issue is also critical. However, now very little data is produced that suggests to what degree architects are delivering outcomes that mitigate climate change.

Discussion: the role of global architectural data

Dynamic data associated with peer review awards, prizes and the fixation on the professional definition of architects is problematic. Qualitative data measuring change does not entirely explain the continuing globalisation of architectural services. Clearly, for architectural firms across the globe there is a need to improve data and the collection, management and governance of data in order to make the data more useful.

International and national data on architects and the architectural profession is limited by the haphazard and ad-hoc way it is collected by national and international entities. For example, data related to the Global South is not often gathered, analysed or reported. Overwhelmingly, available data points to the global architectural industry as being homogenous in its makeup across different states and jurisdictions. The primary feature of this structure is the difference between very large firms and many much smaller firms. An industry segmented between the many, small micro firms and the small minority of very large mega-firms. The number of women, and their status, in the architectural profession also appears to be similar across the globe.

Across the globe architectural award systems, and the symbolic capital it confers, appear to have greater influence over change than data related to industry structure, revenues, profits and labour force composition. Data, such as profit margins, is limited by being more available within firms and this is preventing architects from debating the macroeconomic and financial factors that might impinge on the profession. For knowledge-intensive firms such as architects a mapping of firm size and corresponding profit margins would be a compelling way to begin to understand the dynamics of a fragmented industry.

The composition of the architectural labour force is not often collected or published. In this regard, the work of Parlour in Australia is exemplary and serves as a model for other registration and professional entities. The data gathered and reported in the various ranking systems, about the top ten firms cede very little information about how these firms operate, their profit margins and the incentives that are used to incentivise their owners, managers and workers. Profit margins within architecture are largely a mystery, and this is possibly the result of an ingrained competitive culture of secrecy within the profession. The AIA survey is probably the best publicly available data about the profits of architectural firms in relation to revenues, but this is based on self-reporting. This approach is compounded by the fact that few architectural firms are listed companies with strict reporting guidelines and on-line benchmarking systems are not often analysed or researched.

Data with a strategic relevance is what some might call business intelligence – as evidenced by the plethora of global data and business intelligence providers. If architectural firms are to be entrepreneurial and anticipate future work, then they need to develop a base of research and knowledge in an area. Much has been written about cities and urbanisation in recent years, and the data around the global cities rankings movement has become a focus of both research and hyperbole. So, while architects are intimately involved in the production of cities, there is scant measurement of the role of architecture in these modes of production. As Gruneberg and Folwell (2013), as well as others have argued, there are compelling reasons for the need for a global data system for construction and the built environment.

Parallels in construction management

In construction management, a recurring mantra has been that global measures of construction data remain problematic. This is despite the number of efforts that have been made to look at global industry structure and examine the emergence of professional construction services in China (Ye, Lu and Jiang, 2009; Lu, Flanagan and Jewell, 2013). Nonetheless, this mantra is much the same for architectural data in the worldwide arena. In contrast to architecture, in the allied discipline of construction, numerous economic studies have been applied to global and nationally aggregated global construction data. These studies have sought to explore the mantra of inconsistent data and to find new economic models and explanations. These efforts suggest some of the paths that architects themselves may pursue. Gruneberg and Hughes question the worth for aggregating data at different stages in the linear step by step model of construction processes. They conclude that "aggregate construction statistics taken at different phases in the development process are in practice unlikely to be consistent." They conclude that strategic planning in the construction sector and government policy should be based on the relationship between "inputs, processes and outputs in the construction sector." Similarly, architects could begin to aggregate and report on data that recognises their core activities (design, development, contract administration, etc.). In another call for consistency, Gruneberg and Fraser (2012), writing just after the GFC and using three steel markets (EU, China and the US) between March 2008 and 2010, call for a common unit of measure, such as a construction-specific Purchasing Power Parity measure, in order to measure and compare global construction markets. Again, architects may also look at different PPP measures in order to compare different variables such as fees, wages and project values. Such measures would possibly be insightful in comparing architectural services between the global north and the global south. As Gruneberg and Hughes found, "there has been little attempt to make data on the construction industry consistent throughout the world." This is the same for architecture and, as these authors stress, consistent data is critical in order to assess how different countries might reduce their carbon emissions.

Future research

The picture of architecture painted here is a global profession buffeted by economic forces operating without adequate data. This assertion points to the need for future research that begins to address many of the issues and problems suggested by the patchwork and disconnected silos of data currently describing the global market for architectural services. The emphasis on prize-winning architects and data that is given life with an optimistic future – or is it futuristic? – orientation has come at the neglect of developing a greater understanding of how architects operate in different markets across the globe. More importantly what data needs to be gathered for architects to understand issues around gender, ethnicity, work-life balance and well-being in and across their industry? How can professional architectural organisations begin to gather and share global data and what are the best methodologies and methods to do this? Currently available data suggests numerous pathways of further research. The impact in the 21st century of both globalisation through increasing cross-border trade and the effects of the GFC on both the architectural profession and firms has not been thoroughly researched or covered by various professional associations associated with architecture. Research into architects' profitability and revenues across different markets is also required.

Given the dominance of the large firms in architecture, many lines of research and questions can be raised. Will these firms continue to grow at the expense of smaller firms? How do these firms compete? How do firms use data with different agencies to form a competitive strategy? Perhaps, more importantly, how do these firms operate in a global market, given much of the secrecy about their operations and financial metrics, and do they operate ethically in the global South?

The gaps highlighted here in relation to the way that architects manage and make use of data suggest many new paths of research and questions. Architects are now faced with the emergence and rise of new technologies such as of artificial intelligence (AI), the Internet-of-Things along with advanced methods of simulation and virtual reality, (VR). The rise of so-called big data will be a central corollary of these new technologies. How then should architectural firms of whatever size gather, organise and develop infrastructure around data? How will architects use and manage the data associated with predictive analytics? Moreover, will architects cede their current expertise in design and spatial visualisation to new specialised experts, who will better manage both design and data visualisation?

Conclusion

With the rise of so called big data and the explosion of new data as Jorn Lyseggen, the CEO of Meltwater, a data science company argues, the world is drowning in data (Ganapathy, 2018). More than other professions architects will perhaps be the first to drown in data. Arguably, haphazard data infrastructure and the culture of competitive secrecy seems to be evident in architectural firms. In this context, influence and agency are only given to that data that either supports seemingly vague forecasts of an innovative future and or reiterates existing pedigrees and genealogies within the profession through the star architect system. In the future, for both clients of architects managing data, information and producing knowledge will be critical. Architecture, if it is still called that, may become a socio-technical, practice where the management and creation of data is almost as essential as building physical objects. This eventuality is especially the case, particularly regarding design and design outcomes. It is important that architects do not miss this opportunity to reshape their profession through renewed global data practices.

References

ACE (2016). *The Architectural Profession in Europe, 2016. A Sector Study. Architects Council of Europe.* Available at: www.ace-cae.eu/fileadmin/New_Upload/7._Publications/Sector_Study/2016/2016_EN_FN_070217_new.pdf [Accessed 18.12.18]

AIA (2016). *AIA Firm Survey Report Overview, 2016.* Available at: www.4specs.com/s2a/news/Research_2016-AIA-Firm-Survey-Report-Overview.pdf [Accessed 18.12.18]

AIA (2106). *Diversity in the Profession of Architecture Executive Summary, 2016.* Available at: www.architects.org/sites/default/files/AIA_DiversitySurvey_2016.pdf

APAW (2005). *Architectural Practice Around the World. Research carried out by the International Relations Department of the Collegi d'Arquitectes de Catalunya* (COAC – Architects' Institute of Catalonia) under the auspices of the Professional Practice Commission of the International Union of Architects (UIA) and on behalf of its Spanish section (Consejo Superior de los Colegios de Arquitectos de España – Higher Council of Architects' Institutes of Spain). Available at: www.coac.net/internacional/ang/docs/APAW.pdf [Accessed 18.12.18]

Architectural Record (2017). *Top 300 Architectural Firms 2017 List.* Available at: www.architecturalrecord.com/Top300/2017-Top-300-Architecture-Firms-1 [Accessed 18.12.18]

Bon, R. (1990). The world building market, 1970–1985, in *Proceedings on the CIB International Symposium on Building Economics and Construction Management* (Vol. 1). Sydney, March 14–21, pp. 16–47.

Bos-de Vos, M. and Volker, V. (2017). Constructing business models around identity: Tensions in architectural firms, in Chan, P. W. and Neilson, C. J. (eds.) *Proceeding of the 33rd Annual ARCOM Conference*, 4–6 September 2017, Cambridge, UK, Association of Researchers in Construction Management, pp. 491–500.

Building Design (2018). Foster: I don't know what 'cult of starchitect' means. March 2018, p. 4.

Cannon, J. (1994). Lies and construction statistics, *Construction Management and Economics*, 12(4), 307–313.

CIA (2018). *The World Factbook.* Available at: https://www.cia.gov/library/publications/the-world-factbook/ [Accessed 15.06.19]

Connaughton, J. and Meikle, J. (2013). The changing nature of UK construction professional service firms, *Building Research & Information*, 41(1), 95–109.

CoreLogic (2018). *About Us.* Available at: www.corelogic.com.au/about-us [Accessed 18.12.18]

Euro Monitor International (2018). *About Us.* Available at: www.euromonitor.com/about-us [Accessed 18.12.18]

Ganapathy, D. (2018). *Book review: Outside insight: Navigating a world drowning in data,* by Jorn Lyseggen.

Garcia, C., Ordonez, J. and Pisonera, R. (2017). Global cities rankings: A research agenda or a neoliberal urban planning tool? *Revista Internacional de Sociología RIS*, 75(1) enero-marzo, 2017.

Giffinger, R., Haindlmaier, G. and Kramar, H. (2010). The role of rankings in growing city competition, *Urban Research & Practice*, 3(3), 299–312.

Gluch, P. and Bosch-Sijtsema, P. (2016). Conceptualizing environmental expertise through the lens of institutional work, *Construction Management and Economics*, 34(7–8), 522–535.
Gruneberg, S. and Hughes, W. (2005). UK construction orders and output: A comparison of government and commercially available data 1995-2001, *Journal of Financial Management of Property and Construction*, 10(2), 83–94.
Gruneberg, S. and Fraser, B. (2012). Construction purchasing power parities: Potential roles and limitations, *Building Research & Information*, 40(3), 348–356.
Gruneberg, S. and Folwell, K. (2013). The use of gross fixed capital formation as a measure of construction output, *Construction Management and Economics*, 31(4), 359–368.
Hagen, A. L. (2018). The magic trick of creative capital: Competition, confidence, and collective enchantment among "starchitects". In *Magical Capitalism*, Palgrave Macmillan, Cham, pp. 215–238.
IBISWorld (2018). *Global Architectural Services Industry*. Available at: www.ibisworld.com/industry-trends/global-industry-reports/business-activities/architectural-services.html [Accessed 18.12.18]
Jamieson, C. (2011). *The Future for Architects? Project Report*. London: Royal Institute of British Architects. Available at: http://ualresearchonline.arts.ac.uk/8856/1/The_Future_for_Architects_Full_Report_2.pdf [Accessed 18.12.18]
Janssen, P., Loh, P., Raonic, A. and Schnabel, M. A. (eds.) (2017). Protocols, flows and glitches, in *Proceedings of the 22nd international conference of the association for Computer-Aided Architectural Design Research in Asia (CAADRIA)*, pp. 209–219. © 2017, The Association for Computer-Aided Architectural Design Research in Asia (CAADRIA), Hong Kong.
Lievesley, D. (2001). Making a difference: A role for the responsible international statistician? *Journal of the Royal Statistical Society: Series D* (The Statistician), 50(4), 367–406.
Lu, W., Ye, K., Flanagan, R. and Jewell, C. (2013). Developing construction professional services in the international market: SWOT analysis of China, *Journal of Management in Engineering*, 29(3), 302–313.
Lu, W. (2014). Reliability of engineering news-record international construction data, *Construction Management and Economics*, 32(10), 968–982.
Matthewson, G. (2012). "Nothing else will do": The call for gender equality in architecture in Britain, *Architectural Theory Review*, 17(2–3), 245–259.
Matthewson, G. (2015). *Dimensions of Gender: Women's Careers in the Australian Architecture Profession* (PhD Thesis), School of Architecture, The University of Queensland. https://doi.org/10.14264/uql.2015.1071
MSCI (2018). *Real Estate Investing*. Available at www.msci.com/real-estate [Accessed 18.12.18]
OECD (2007). Sixth Services Experts Meeting Domestic Regulation and Trade in Professional Services Paris, in 2007 Architectural Services in Global Trade in Professional Services by Russell V. Keune, *FAIA Architect*, Arlington, VA. Available at: www.oecd.org/site/tadstri/40778733.pdf [Accessed 18.12.18]
Parlour (2016). *Parlour Census Report 2001–2106*. Available at: http://archiparlour.org/parlour-census-report/
Ponzini, D. and Nastasi, M. (2016). *Starchitecture: Scenes, Actors and Spectacles in Contemporary Cities* (Vol. 1), Monacelli Press, New York, pp. 1–216.
Raisbeck, P. and Adams, L. (2018). September. They're coming at you: Latent and active design agency in a robotic design studio, in *Proceedings of the 34th Annual ARCOM Conference*, pp. 401–409.

RIBA. *Future Trends Survey, 2017, January*. Available at: www.architecture.com/knowledge-and-resources/resources-landing-page/future-trends-survey-2018 [Accessed 18.12.18]

RIBA (2017a). *RIBA Benchmarking 2017 Report Prepared for the RIBA by the Fees Bureau.* Executive Summary. Available at: www.architecture.com/-/media/gathercontent/business-benchmarking/additional-documents/ribabenchmarking2017executivesummarypdf.pdf [Accessed 18.12.18]

RIBA (2017b). *Global Talent Global Reach, Frontier Economics, 2017, December*. Available at: https://www.architecture.com/-/media/gathercontent/core-cpd/additional-documents/ribaglobaltalentglobalreachreportpdf.pdf

Sklair, L. (2017). *The icon project: Architecture, cities, and capitalist globalization*, Oxford University Press, Oxford.

Ruddock, L. (2002). Measuring the global construction industry: Improving the quality of data, *Construction Management & Economics*, 20(7), 553–556.

SNL Real Estate (2018). *SNL Helps Solve the Top Problems Facing Global Real Estate Analysts and Investors*. Available at: www.snl.com/marketing/microsite/problemsSolved/ [Accessed 18.12.18]

Statista. Architects. Available at: www.statista.com/search/?q=architects+&qKat=search [Accessed 18.12.18]

UIA (2018). *Architectural Professions Around the World*. Available at: https://apaw.uia-architectes.org/ [Accessed 18.12.18]

Ye, K., Lu, W. and Jiang, W. (2009). Concentration in the international construction market, *Construction Management and Economics*, 27(12), 1197–1207.

Part IV

Comparing construction industry performance from a financial perspective and in terms of industry output

9 Make/buy decisions in international construction industry firms

Alex Murray and Alexandr Kulakov

Introduction

Firms are one of the fundamental economic units and are ever-changing. They are born, grow, adapt, marry, breed, divorce and die. Their constancy and commercial success are determined by both the external economic environments in which they operate, as well as the internal decision-making and processes they foster. When it comes to measuring the health of the units we care about most, the practice of medicine has developed a vast array of procedures and related statistics to monitor and help heal bodily ills. BMI, blood pressure, cholesterol levels, MRI scans, biopsies and DNA sequencing all provide more information to help improve human health. Medical professionals are highly specialised in their knowledge about the determinants of well-being, able to prescribe treatments based on contestable evidence as to their effectiveness. Such sophisticated medical practices developed over many thousands of years from ancient shaman healers to the range of modern day experts from anaesthetists to urologists. While the profession of the economist has not had the benefit of such timely recognition, there have developed a similarly diverse variety of experts on how to monitor and prescribe treatments for firm success – consultants and managers in production and procurement, marketing and sales, logistics, legal and regulatory compliance, human resource management, administration and data management, financial management (the list goes on).

One profession that is highly regarded in monitoring the health of firms is that of the accountant. This profession out dates that of the economist with early references dating back to the early 15th century with Luca Pacioli's development of double entry bookkeeping. A core competence of the profession includes the ability to record the monetary implications of firm activities. In this respect, an accountant is much like a radiologist, providing thorough examinations of the patient without necessarily having within their remit the decisions to improve the patients' treatment. Measures of profitability and judgement on risk exposure become the equivalent to stethoscopes and informed medical opinion. Decisions based on prognosis are left to leading physicians, or rather the management and shareholders of the firm.

One might question whether the accounting profession is at all worth comparing to that of practicing medicine. What is the equivalent of the Hippocratic oath for accountants? Accountants are charged with providing a 'true and fair view of the assets, liabilities, financial position and profit or loss' (Section 393 of the Companies Act 2006) but it should be remembered that it is the directors of the company that sign off on the final accounts and take liability for their exactitude. It might best be left to the administrators and liquidators of failed companies to judge the appropriateness of accounting decisions, much as one might trust the coroner's report for hints of medical negligence leading to premature death.

This chapter demonstrates some of the insights an examination of the published accounts of construction firms can provide. A brief method explains how we sample 320 publicly limited companies (PLC) across the United States, Japan, the UK and France. The core theme of this chapter concerns the make/buy characteristics of business models. This considers the decisions and results of firms, who either produce their output internally (make) or sub-contract production of intermediate output to other firms (buy).

A key proposition is that a single firm's accounts provide a glimmer of insight on aspects of its business models. Further, bright shards of light across industries are made visible via observation of large sets of firms' accounts. The use of well-defined continuums based on continuous accounting ratios allows the analyst to comment objectively on whether individual firms exhibit the normal economic characteristics of firms within their wider industry. This chapter will reflect on the unique challenges of using accounts to grasp an insight into construction firms.

While there is discussion of wider theory, some knowledge is assumed, specifically the theory of the firm, appreciation of terms, such as stocks (assets and liabilities) and flows (revenues and costs) and more generally, the activities of large, corporate, main contractors and developers. The dead ends and pitfalls of accounts are also highlighted to develop an appreciation for the limitations and biases involved in their use. The reader of this chapter should gain basic tools for sampling and analysing firm accounts.

Finally, given the inclusion of Carillion PLC within the dataset, up until its compulsory liquidation on 15 January 2018, the second largest UK construction contractor by turnover, commentary will invariably highlight their results. Balfour Beatty PLC, the largest UK construction contractor will also be a focus of some commentary. Their predominant buy business models and common long-term use of short-term cash flow management is a key factor in the demise of the Carillion and near failure of the Balfour Beatty.

Unit of analysis – the firm

While much study and measurement of construction activity tends to focus on the project as the unit of analysis, economists tend to consider this unit as inferior to that of the firm, (Runeson and Valence, 2015). There are a few reasons for this:

1 The firm constitutes a permanent and common form of organisation for investment in production and capacity. Projects are temporary and

virtual – the resources available to them depend on decisions made at a higher level within the firm, be that the firms' management and/or shareholders.

2 Projects are the way demand is segmented by customers, not how supply is organised, managed and delivered.

When examining industries, definable as sets of firms that share some common means of technology in their production processes to form the supply side of economic output, the firm becomes the obvious unit for comparison. The firm constitutes a boundary of interest around those core activities, over which investors and managers have some level of control. This is not the case with a single construction project for larger buy firms. Whereas Tier 1 contractors or contract managers have a dedicated focus for the projects under their care, from the level of the firm, there are decisions to be made about optimising the commercial success of a portfolio of projects that will necessarily involve ranking individual projects in terms of relative importance. In the context of large diversified contractors, the management of the corporate cash flows resulting from work on numerous projects is a pertinent example of this, such as delaying payment to a non-critical supplier in one project to ensure earlier payment to a critical supplier in another project.

The single firm may not always possess this level of autonomy. In the context of a large, corporate PLC one must consider the numerous subsidiaries nested within the corporate group (as projects are nested within and across, sets of firms). The corporate group management might consider the performance of subsidiaries in a similar way as a programme manager would look at projects. A happy consequence of, and relevant factor in, using the firm as the entity of interest here, includes the compatibility of accounts as a source of data for analysis. Published accounts are derived from and based upon precisely this unit. These accounts are separate from the management accounts of firms that provide more detail but relate to particular projects or firm activities. Management accounts tend to be structured in ways that the firm chooses as more appropriate for monitoring and decision-making. As such, they do not necessarily exhibit common formats or structures that allow for large sample comparative analysis. While comparability can be an issue when using published accounts, especially when accounting standards applied vary, there are opportunities for timely insight from their examination.

Data source – Osiris

The data source used here for accessing global PLC accounts is referred to as Osiris (2018). Bureau van Dijk (BvD) the provider of this platform, collates, 'treat, append and standardise' the accounts of companies from around the world, as well as provide information about corporate ownership structures, directors, auditors, mergers and acquisitions activity and other aspects of firm operations. BvD was acquired from the Swedish private equity firm EQT for $3.3 billion (EUR) in August 2017, by Moody's, a leading provider of credit ratings and consultancy services.

Osiris is a specific product providing global PLC firms. BvD provides a wider suite of products with more specific geographical scope but deeper access in terms of additional coverage of limited companies (FAME: UK public (PLC) and private (Limited), Orbis, – international public and private, Zephyr for mergers and acquisitions and foreign and direct investment (FDI) deal information.

> Bureau van Dijk's solutions support the credit analysis, investment research, tax risk, transfer pricing, compliance and third-party due diligence needs of financial institutions, corporations, professional services firms and governmental authorities worldwide.
>
> (Moodys, 2017)

Sampling firm accounts

The ability to design complex search criteria within the BvD product range is one of their most appealing features. A variety of search steps can be defined based on the availability and value of a full spectrum of financial variables and firm characteristics, as well as data on location, ownership and industrial sector using standard industrial classification (SIC) codes. Users can also define their own concepts made up from individual accounting lines against which to sample firms and extract data. The use of Boolean operators can be applied to develop sophisticated requirements for bespoke time series datasets. As ever, one should bear in mind the survivor bias that is inherent with requiring samples of firms based on consistent reporting of financials over many years.

The natural place to start designing a search strategy is based on the reporting of the variables that the analyst is looking to inspect. There are significant trade-offs between the availability of variables and the coverage that the resulting sample provides over sets of firms within the industry or the wider economy (the population). These should be thoroughly investigated before the analyst finalises the sample of firms to be used.

The availability of financial data varies greatly depending on the concept, with larger, more aggregated concepts having greater availability over more diverse samples of firms. Whether a firm reports a variable is driven, in the main, by their size and also their share listing status. In the UK, the primary requirement to report accounts is driven by the size of the firm according to the Companies Act, 2006. Firms are not required to report even basic accounts unless they meet at least 2 of the following criteria:

1. Turnover – more than £5.6 million
2. Balance sheet total – more than £2.8 million
3. Number of employees – more than 50

The reporting requirements in individual countries varies depending on their legislation. The benefit of looking at PLC firms across multiple countries is the

Table 9.1 Search criteria and resulting samples

Step	*Requirement*	*Step result*	*Search result*
1.	Listed/Unlisted companies: Publicly listed companies	61,536	61,536
2.	Status: Active	64,954	61,180
3.	World region/Country: G8	39,729	20,207
4.	NACE Rev. 2 (Primary codes only): 41 – Construction of buildings, 42 – Civil engineering, 43 – Specialised construction activities	2,557	411
	Boolean search: 1 And 2 And 3 And 4	TOTAL	411

greater consistency in the size and diversity of firms given their status and hence the availability of many, though not all, variables for analysis.

The search criteria applied to reach the following samples did not impose any requirements for variables to be available. The search criteria was applied, and the resulting samples are detailed in Table 9.1 below. As is indicated, Osiris includes over 60,000 publicly listed companies globally, just under 40,000 of which are within the G8 economies and over 2,500 of which are within their construction industries according to the NACE SIC system. These requirements applied together produce an initial sample of 411 firms.

The G8 economies are comprised of the USA, Japan, Russia, France, Germany, Canada, Italy and UK. Following review of the initial sample, and to aide focus, the analysis concentrates on the 4 economies with sample sizes as follows: USA (n=100), Japan (n=174), UK (n=31) and France (n=15) making up a maximum sample size of 320 where all firms report the variables of interest. While the sample sizes for some of the other economies were much larger than for France, (Canada had 18, Russia had 61, Germany had 6 and Italy had 6), it was hard to ignore the fact that the French sample included the three largest multinational construction companies of Vinci, Effiage and Bouygues. The sample of Russian firms exhibited large numbers of firms with peculiarly negative profit margins and was discounted for concerns over data quality. Analysis will provide a snapshot across the samples focussing on 2015 results given the considerable reduction in availability of 2016 data at the time of sampling (April 2018).

Accounting indicators of position on make/buy continuum

Accounts provide indicators over a range of economic concepts. For example, accounts provide measures of the extent to which a firm makes in-house, taking on the processes of value adding activity required to produce the eventual output for sale. Alternatively, the accounts reveal the extent to which a firm predominantly buys intermediate output from other firms. The application of make/buy concepts is particularly relevant for the analysis of firms within the construction sector, given the temporary nature and varying length of supply chains that deliver construction output. While the complexity of supply chains might be considered lower than in other industries, such as automotive or aeronautical manufacturing, a relatively unique feature of construction supply chains is they are often temporary in nature, given the project structure of demand.

At one extreme of this make/buy continuum a Tier 1 contractor may choose to subcontract almost all of the production process, the output of which it eventually sells to its clients, with its direct employees providing the project management element alone, to co-ordinate the packages of construction output. A firm pursuing this strategy may be characterised by high cost of sales (CoS) relative to turnover (T) and low net value added (NVA) to turnover (NVA, measured as the total remuneration of employees plus profit before interest and tax (PBIT), as the respective incomes to labour and capital). This is a consequence of more of the tier 1's costs being variable with their output, as subcontracting reduces the fixed costs associated with internal productive capacity. The relevant equivalent accounting concepts for the economists' view of variable and fixed costs are CoS and administrative expenses (AdExp, also known as overheads).

Tier 1 contractors try to minimise their fixed costs in part to reduce the risk of losses in periods of low demand during recessions. They achieve this commercial outcome through sub-contracting. This cost structure can be highly beneficial in the long run, especially in industries characterised by volatile market demand through the business cycle, as occurs in construction. This is part of the wider economic environment that explains the emergence of this typical tier 1 contractor commercial practice. When Tier 1 firms fail to win contracts, either because demand has reduced in the market or their bidding strategy has proved unsuccessful, their order books shrink, and subcontracting costs diminish with output. When a firm's business model relies on supplying higher tiers (Tier 2 firms and lower make for Tier 1 firms to buy), a larger proportion of the makers' costs will be fixed in nature (AdExp), to account for the element of their productive capacity that is more difficult to switch off when demand is low. The fixed cost element in the cost structure between construction processes of course varies greatly. The more capital intensive a process is, the higher is the fixed cost element, be this either in the cost of direct resources or indirect finance costs. Construction processes tend to be labour intensive, and the use of casual labour in construction processes means the cost for employing firms can be highly variable.

Lower value added, (the source of wages and profits), to turnover results from the lost opportunity for firms that sub-contract to earn profit on the production of output for the final client. Profit on work that could have been undertaken in-house at one level of the supply chain, is now undertaken over two or more levels and so is distributed between more *layers*. Firms that predominantly subcontract grow their turnover more quickly than firms that grow through organic arithmetic increases in in-house capacity through sustained investment. Increasing subcontracting further reduces NVA/T, through larger increases in T than NVA.

The profit and loss statement, or the statement of consolidated income under International Financial Reporting Standards (IFRS), details the costs (outflows) and revenues (inflows) for the firm. Starting with turnover and progressing through the various concepts of profit through deductions of different types of costs, the ultimate bottom line provides a net profit concept after all costs (both resource and finance) have been accounted for.

Direct remuneration of employees (Rem) is often the foremost source of expense to those construction firms that make, given its labour intensity. Employment costs of subcontractors are included, or subsumed, under CoS for the firm and where considered as a proportion of CoS, provides another useful business ratio to indicate where a firm sits on the make/buy continuum. Firms that show higher Rem/CoS values tend to be towards the make end of the continuum. When a firm subcontracts (buys) a labour intensive process, the cost of the contract becomes a non-Rem CoS for the purchasing firm. The supplier firm then accounts for the labour intensive process by showing higher Rem/CoS in their own accounts, unless they themselves are further sub-contracting the production of course. Unfortunately, consistent data on Rem for employed labour and the number of employees (Emps.) is not so widely reported, other than for the very largest firms. One can also deduct Rem from CoS to reach the concept of *Purchases from other firms* (PfOF = CoS – Rem). This concept can be used as a more sensitive normaliser for calculating creditor days than the standard denominator of turnover (Ive and Murray, 2013). As buy firms can generate much higher turnover than make firms, they will appear to look like more prompt payers (with lower creditor days) than would otherwise be the case.

Where number of employees and remuneration expenditure are available, another perspective on make/buy is available through analysis of the ratios T/Emp and Net Value Added/Emp. One expects the first ratio to increase with a buy strategy, as employees are managing the subcontracting of final output rather than producing it themselves. For example, where a firm is predominantly undertaking in-house a non-specialist labour intensive process, the turnover per employee per year is required to cover their remuneration, any minor capital element, plus materials and profit. Contrast this with an intensive subcontracting firm whose employees are highly skilled and well paid professional project managers, who tender and package up work to pass down to lower tiers. This firm's turnover must cover the payments to employees and for all subcontracted work, minimal depreciation (as capital will be owned by subcontractors) and profit. Depending on the scale of the operation and how productively project managers can monitor and manage external suppliers, the turnover per employee of the buy firm will be many times greater than those of make firms.

Where a firm pursues a buy strategy, the high proportion of turnover per employee creates a scenario whereby just a small negative margin can magnify losses to negate the positive remuneration figure and render this ratio negative overall.

Balance sheet headlines

Before progressing on to an analysis of the data, we should acquaint ourselves with the headline balance sheet concepts. Total assets (TA), is the aggregation of fixed assets (long-term less liquid assets) and current assets (convertible into cash within a year). TA include the stock of assets firms require to deliver output. The liabilities side of the balance sheet is dominated by debt, D, or long-term liabilities and equity, E, or shareholders funds, as in many business models the two main forms of finance that maintain solvency. The final headline concept of the balance sheet, that of current liabilities, CL, is defined as sums owed within the year. These current liabilities are deducted from total assets, which brings us to the fundamental balance sheet equation, TA – CL = D + E, where total assets fewer current liabilities is equivalent to debt and equity. Both sides of the equation are alternative perspectives on a firm's capital employed (K). TA – CL is the operating perspective, that is, what value of assets does a firm own in excess of its short-term liabilities required to remain solvent. The right side is the financing perspective of capital employed, showing the balance between debt and equity as the long-term sources of finance.

Make/buy through 3-part Du Pont system

Besides considering how bespoke ratios may be designed to compare firms on the make/buy continuum, an alternative approach is to reflect on the value of other more commonly used accounting ratios from a *make/buy* perspective. The following section considers the core ratios that determine a firm's return on capital employed, ROCE, using global PLC accounts for analysis of and reflection on the make/buy framework.

The 3-part Du Pont system illustrates how the return on capital employed (PBIT/K) breaks down into the three core ratios of:

1. Profit margin (PBIT/T)
2. Asset turnover ratio (T/TA)
3. Current gearing (TA/K)

In Equation 1 (the 3-part Du Pont accounting identity) these three ratios are multiplied together to determine Return on Capital Employed (ROCE), showing how increasing any one, keeping everything else equal, improves profitability. There are various economic theories able to explore the potential relationships between these 3 core ratios, exploring the trade-offs inherent business models and alternative commercial strategies. The following commentary seeks to draw out these trade-offs inherent with the firms position on the make buy continuum.

$$ROCE = \frac{PBIT}{K} = \frac{PBIT}{T} \times \frac{T}{TA} \times \frac{TA}{K} \qquad (1)$$

Profit margin – the downside risks of buy strategies

One major downside of pursuing buy business strategies is reduced profit margins resulting from forgoing the opportunity to add value internally to the eventual output sold. A merchant trader is the archetypal buy strategy firm, in which profitability hangs almost completely on the ability to charge a higher price for units sold (outputs, O), than the cost of their purchase (inputs, I) (Gruneberg and Ive, 2000). As in any other enterprise, the direction of profitability, as a measure of a flow of profit on a stock of assets or a form of financial capital, depends on achieving positive relative prices ($O_p > I_p$). However, whereas firms typically undertake some value adding productive process, transforming a quantity of inputs (I_q), often including intermediate outputs from other firms, into quantities of more valuable outputs (O_q), merchants' productive transformation involves little more than the moving of goods purchased from one location to another. As a result, the profitability of a firm does not depend upon how productively it can transform its inputs into outputs, but it will depend on the costs incurred from logistics in search of arbitrage. From this extreme, we can consider the differences between merchants and sub-contracting firms as less discrete, with buy strategy firms considered closer to merchants than they are to make firms.

Looking at our samples of global PLC firms and correlating profit margin with a key make/buy indicator, CoS/T, we see each economy's sample demonstrates a negative relationship, as theory would predict. As firms' CoS/T ratio approaches 1, that is, variable cost outflows become equal to sales inflows, margins compress and approach zero. In the larger sample of Japanese PLCs there is a lower negative effect on margins with increasing variable cost, though this may in part be the result of the much lower proportion of firms with lower ratios of CoS/T of below 0.75. As such, the line of best fit or the trend line, is more influenced by most of the sample that exhibit more buy characteristics with CoS/T > 0.75.

The accounts of PLC firms tend to suggest that such firms are more buy than make in nature. Turnover growth achieved through buy strategies supports their path towards trading publicly. As such, we would expect our sample to have cost structures that have higher CoS/T than firms in the wider industry. The relationship between margin and CoS/T is unlikely to be purely linear. Exploration of these relationships requires much larger samples than those presented here, including wider consideration of limited firm accounts.

Asset turnover – the margin trade-off

Buy firm strategies can achieve increases in asset turnover ratios by reducing the need for assets to produce output by using subcontractors instead. The sources of increased turnover relative to assets involve separate effects. First, turnover can grow more quickly with subcontracting compared to pursuing organic growth strategies, as the buy strategy foregoes the need to either accumulate retained profits or raise additional debt or equity to finance growth in productive capacity. The effect on the amount of assets a firm owns from a move towards buy strategies depends on the economic characteristics of the process being subcontracted. Construction activity is generally labour intensive, but some processes, especially the early phase demolition and ground works of large scale re-developments, require significant plant and equipment. Whereas large PLC contractors tend

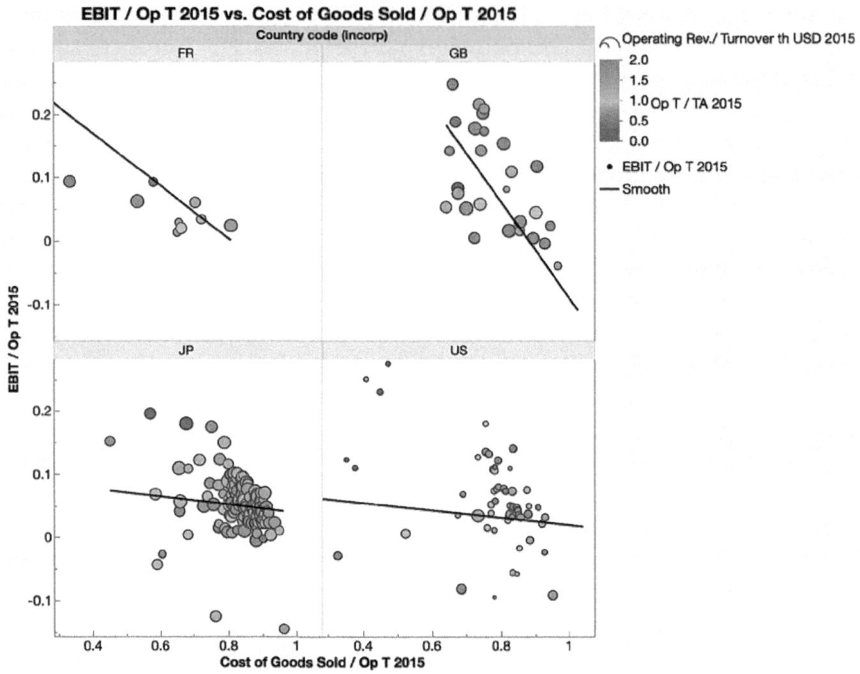

Figure 9.1 The margin/cost structure trade off

to own some plant to deliver this type of work in-house (make), many other firms forgo this need to own such assets by leasing them as and when required. This practice means the potential for reducing the need to own assets via buy strategies is smaller than it would be than if the typical make firm tended to own such assets, rather than lease them. The growth in turnover relative to assets through buy strategies might be referred to as outs tensive growth. While it may involve reduced use of inputs, in this case capital assets, to achieve similar levels of outputs (the definition of intensive growth), for the Tier 1 firms, the inputs are predominantly intermediate output supplied by lower tier suppliers.

There is an inherent lower limit to the ratio of the relative value of assets to turnover, even through extreme buy strategies. As firms generate output and turnover via sales in business-to-business transactions, they issue invoices to administer payment. Prior to receipt of payment, a firm records the money owed by clients as an asset on their balance sheet. This is commonly referred to as trade debt or receivables. As a result, it will have relatively fewer assets to turnover than firms who make in-house. In this way some contractors can gear up their assets through active subcontracting, generating many more times the value of turnover to assets than would be possible producing their output completely in-house. This benefit of subcontracting comes at a price in terms of a negative effect on profit margins. This is observed below in Figure 9.2. The colouring of observations in Figure 9.2 relates to our first measure of profitability that of PBIT on TA, otherwise known as the return on total assets (ROTA). The greener the shading the higher the return on total assets. ROTA is the first profitability concept calculated as the product of margin and asset turnover (the axes in Figure 9.2). This analysis illustrates the alternative commercial strategies of firms that sell high quantities at low prices, such as the low margin, high T/TA, which is a typical strategy of Tier 1 contractors. The alternative strategy is to sell lower quantities at higher prices, producing high margins and a low T/TA, a typical strategy of developers.

In Figure 9.2, the top left cluster of green discs for the UK sample includes a range of the largest and best-known real estate developers (mainly residential) in the UK, including Taylor Wimpey, Bovis Homes, Barratt, Persimmon and Berkeley. In the graph, the size of the dots reflects the size of the firms' balance sheets compared to contractors with the size of each dot weighted by each firm's total assets. The balance sheets of developers tend to be dominated by the value of their land holdings as a long term fixed asset. Their generally brighter green colour illustrates how their ROTA is generally higher than that of contractors. Developers tend to achieve much lower asset turnover ratios of 0.6 to 0.8 compared to those PLC firms more focused on contracting, where asset turnover

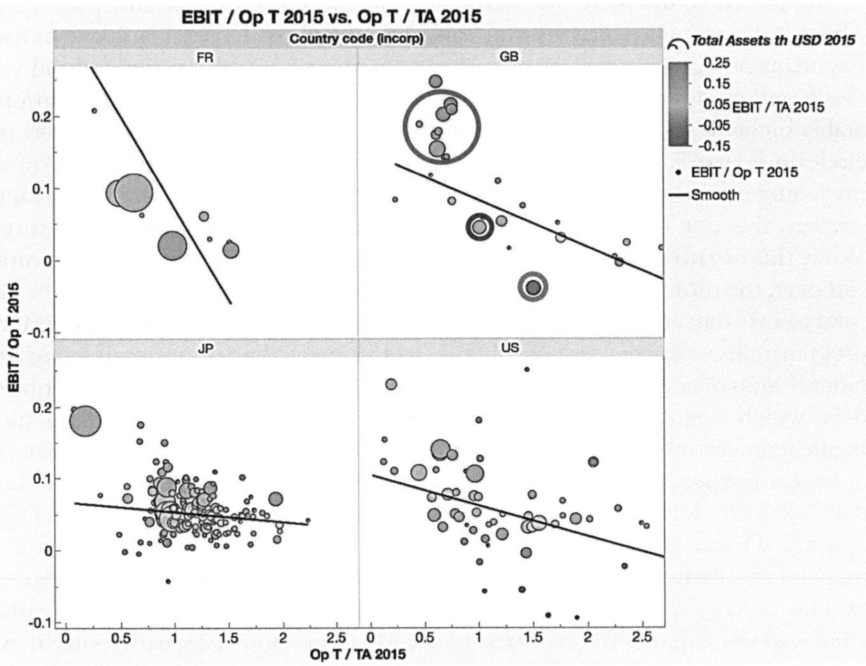

Figure 9.2 Return on total assets – margin by asset turnover

ratios were invariably greater than 1. Developer profit margins were considerably higher at 15% compared to contractors with margins typically around 5% or lower.

The ownership of land is of course a necessary input into the development process and this limits the pursuit of buy strategies in real estate development. Historically, many house builders have maintained significant *in-house* capacity to undertake the process of constructing real estate. In more recent years, many large developers have focused their efforts on the *core* processes of purchasing, financing, gaining planning permission and the marketing and sale of real estate, while outsourcing much of the actual construction processes. Given that land provides a good form of collateral as an asset that tends to increase in value over the long-run, developers can achieve much higher levels of long-term gearing (D/K) compared to construction contractors.

Any firm that is diversified across both construction contracting and real estate development will exhibit an asset turnover ratio and other accounting ratios, that reflect neither of these activities particularly accurately. This is one problem of using the consolidated accounts of large complex firms – the process of consolidation muddies the waters limiting the insight into the diversity of economic characteristics among the various subsidiaries. For example, there were 2,913 subsidiaries recorded within the Vinci corporate group, the largest of the French major contractors. The ratios of the corporate group are unable to reveal the range of activities of this multitude of firms.

The red circle in Figure 9.2 highlights Balfour Beatty PLC's results for 2015. This was a particularly bad year for this firm, one of the largest UK contractors. Reporting a negative profit margin of -3.95% and recording a negative EBIT of -$408 million, they nevertheless generated a turnover of $10.3bn and a considerably higher asset turnover ratio than their key competitor Carillion (the blue circle in Figure 9.3). Balfour Beatty's 2015 results demonstrate the perils of a predominantly buy strategy that subcontracts most of the output. Because of this strategy, the Tier 1 firms cease to retain full control of their costs and delivery. While this negative profit margin might only seem a small proportion of the firm's turnover, the turnover of a buy strategy firm is significantly inflated relative to its total assets compared to that of a make strategy firm and even slightly negative profit margins pose a real risk of commercial loss translating into overall financial failure. Moreover, much of the asset base of a buy strategy firm is in fact trade debt, which is money owed to it from the prior sale of output. This makes the fragile financial position of buy strategy firms even more precarious.

By comparison, Carillion's profit margin in 2015 was a relatively healthy 4.4%. It had a low asset turnover ratio for a contractor of 1.02, with a ROTA of 4.5%. This compares to a typical ROTA for pure developer firms of approximately 13% (derived from a profit margin of 20% and asset turnover of 0.65 based on Figure 9.2). However, contractors' profitability in terms of return on capital employed (ROCE or PBIT/K) benefits greatly from another aspect of cash flow management within the Du Pont framework.

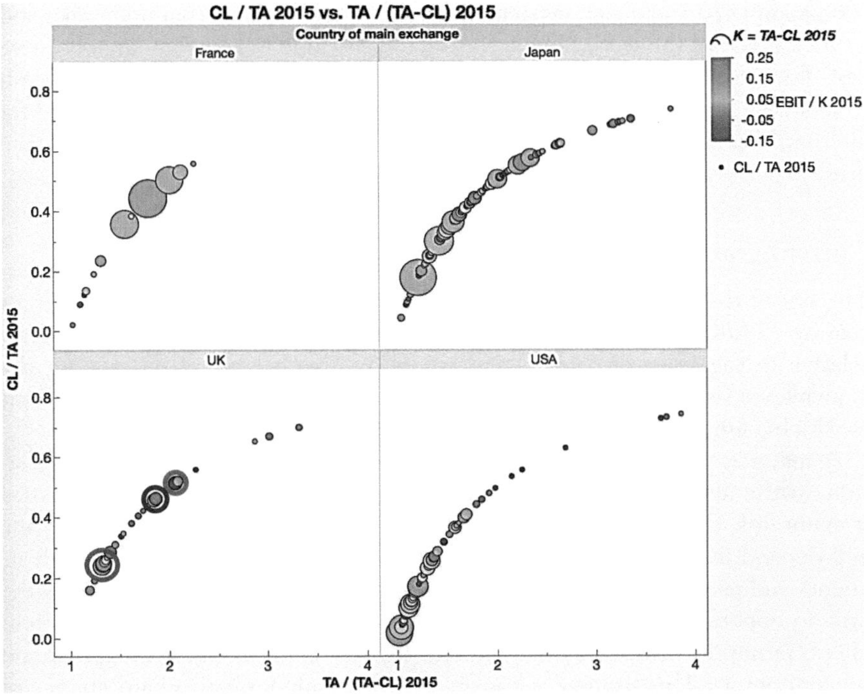

Figure 9.3 The geometric relationship between current gearing (TA/K) and CL/TA

The manipulation of supplier credit to finance production

One of the benefits of pursuing a buy strategy is the ability to access supply chain finance, otherwise known as trade credit or cash farming. When a firm subcontracts the production of its output to another firm, the negotiation around when payment for goods and services is required typically takes place before supply occurs. Where the potential purchaser, say, a Tier 1 contractor, engages with lower tiers to tender for work, the Tier 2 or lower supplier may receive a large proportion, sometimes a majority, of their sales revenue from that single Tier 1 firm. This can be for work on different projects, in which case the sums owed by the Tier 1 firm will depend on numerous work packages over a range of active construction sites and contracts.

All work done on site will be subject to sign-off and review and in due course, the Tier 1 contractor will request interim stage payments from the developer, their client, to fund the works. The rate at which these cash flow payments cascade down to lower tiers in the supply chain is something over which Tier 1 contractors have a great deal of control in most forms of procurement and project delivery. By pursuing payment from clients as soon as possible after work has been completed and delaying payment to the lower tier firms that undertake and finance much of the work, Tier 1 contractors are able to generate large positive cash flows for their own benefit. The use of these accumulated stocks of cash to maintain solvency in financing corporate assets directly reduces the need for alternative forms of finance, namely debt and equity, as the two components of a firm's *financial* capital employed.

Current gearing – TA/K

The last of the ratios in the 3-part Du Pont framework is referred to as current gearing (TA/K). This ratio measures the value of all assets, fixed and current, relative to the value of debt, D and equity, E. The balance sheet sets out the equivalence between TA and D + E + CL and the ratio TA/K measures the extent to which a firm's assets are financed by CL.

A major factor that determines a firm's level of current gearing is its position on the make/buy continuum and the related level of supply chain finance it maintains. For a firm that pursues buy strategies, the value of current gearing will depend increasingly on the payment practices the firm negotiates with its clients and particularly suppliers. Increasing the use of subcontracting gives the firm an opportunity to generate a positive cash flow by pursuing payment from clients promptly, while delaying payments for work done by its own suppliers and subcontractors. This strategy is known as cash farming, supply chain finance or the strategic management of organisational cash flow (Kenley, 2003). The result is like filling a bucket with water more quickly than it drains out, allowing the accumulation of cash.

While at some point, funds will be required to pay suppliers, in the meantime, this cash provides solvency and helps finance the assets and investments in working capital required for other projects within the firm's portfolio. The effect on the balance sheet is an increase in the value of trade creditors (trade payables) as well as accrued liabilities in line with accruals principles – to allocate costs and revenues to the period in which the activity that lead to them occurred.

As this practice of delaying payments to suppliers increases current liabilities, it allows the firm to finance a larger stock of assets than reliance on debt and equity alone would permit and so increases the ratio of TA/K. In this way buy strategies are effective for firms to avoid the constraints of access to finance for turnover growth (Gruneberg and Ive, 2000). Such strategies also allow firms to avoid the productive capacity constraint on growth by using that of other firms via the purchase of their intermediate output. However, buy strategies do not assist in overcoming the demand constraint. In fact, buy strategy firms must foster sufficient demand for their services, if they are to achieve sustained turnover growth. The inability to maintain turnover growth brings increased risk of insolvency, especially if turnover starts to reduce. As turnover declines, net cash flows reduce but the need to settle costs on previously higher levels of turnover remains. In attempting to meet its legal obligations, buy strategy firms may be tempted to price work much closer to, or even below outturn cost, a factor leading to thin or negative profit margins.

The ability to achieve large increases in turnover through buy strategies, while facing constraints in sourcing sufficient staff to manage the increased subcontracting of output is consistent with the view of Penrose and Slater (1980). They suggest that firm growth is as much about expanding managerial capacity as it is about sourcing skilled or unskilled labour via sub-contracts. To pursue buy strategies, contractors must engage with larger and larger tenders and build a reputation for being professional managers. This requires development of expert project management teams, who can successfully win bids, deliver projects through high value and complex subcontracting and the building of relationships within long supply chains, as well as managing commercial risk and minimising cost over runs.

Figure 9.3 plots PLCs from France, Japan, the UK and the United States against the two concepts of current gearing (TA/K, measured on the horizontal axis) and the proportion of TA that are financed by CL (CL/TA as measured on the vertical axis). These ratios are fundamentally linked by the arithmetic of the balance sheet, hence the consistency of the observations of the firms along the curve. Balfour Beatty stands out in the UK samples for its very poor ROCE in this year (-12.3%), indicated by the red coloured circle in Figure 9.3, concurrently showing higher than average current gearing (2.06) and so by definition, higher than typical levels of CL financing of assets (0.514).

This low profitability is linked to the high use of CLs to finance assets and the commercial risks that excessive subcontracting entails. When firms subcontract, they move the control of many aspects of production out of the firm. While contracts are used to define and enforce terms, the risk profile of construction projects frequently test, and sometimes break, the limits of contracts. Disputes may arise between Tier 1 and Tier 2 contractors due to poor initial costing of work or lack of clarity in defining responsibilities for delivery. Regardless of who is legally at fault, delays and cost overruns leave Tier 1 firms exposed to considerable losses.

There is an inverse relationship between profit margin and current gearing, in part due to the higher prices charged by suppliers, who need to cover their own interest charges incurred while awaiting payment. These higher prices from the Tier 2 firms translate into lower profit margins for the Tier 1 contractors through their higher Cost of Sales, CoS, (due to the direct cost of subcontracted works). This higher resource cost facing the Tier 1 firm is compensated for by lower finance costs due to resorting to supply chain finance, which reduces the use of debt and equity and improves overall profitability for the Tier 1 firm, as a result of this buy strategy despite lower margins, compensated for by a much higher sales turnover. Make/buy frameworks can demonstrate how one firm's finance costs (the additional interest charges of the Tier 2 net supplier of trade credit) translate into another firm's resource costs (the higher CoS of the Tier 1 net recipient of trade credit). Ive and Murray (2013) found that the 'implied rate of interest' paid by users of trade credit finance was low, below ROTA, such that the more they borrowed using trade creditors, the higher was their own ROCE.

This seems to bear out from visual inspection of the Japanese sample in Figure 9.3 above. This sample clearly has more firms with higher levels of current gearing than in other economies. Those firms with higher current gearing (TA/K > 2) exhibit the highest levels of ROCE, illustrated by the brighter green colouring of the discs of Japanese contractors. This demonstrates that while *buy* strategies can bring commercial risks in terms of tighter margins and potentially lead to losses, the use of CL to replace D and E can be a highly effective strategy to improve firm profitability.

Limitations and further research

Accounts provide little or no information on the identity of trading partners, namely those firms, with whom firms do business. Some firms provide information on their customers and their suppliers within data fields within BvD products. However, there is no systematic data source that enables networks of supply chains to be constructed within and between projects across industries, other than through case study research with the agreement of supply chain members. Accounts provide ample data on the firm, as the node, but little insight on the supply and demand relationships between firms, the ties that make up supply chains. One benefit of project-based analysis is that it reveals these ties to some extent. However, without such coverage over industries, the systematic study of supply chains is limited.

Buy and large bias – non-random missingness

The requirement that only larger firms publish detailed accounts, depending on the specific national legislation, creates an inherent bias in the insights achievable via accounting data. The pursuit of buy strategies allows firms to grow and maintain larger levels of turnover than would be the case for make strategy firms. In pursuing broad samples of firms across industries, analysis tends to generate samples of firms that are more buy in nature. This buy bias may be more troublesome in construction industries than in other sectors of the economy, given the predominance of large numbers of small and very small firms. This limits the coverage of firm accounts over aggregate output, as well as precluding insight into the smaller, predominantly *make* strategy firms. Analysis should remain open to the possibility of markedly different business models and ratio values in unobservable firms within the industry. In this sense, accounting data on small firms is *Missing Not At Random (MNAR)*, with the unfortunate consequence that their form and value are not amenable to imputation based on the measures of larger firms within the wider industry.

Conclusions

Company accounts provide a reliable basis for economic insight into the varying business models of firms across industries. The variety of accounting concepts that allow one to observe, provides ample fertile ground for further research.

The focus on make/buy aspects of international construction PLCs is only one of many alternative economic frameworks that can be used to analyse accounting data. Nevertheless, as has been pointed out, there are limitations concerning the representativeness of only relatively large firms, when using firm accounts for industrial measurement in the construction sector. While these analyses can claim to have captured the population of construction industry PLCs in the respective economies, what they achieve in breadth, they lack in depth due to the scale and complexity of corporate structures.

From the analyses of the four economies, we see a consistent margin compression effect as firms exhibit indicators of increasingly buy strategies. While such firms can use these strategies to achieve significant turnover growth over short periods of time, the commercial risks of drifting into even slightly negative margins on this inflated turnover include sudden firm insolvency. This risk of failure is magnified by the ability of *buy* strategy firms to maintain such small balance sheets, as the buffer for absorbing risk, using unsecured supply chain financing.

Carillion's involuntary liquidation on 15 January 2018 demonstrated how fragile even the largest of construction contractors can be. Their pursuit of buy strategies was instrumental in achieving many years in both their commercial success and their commercial demise. Recording a turnover of £4.4 billion and a profit margin of 4.7% for their accounts to the end of 2016, the firm's cost overruns on a small number of large contracts completely exhausted its equity which had stood at £701m in 2016. The profit warning of the 10 July 2017 announced provisions for losses on three UK PFI contracts as well as works in the Middle East. The combined PFI cost overruns accounted for the minority of this overall sum, of approximately 27% (NAO, 2018). By the autumn of 2017, these provisions had risen in value to £1.1 billion. The accumulation of such high losses is only conceivable against the levels of output and risk transfer made possible via buy strategies. Carillion's 2016 assets of £4.4 billion were financed by £1.5 billion in debt and £2.2 billion in current liabilities, in addition to equity, demonstrating their reliance on short-term financing using supply chain finance practices, which are typical of buy strategy firms.

While some firms are prominent and visible given their large turnovers, there are a vast number of medium and small firms, whose share of productive output cannot be ignored in understanding the construction industry. In 2015, for example, as much as 39% of UK construction output was produced by firms employing between 0 and 19 employees, compared to 38% employing more than 100 people or having turnover greater than £100 million (Office for National Statistics, 2018). Based on an analysis of the accounts of only a relatively small number of relatively large contractors, our insight into the economic diversity and activities of firms in construction provides a limited understanding of industrial organisation in general and the role of small and medium firms specifically.

References

Companies Act (2006). [Online] Available at: http://www.legislation.gov.uk/ukpga/2006/46/pdfs/ukpga_20060046_en.pdf [Accessed 20.09.2018]

Osiris (2018), *Bureau van Dijk*. [Online]. Available at: https://osiris.bvdinfo.com/ [Accessed 20.08.18]

Gruneberg, S. L. and Ive, G. (2000). *The Economics of the Modern Construction Firm*, Palgrave Macmillan, Basingstoke.

Ive, G. and Murray, A. (2013). *Trade Credit in the UK Construction Industry: An Empirical Analysis of Construction Contractor Financial Positioning and Performance*, Dept. of Business, Innovation and Skills, London.

Kenley, R. (2003). *Financing Construction: Cash Flows and Cash Farming*. Routledge, London.

Moodys buy BvD [WWW Document] (n.d.). URL http://ir.moodys.com/news-and-financials/press-releases/press-release-details/2017/Moodys-to-Acquire-Bureau-van-Dijk/default.aspx [Accessed 06.08.2018]

National Audit Office (2018). *Investigation into the Government's Handling of the Collapse of Carillion.*

Office for National Statistics (2018). *Output in the Construction Industry*. Available at: https://tinyurl.com/y5n7fcxb

Penrose, E. T. and Slater, M. (1980). *The Theory of the Growth of the Firm* (Second Edition), Basil Blackwell, Oxford.

Runeson, G. and de Valence, G. (2015). A critique of the methodology of building economics: Trust the theories, *Construction Management and Economics*, 33, 117–125. Available at: https://doi.org/10.1080/01446193.2015.1028955

10 A comparison of the construction output of the G7 countries

Stephen Gruneberg

Introduction

The need for international statistics on construction is compelling and important. Policy makers, construction companies, developers and investors need numerical information on construction before decisions can be taken. Apart from qualitative information, statistics and numerical data can form a rational basis for sound decision making. Buildings can survive, with maintenance, for up to several hundred years or more. The impact of infrastructure investment can also last for hundreds of years. In the relatively short term, the capacity of contractors to meet demand for buildings requires data, if the workload of construction firms is to be managed in an orderly fashion. The alternative is to respond to changes as and when they occur, moving from periods of unemployment and over-supply to periods of excessive demand and inflationary pressures on construction and labour costs.

Unlike national income accounts, national construction statistics are not necessarily consistent when comparing countries, making it problematic, if not impossible, to compare like with like. Differing definitions, systems and measures in national statistics mean that it can be extremely difficult to find consistency in measures of construction in different countries. The formal definition of UK construction, for example, given in the notes to the national income accounts, includes civil engineering projects, including infrastructure, house building, demolition, road building and the installation of mechanical and electrical products and plumbing. The hiring of construction equipment is also included.

Inconsistency of international construction data poses a major difficulty when attempting to make cross-border comparisons. Differences in defining terms and measuring output and differences in the roles, duties and responsibilities of the various participants in the construction production process all add to data confusion at an international level. In view of the contradictions and confusion in the data, one might conclude that there is little point in referring to official published data at all at an international level.

In fact, this is not the case. Even though international data may not be perfect, it nevertheless forms a starting point for discussion and debate. It raises questions and issues and it indicates the scale of the problems facing policy makers and those in the industry. In other words, the data is indicative of the scope of activities, the economic size of the industry and the relative performance of contractors in different countries. This statistical information can act as a basis for discussion, policy making and strategy. Indeed, it can also serve to raise questions about the data and expectations and begin the process of improving the quality of construction statistics to examine change in the construction industry over time at an international and global level.

Published data is often subject to revision. Revisions can occur for many good practical reasons on the assumption is that the data is ever more reliable as a result. Data is collected through various channels and respondents in some of the smaller establishments may not always be able to complete forms and questionnaires as accurately as assumed, given the practical difficulties, time and work pressures that arise on a day to day basis. Also, data may need to be revised as more information arrives after the deadlines set for data have passed. The result is the need to publish revisions that occasionally require major adjustments to the data.

It could also be argued that even within one country, the most recent statistics are not always reliable or accurate. For example, Table 2.4c of the published UK construction output data shows the value of new housing in 2014, (published in 2016), was adjusted the following year, see Table 10.1.

Although these adjustments appear to be minor, ranging from £2 million to £15 million, much larger modifications are not uncommon. For example, Table 10.2 shows the value of other buildings and structures for 2013 was raised by almost 11 per cent from £69,878 million in 2013 to £77,394 million in the revised figure.

UK national income data carry a warning stating that expectations of accuracy using early estimates of data are often not met, due to the need to deliver data in a timely fashion even though the data may not be complete at the time of publication. Estimates can be expected to contain statistical errors as a result of uncertainty due to sampling and modelling data, which involves the need to make unavoidable assumptions about the data. According to the Office for National Statistics (1997), estimates for the previous three years may have been revised.

Table 10.1 Public and private new housing 2013–2015 in £million

Year	*New Housing 2013–2015*		
	Original	*Revised*	*Difference*
2013	22 405	22 405	0
2014	29 405	29 407	+2
2015	31 175	31 190	+15

Sources: Construction Statistics Annual, Number 18, 2017 edition, Table 2.4c Value of construction output by type of work, New Work for Public and Private Sectors, Great Britain, Current Prices

Table 10.2 New dwellings and other buildings and structures in £million

Year of publication	*2015*	*2018*	*Difference*
	Original	*Revised*	
New dwellings (in 2013)	58917	56406	-4.3%
New dwellings (in 2014)	68632	63644	7.3%
Other buildings and structures (in 2013)	69878	77394	10.8%
Other buildings and structures (in 2014)	74918	80166	7.0%

Sources: Table 8.3 Gross fixed capital formation in 2015 at current purchasers' prices, analysis by type of asset, Blue Book, 2018

Similarly, international sets of data are also subject to revision. For example, the UNStat table of "GDP/breakdown at constant 2005 prices in US Dollars (all countries)" uploaded in December 2015, was revised in 2016 for 2015 data (accessed May 2017). The revision shows major changes to gross fixed capital formation (GFCF) data in certain countries as far back as 1970.

Naturally, one would expect the statistical agencies to make public their revisions. The problem lies with ignorance and the set of assumptions that lead users of the data to see data as being in some sense "factual" and therefore accurate and reliable. Caution is always required when interpreting international data. Not only is recent data open to revision, even older data can also be revised with the benefit of hindsight.

The UK benchmark model and how it is calculated

Since the 1980s, several authors have attempted to raise the issue of international construction measures, including Drewer (1980), Bon (2000), Ruddock and Lopes (2006), Meikle and Gruneberg (2015). All these authors have taken one or other aspect of construction and attempted to compare results from an international point of view. One problem in measuring construction output in all these papers is that the expectation of what is actually measured often bears little resemblance to what is actually delivered. To overcome the inconsistencies in construction data between countries a UK Benchmark Model (UKBM), discussed here, can be used to estimate and compare the performance of construction industries in different economies. The UKBM makes use of the advances made in re-classifying economic activities consistently and internationally through both NACE Rev 2 and ISIC Rev 4. NACE is the European Classification of Economic Activities, (Statistical Office of the European Communities, 2006) and is the shortened acronym of the French, la Nomenclature des Activités économiques dans la Communauté Européenne or Nomenclature statistique des activités économiques dans la Communauté européenne, which translated into English becomes "the statistical classification of economic activities in the European Community" (Eurostat, 2008: 5).

ISIC Rev 4 is the International Standard Industrial Classification of All Economic Activities, (United Nations, 2008) and is used to produce the global system of measuring the national income of every country. The UN System of National Accounts (SNA) and more specifically the European System of Accounts (ESA) form the basis of, for example, the United Kingdom accounts. The SNA forms an internationally consistent set of national accounts, which use agreed concepts, classifications and accounting rules. It provides the framework for reporting economic data, enabling international comparisons of national income and economic performance. However, Lee (2011) warns about the distortion of data arising from the "underground economy" and notes that data on the construction industry is particularly vulnerable from this source.

Nevertheless, the UK construction industry is only an example to illustrate the principle of using a benchmark model. Indeed, much work will be required to establish in the longer term, which country or collection of countries would be best suited to use as a basis for comparison. Indeed, in their chapter on the UKBM model Meikle and Gruneberg (2015) point out that regional differences in construction may make international comparisons more reliable, if the underlying model of construction was not based on one country alone and that different models were applied to different regions of the world to take into account differences between countries in Asia, Africa, South America, North America, the Middle East and Europe.

Estimates of construction output are usually taken from construction industry statistics or the national income accounts based on the contribution of contractors to the building process. In the UK, the Monthly Business Survey questionnaire, sent out by the Office for National Statistics, new construction work includes demolition and site preparation, while repair and maintenance includes improvements, major alterations, extensions and work carried out to maintain a building to its existing standard, in short, all work on existing stock. In principle, projects involving renovation, reconstruction or enlargement are included in GFCF, if they increase capacity or extend the life of an existing asset.

Improvements are distinct from repair and maintenance, which is a form of consumption and not fixed capital formation. Unfortunately, the distinction is not always clear as repairs are often carried out to "improve the performance or extend the life of an asset" (The Stationery Office, 1998, National Accounts Concepts, Sources and Methods, p. 103), in which case the work is included in the definition of fixed capital formation. The cost of transferring building ownership includes lawyers', architects' and surveyors' fees, estate agents and auctioneers and these costs are in principle also included in GFCF but as land is not produced, it is excluded from gross fixed capital formation. When completing the survey, construction firms are asked to include materials and direct labour but to exclude payments to subcontractors, labour only subcontractors, architects and consultants. The value of land and VAT are also excluded from the value of construction output.

Structures and other built assets are work-in-progress until they are transferred to the eventual user or developer. GFCF is measured in terms of the value of the transaction, when the ownership of the asset is transferred. Before the transaction has occurred, the assets are considered as work-in-progress. Buildings and infrastructure are valued at purchasers' prices plus the cost of transferring ownership incurred by the purchaser. If there is no change in ownership fixed capital output is equivalent to gross fixed capital formation, valued at the estimated basic price of the finished structure or the cost of production plus a mark-up. According to Lee (2011), gross fixed capital formation (GFCF) is investment in fixed assets and relates to the productive capacity of a country. A fixed asset is durable and lasts more than one year. This distinguishes fixed assets from current assets, such as materials, which are used up in the production process. Fixed assets include computers, cars and aircraft, plant and machinery and investment in buildings, structures and dwellings, which form an important element in GFCF tables. Even mobile homes, caravans and houseboats are included in GFCF, if they are used as principal residences.

According to Gruneberg (2008), GFCF is comprised of new plant and machinery and new construction. The construction element of GFCF can be found by combining new dwellings, (excluding land) and other buildings and structures in Table 8.5 of the UK National Income Accounts. According to the National Accounts Concepts, Sources and Methods, the measurement of capital formation of new assets is valued at purchasers' prices, when ownership is transferred. This includes all costs and taxes incurred through the change of ownership. Sales of existing assets are valued after deducting the cost of transfer paid by the seller. Own-account production of fixed assets is valued at basic prices, (the selling price net of taxes and subsidies) or, if not possible to calculate, the cost of production is used. As ever, when considering the detailed methods of measuring the value of fixed assets, it can become obscure and difficult to record. For example, if the sale of a built asset is to a non-resident, the sale is "sometimes deemed to be to a notional resident, whose equity is then purchased by the non-resident as a financial asset." (National Accounts Concepts, Sources and Methods, p103). This national income accounting convention is applied to buildings.

Repair and maintenance is approximately 40 per cent of construction output, though of course this percentage varies from year to year. As GFCF refers to new build only, an adjustment is needed in order to include repair and maintenance to find the total value of construction output. Fortunately, Table 2.8 in the Construction Statistics Annual presents both new build and repair and maintenance, which enables the percentage share of each to be estimated. It is important to note that although the time series below span from 1987 to 2017, the coefficient of GFCF used in the model is only based on the average of the years from 2009, (when the series began to recover from the shock of the financial crisis of 2008), to 2017, the latest year available.

To calculate the coefficient of new build to find the value of all building work including new build and repair and maintenance, we use the geometric mean of the inverse of New Build divided by All Build from data in Table 2.8, Construction firms: value of work done by trade of firm and type of work at current prices, Great Britain, in Construction Statistics Annual. With the help of this coefficient, total construction including repair and maintenance can therefore be calculated from new build alone. This can be estimated using the inverse of the fraction of repair and maintenance over total construction in Table 2.8. In the UK benchmark model, this ratio becomes the coefficient of new build in the UK National Income Accounts GFCF Table 8.5, which provides the value of aggregate construction, including both repair and maintenance and the whole supply chain.

This benchmark modelling approach makes use of the construction components of GFCF to enable a direct comparison of construction industries in different countries. If the measure of construction output understates the size of construction activity and its relative importance to the economy, when the construction industry is stimulated by investment the impact of that investment will tend to be greater than anticipated. This can lead to shortages of skills and materials and consequential inflationary increases in costs, delays and disputes.

Although it has often been argued that the multiplier effect of construction is responsible for stimulating the economy, we would suggest that it is the investment behaviour of developers, who take advantage of the opportunities created by, for example, infrastructure improvements that encourages further rounds of investment. This is distinct from the multiplier effect, which is based on further rounds of consumption expenditure because of capital investment. This is not to say that investment in construction does not have an impact on the economy, but this impact is not only due to a Keynesian type of multiplier effect, but is the result of a combination of the stimulation of consumption expenditure, the mobilisation of the construction supply chain and the activities of developers to capture the gains in property and land values through the improvements in a locality due to investment in infrastructure or urban regeneration brought about by subsequent rounds of investment in the built environment.

The UKBM can be used to compare the relative construction performance of different countries throughout the world. In this chapter, the model uses UK construction data, but an equivalent method based on another country's data could possibly be equally well used for the same purpose. Indeed, there is no one way of establishing a comparator. For example, the benchmark could be based on the average of one country over a number of years, or the average of a basket of countries either in one year or over several years, either using exchange rates or purchasing power parities (PPP), which is the preferred method described by Langston, (see Chapter 5). Whichever benchmark model is selected, it enables all countries to have a common denominator for the purpose of drawing comparisons.

To compare the UKBM method and ISIC-F, the countries of the G7 have been used. The members of the G7 are Canada, France, Germany, Italy, Japan, the United Kingdom and the United States. This comparison applies UK construction statistics and data from the UN national income accounts to form the UKBM model in contrast to the ISIC-F data in UNStats. It is likely that changing methods of building will require careful monitoring when making international comparisons. Because modern methods of construction and technological developments are continuously developing, the skills needed and the demand for labour are also in a continuous state of flux, adapting to new circumstances and this trend looks certain to continue for the foreseeable future. Prefabrication, on-site robotics, on-site drones, new materials and construction products, Building Information Modelling (BIM) and 3-D printing indicate the potential for changes in the industry.

Nevertheless, the conventional value added approach to estimating the contribution of construction to national income remains valid for finding the gross domestic product (GDP) but this is a specific purpose, namely the calculation of national income, important as it is, that lies beyond an accurate and useful analysis of the construction industry *per se*. The relevance of the data used depends on the question asked or the uses to which the data is put. The value-added approach is only a method of measuring and aggregating all activities in an economy to avoid double counting in the process. The disadvantage of using the value added approach to measure the size of the construction sector is that it does not take into account the value of the total contribution of construction to GDP as it ignores aspects of construction such as the contribution of the construction professionals including structural engineers and architects, who together form a sizeable share of the value of total construction output. It should, however, be noted that the ONS construction statistics specifically includes materials used and is therefore not based on a value-added approach. Fortunately, the difficulties found in calculating the value of total construction output as a measure of the size of the construction industry can be overcome to a certain extent by using an approach similar to the UKBM model method.

Benchmark models may use a variety of approaches. There is a need to establish an approach that is consistent and theoretically acceptable. A debate needs to be had to agree in principle which method to use. For example, average data may be taken from one or more countries to assess the breakdown of construction by type of output or type of firm. Fortunately, because of ISIC-F and NACE, international sets of national income accounts and construction data are consistent and can be used to make global comparisons. National income accounts are published by the World Bank and the United Nations, where data on every country's GFCF can be found. Each country's national income accounts are measured both in their national currency and in US dollars converted using exchange rates. At the time of this writing, all countries' national income accounts at constant US dollars are given in 2010 US dollars, updated from the previous set in 2005. Increasingly, purchasing power parities (PPPs) are being adopted to make international comparisons, as an alternative to exchange rates. Although there are valid theoretical objections to using exchange rates to compare construction output in different countries, it is nevertheless a consistent, if limited, approach to measuring construction output in different countries, albeit inaccurately.

At the centre of the UK benchmark model is GFCF, adjusted to include repair and maintenance for the entire construction supply chain. The same ratio of total UK construction over UK GFCF is then applied to whichever nation's GFCF is to be measured. This does not provide a definitive basis for the size of construction in the target country but in the absence of reliable data, it can be a useful starting point to have an approximation of the size of construction, until evidence is found to the contrary.

The size of construction output can be estimated using the ratio of construction output over GFCF. More specifically, the ratio of total build (including new build and repair and maintenance) over GFCF is used and this becomes the coefficient of GFCF of the target country to find its total annual construction output from GFCF. Similarly, once the total UKBM construction output is established, this can be used to estimate the share of different building types, using ONS, Construction Statistics, Table 2.4, value of construction output by type of work, published annually. The proportion of each building type becomes the coefficient used to multiply total output to find the estimate of that building type in any given country. The total output figure can also be used in a similar way to estimate the share of output produced by the different types of firms from the ONS Construction Statistics, Table 2.8 Private contractors: value of work done by trade of firm. Finally, using demographic data, construction output per capita can also be estimated.

It is important to note that GFCF is an expenditure measure of construction. This means that it is found by calculating the value of investment in all new build, excluding land. This figure therefore includes materials and the whole construction supply chain. In addition, the benchmark model includes repair and maintenance. For this reason the time series of the UK benchmark model is greater than the ISIC-F values, which are based on a much narrower definition of the value produced by the building industry, which includes materials and components used in the production process but not the inputs of independent designers, structural engineers and quantity surveyors.

As the UKBM uses GFCF and the GFCF of all countries can be found in UNStats, the coefficient derived from the ratio of construction to GFCF can be used to estimate annual construction output from the GFCF data. Using the UKBM to estimate national construction output serves as an alternative to the ISIC-F (Construction) output series. The following graphs compare the UKBM and ISIC-F measures of construction output.

Net investment

Before turning to the research results, there are underlying trends that can distort understanding of the actual construction processes taking place. Construction demand is derived from investment demand, which in turn is derived from expectations about future needs. Investment may be divided into replacement investment and net investment. Replacement investment in construction may be new build or renovation work. Such investment replaces buildings and structures that have reached the end of their useful lives. The buildings may be obsolete, meaning that although they may be standing the cost of their maintenance and repair is greater than the rental earned, or the rental is insufficient to retain the property profitably. As a result, insufficient funds are used to maintain the built assets and they gradually decline into dilapidation over time. New buildings and structures are built to replace them.

In practice, from the point of view of the economy, a new building may be constructed but it is not always possible to tell whether the new building is an addition to the total stock of buildings or only a replacement for a demolished building elsewhere. If the new building is adding to the total stock of buildings in an economy, then economists refer to that kind of investment that increases stock or capacity, as net investment. If the new building or structure simply replaces another building that has been demolished, without increasing the total stock, then that building has only compensated for wear and tear on the built environment.

It is worth bearing in mind that just because so much of construction output may be net investment, new build output does not necessarily increase the stock of residential buildings or places of employment, or infrastructure, even when additions to stock are produced in one location, while quite unknown and unrelated buildings are demolished in another place. The net effect in that case is no economic gain to be had from the new construction beyond replacing worn out buildings.

However, it also needs to be understood that as buildings are durable and can provide work spaces and residences for up to centuries, and that the process of replacement is an ongoing process in construction, it is quite possible that construction may be increasing the stock of the built environment without increasing the annual output of buildings and infrastructure from one year to the next. This is because the building industry has the capacity to replace existing buildings and even add to stock, without necessarily increasing annual construction output from one year to the next. This means that total construction output can be the same as in a previous year but in each year additions to stock may be produced increasing the economy's capacity and hence, enabling the rest of the economy to grow. Simply looking at annual figures for construction output does not reveal the effect and impact of construction on the economy. That impact depends on the extent to which construction output is net output (adding to stock) and how much is replacement investment.

Results and discussion

In all the figures below, construction output, based on the benchmark model, is shown as a solid line. The UN data, shown as a dashed line, is based on construction industry output by contractors and specialist contractors only, based on firms in the International Standard Industrial Classification F (ISIC-F). In all the figures below, the data is recorded in billions of US dollars at 2010 prices. In all the time series of the G7 countries, the UKBM based data is greater than the official ISIC-F based data, reflecting the fact that the benchmark data measurement includes the whole supply chain, building materials and components and the professional inputs of designers, structural engineers and others, whose total fees amount to approximately 10 per cent of total building costs.

Table 10.4 summarises the findings of the comparison of the construction trend lines from 1970 to 2017. The R^2 statistics for the UKBM figures appear in general to be higher than the ISIC-F data, implying that a higher proportion of the UKBM data can be accounted for by the trend line compared to the ISIC-F model. Table 10.3 also shows that the coefficient of x in the equation of the trend lines of the UK benchmark model, (an indicator of the growth rate), is invariably higher than the coefficient of x of the published ISIC-F figures. An extreme case is that of the United States, where the trend growth of the UKBM is given as 47.92 compared to 3.19 for the ISIC data.

Comparing the relative changes in the construction industry as measured by the ratio of the UKBM model of construction output compared to the ISIC F model in Table 10.4, confirms a significant increase in the difference between the UKBM model compared to the ISIC-F model over time. In 1970, the ratio of UKBM over ISIC for the G7 countries was between 1.17 and 1.84 but, by 2017, the differences between the two measures had increased to between 2.4 and 4.64 times, more than doubling the differences between the two measures. A similar pattern can be seen in all 7 members of the G7 below, reflecting a global trend of increasing use of technology and high-level training and skills. Many factors may account for this growing discrepancy between the two measures of output, including the increasing importance of those elements not captured by the more

Table 10.3 G7 construction industry trend growth rates 1970 to 2017

Country	*UKBM 1970 to 2017*		*ISIC-F 1970 to 2017*	
	Coefficient of x	R^2	*Coefficient of x*	R^2
Canada	5.60	0.932	1.77	0.871
France	6.31	0.943	0.42	0.314
Germany	6.38	0.922	0.93	0.510
Italy	3.36	0.671	0.05	0.006
Japan	11.85	0.545	−0.87	0.033
UK	5.01	0.936	1.38	0.827
US	47.92	0.95	3.19	0.262

Table 10.4 The relative size of G7 construction industries as measured by the UKBM model and ISIC F model in 1970 and 2017

Country	*UKBM/ISIC-F in 1970*	*UKBM/ISIC-F in 2017*
Canada	1.62	2.41
France	1.84	3.75
Germany	1.84	4.2
Italy	1.70	3.4
Japan	1.74	3.32
UK	1.62	2.4
US	1.17	4.64

traditional measures of construction, namely the intellectual inputs to the built environment over time, including planning costs, technology and the value and contributions of the building professions, as construction has become increasingly complex, technological and skilled.

According to Figure 10.1, the UKBM of Canada's major period of expansion appears to have been between 1996 and 2008. By 2017, it was barely higher than it had been in 2008. A similar pattern emerges in the data from all G7 countries (Figures 10.1–10.7). Minor differences emerge such as a long-term decline in real construction output as measured by ISIC-F in Germany and Japan. However, there is evidence in both countries that this decline has reversed in recent years. Using the UKBM both countries experienced strong but volatile growth since 1970.

The question remains, however, which is the more reliable measure of construction performance, the ISIC-F data or the UKBM model? To answer this question more research is needed. Nevertheless, the UKBM model offers an approach that considers the whole supply chain, including construction material and component suppliers, architects, structural engineers and surveyors, subcontractors and specialist contractors.

In all the figures, (Figures 10.1–10.7), the growth rate of the UK benchmark model as measured by the coefficient of x in the regression line equations of both time series is greater than the published ISIC-F data. This tendency to grow faster than the contractors alone and the materials used in the construction process indicates that as modern methods of building, increasing prefabrication and more sophisticated components are brought to site, the UKBM indicates that contractors have been providing a diminishing share of the work on site, as a higher proportion of building inputs are produced in factories off-site.

The more rapid growth in the value of construction output in the UKBM model may be accounted for, by a greater share of the value of output coming from the supply chain, (including designers and engineers), rather than the contracting side of construction.

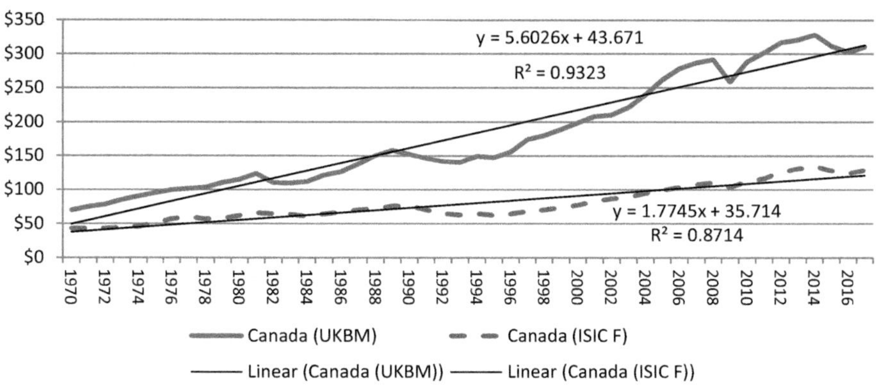

Figure 10.1 Construction output in Canada at constant 2010 US $bn, 1970 to 2017

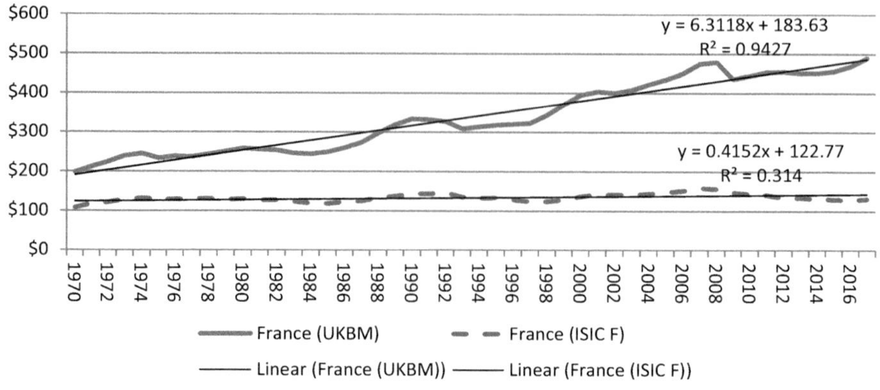

Figure 10.2 Construction output in France at constant 2010 US $bn, 1970 to 2017

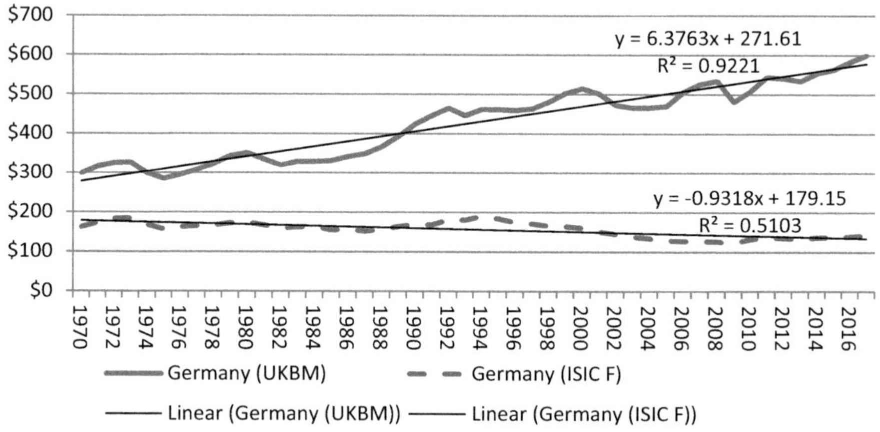

Figure 10.3 Construction output in Germany at constant 2010 US$, 1970 to 2017

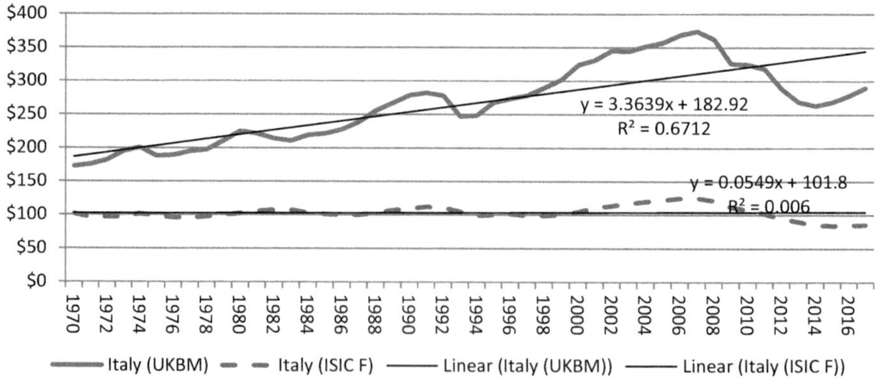

Figure 10.4 Construction output in Italy at constant 2010 US$bn, 1970 to 2017

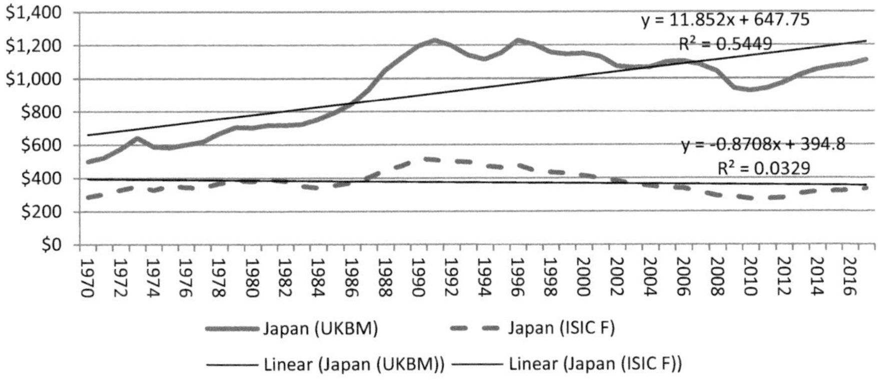

Figure 10.5 Construction output in Japan at constant 2010 US$bn, 1970 to 2017

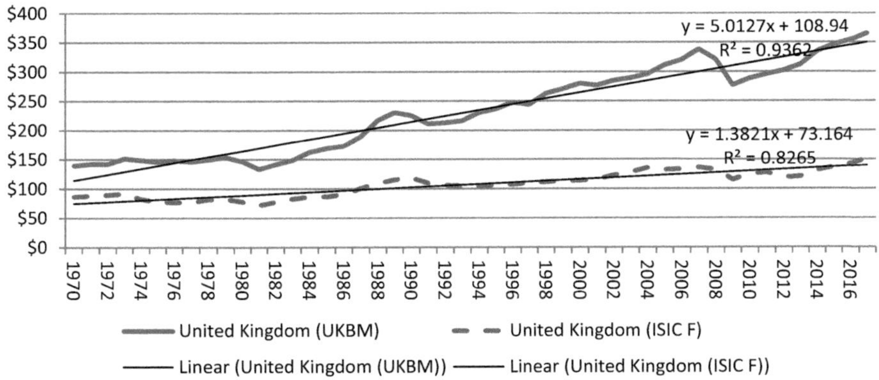

Figure 10.6 Construction output in the UK at constant 2010 US$bn, 1970 to 2017

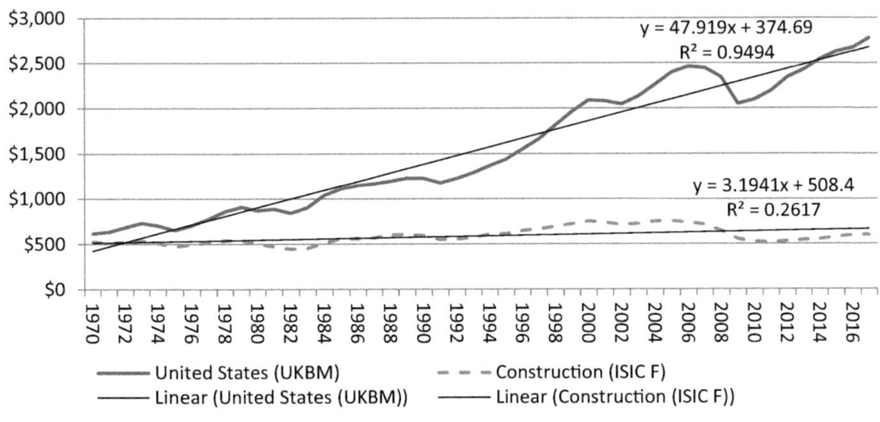

Figure 10.7 Construction output in the US at constant 2010 US$bn, 1970 to 2017

In Figure 10.2 the UK benchmark model shows growth in construction output in France, while the value of output from contractors remained static between 1970 and 2015, as prefabrication, standardisation and other modern methods of working replaced work on site.

In Figures 10.1–10.7, the growth of the benchmark model rather than the output of firms classified to ISIC-F could be interpreted as showing the growth of construction may be correlated more with the growth of GDP than had previously been thought, due to omitting the changing nature of production in the construction sector. This new approach may highlight a new interpretation of what the figures mean and what narrative emerges from the statistics bearing in mind there is always a residual margin for error.

Table 10.5 summarises the actual change in the value of construction output at 2010 prices between 1970 and 2017 and the growth in construction output between 1970 and 2017 using the UKBM model. The expansion of annual construction output in the G7 countries from 1970 to 2017 ranged from an increase of only 68 per cent in Italy to 351 per cent in the US. Table 10.6 compares the same years using the ISIC-F data, where the change in annual construction

Table 10.5 Change in construction output 1970–2017 using the UKBM in US $bn at 2010 prices

	UKBM in 1970 in US$bn	*UKBM in 2017 in US$bn*	*Growth of UKBM 1970–2017*
Canada	70	311	345.78%
France	197	490	148.29%
Germany	299	600	100.77%
Italy	173	290	68.02%
Japan	499	1,109	122.16%
United Kingdom	140	365	161.85%
United States	616	2,778	350.84%

Table 10.6 Change in construction output 1970–2017 using ISIC-F in US $bn at 2010 prices

	ISIC-F in 1970 in US$bn	*ISIC-F in 2017 in US$bn*	*Growth of ISIC-F output 1970–2017*
Canada	43	129	199.36%
France	107	131	21.89%
Germany	162	143	−11.93%
Italy	101	85	−15.79%
Japan	286	334	16.71%
United Kingdom	86	152	76.23%
United States	526	598	13.68%

output declined from $101 billion in Italy in 1970 to $85 billion in 2017, a decline of almost 16 per cent in the size of the Italian construction output compared to Canada where annual construction output rose from $43 billion in 1970 to $129 billion in 2017, an increase of almost 200 per cent. Nevertheless, the US remained by far the largest construction market in the G7 in 2017 at $598 billion at 2010 prices, though it had only increased in size by $72 billion, an increase of only 14 per cent since 1970. It was the smallest construction market in the G7 in 1970, Canada, that had expanded the most.

Concluding remarks

As with any set of data, its usefulness depends on to what use it is put. In theory it is hoped that being able to use the data internationally, it will aid policy makers to monitor construction, measure the capacity of construction industries to undertake work and compare the performance and productivity of construction industries in different countries. In many ways the UKBM model is only an approximation and is only indicative of the scale of construction in any one country. However, the UKBM model may well be able to answer questions, measure and compare the impact on an economy of investment in the built environment. By using established construction industries as a guide and proxy for variables in a third country's construction industry, the UKBM could be used to monitor through proxy measures the success or failure of policies and investment in construction and infrastructure.

This chapter has highlighted some unexpected results. Why for example, is construction in the US growing rapidly using the UKBM model, while its ISIC-F measure seems to grow very slowly by comparison? It is by no means clear which series is more accurate. It is possible that unrecorded construction has in fact enabled the construction industry to grow at a far higher rate than that reported by firms in the industry. Clearly more research is required to establish which data sets best serve the measurement of capacity in the construction industry and its ability to meet demands made of it.

Finally, the UKBM model is an estimate based on proxies for construction, namely the ratios of the UK based statistics. This measure assumes that in the absence of more reliable data the figures of the UK benchmark are indicative of the figures of all construction industries. This is a highly spurious assumption, as there is no basis for assuming that construction industries share similarities in terms of the proportion of output to GFCF, share similar distributions of building types or similar ratios of different types of firms as a proportion of all firms and similar patterns of skill sets and productivity. Indeed, it is predictable where wages are low, productivity will also be low. The results are therefore only indicative at this stage and further research is needed to be able to produce more reliable models of construction. What the UKBM model provides is a starting point for gathering more internationally consistent data, the quality of which can be improved over time, for example, with the use of purchasing power parities (PPPs).

References

Bon, R. (2000). *Economic Structure and Maturity*, Ashgate Publishing Ltd, Aldershot.

Drewer, S. (1980). Construction and development: A new perspective, *Habitat International*, 5(3), 395–428.

Eurostat, European Commission (2008). *NACE Rev. 2, Statistical Classification of Economic Activities in the European Community*, European Communities, Oxford.

Gruneberg, S. (2008). Modelling the UK built infrastructure market using gross fixed capital formation, *24th Annual ARCOM Conference*, Cardiff.

Lee, P. (2011). *UK National Accounts – A Short Guide*, Office for National Statistics. Available at: www.nationalaccountsshortguid_tcm77-225120.pdf [Accessed 10.01.2019]

Meikle, J. and Gruneberg, S. (2015). Measuring and comparing construction activity internationally, in Best, R. and Meikle, J. (eds.) *Measuring Construction Prices, Output and Productivity*, Routledge, Abingdon.

Office for National Statistics (1997). *United Kingdom National Accounts: Concepts, Sources and Methods*. Available at: www.ons.gov.uk/ons/rel/naa1-rd/national-accounts-concepts–sources-and-methods/1998-release/national-accounts-concepts – sources-and-methods.pdf [Accessed 14.01.2019]

Ruddock, L. and Lopes, J. (2006). The construction sector and economic development: The 'Bon Curve', *Construction Management and Economics*, 24, 717–723.

The Stationery Office (1998). *United Kingdom National Accounts Concepts, Sources and Methods*, The Stationery Office, London.

Statistical Office of the European Communities (2006). *NACE Rev 2, European Classification of Economic Activities*. Available at: http://novebojeznanja.hr/UserDocsImages/Dokumenti%20i%20publikacije/Dokumenti%20i%20publikacije%20referirani%20u%20SOZT-u%20(popis%201)/179a%20NACE%20Rev.%202%20Introductory%20Guidelines.pdf [Accessed 21.01.2019] https://unstats.un.org/unsd/snaama/index [Accessed 16.01.2019] file:///C:/Users/Stephen/Downloads/conceptssourcesmethod_tcm77–215625.pdf [Accessed 13.01.2019]

United Nations Department of Economic and Social Affairs, Statistics Division (2008). *International Standard Industrial Classification of All Economic Activities (ISIC) Revision 4*, United Nations, New York. Available at: www.bundesbank.de/resource/blob/612626/067f5294c6df434ea4528bdb62551f9b/mL/isic-rev-4-data.pdf [Accessed 21.01.2019]

Index

For Product Safety Concerns and Information please contact our EU representative GPSR@taylorandfrancis.com Taylor & Francis Verlag GmbH, Kaufingerstraße 24, 80331 München, Germany

Batch number: 10726532

Printed by Printforce, the Netherlands